D0443888

Of Spirits and Madness

Of Spirits and Madness

An American Psychiatrist in Africa

Paul R. Linde

McGraw-Hill

New York Chicago San Francisco Lisbon London
Madrid Mexico City Milan New Delhi
San Juan Seoul Singapore Sydney Toronto

To Laurie,
who just knew that I would love going to Africa.

Library of Congress Cataloging-in-Publication Data

Linde, Paul R.
Of spirits and madness: an American psychiatrist in Africa / Paul R. Linde.
p. cm.
ISBN 0-07-136734-9
1. Mentally ill—Zimbabwe—Harare—Case studies. 2. Linde, Paul R.
3. Psychiatrists—United States—Biography. 4. Psychiatry,
Transcultural—Zimbabwe—Harare. 5. Spirits. 6. Zimbabwe—Religion. I. Title.

RC451.Z55 L563 2001
616.89'0096891—dc21
[B] 2001032656

McGraw-Hill
A Division of The McGraw-Hill Companies

1 2 3 4 5 6 7 8 9 0 DOC/DOC 0 9 8 7 6 5 4 3 2 1

ISBN 0-07-136734-9

This book was set in Sabon by MM Design 2000, Inc.
Printed and bound by R. R. Donnelly & Sons Company.

McGraw-Hill books are available at special quantity discounts to use as premiums and sales promotions, or for use in corporate training programs. For more information, please write to the Director of Special Sales, Professional Publishing, McGraw-Hill, Two Penn Plaza, New York, NY 10121-2298. Or contact your local bookstore.

This book is printed on recycled, acid-free paper containing a minimum of 50% recycled, de-inked fiber.

Contents

Preface

> *"Telling stories can be healing. We all have within us access to a greater wisdom, and we may not even know that until we speak out loud.*
>
> *Listening to stories also can be healing. A deep trust of life often emerges when you listen to other people's stories. You realize that you're not alone; you're traveling in wonderful company. Ordinary people living ordinary lives often are heroes."*
>
> —Dean Ornish, M.D.
> In the Foreword to
> *Kitchen Table Wisdom* by
> Rachel Naomi Remen, M.D.

In my mind, I was just going along for the ride when I agreed to go to Africa with my wife, Laurie. Trained in pediatrics, she knew her life dream: to work as a doctor in Africa.

What would I do in Africa? I was trained as a psychiatrist, for heaven's sake. I thought about faking it as a general practitioner in the bush. I considered a stint submitting travel articles or trying my hand at writing fiction. While Laurie saved the lives of African children, I envisioned myself alone—sweating, drinking potent "crash" coffee in the morning and African lager in the afternoon, pecking away at the keys of a rickety typewriter for hours at a time.

But eventually I woke up from that dream and began a search for international opportunities to work as a psychiatrist. For more than a year ahead of our tentative departure date, Laurie and I tried valiantly to line up jobs overseas. Having waded through reams of international red tape to no avail, we grew tired of waiting and packed up our lives and flew off to Bali to begin a languid tour of Southeast Asia. Our plan was to make our way to Zimbabwe, where we had a few tenuous leads and the medical school was perpetually trying to recruit more faculty members. At best, we'd find work. At worst, we'd travel around Africa until the money ran out.

After our arrival in Harare, Laurie got hired quickly. I blundered into a job as a government psychiatrist for Zimbabwe's Ministry of Health. Sometimes things work out better if you don't plan too hard. When a labor strike by the nation's junior doctors stretched into its second week, we were pressed into duty. Our work permits, previously stuck in a bureaucratic quagmire, magically appeared. I plunged into my job at the Harare Psychiatric Unit, a department of Harare Central Hospital, and ran headlong into culture shock and a crushing workload, the combination making for a baptism by fire.

At first, my clinical experiences in Africa just hit me in the head, forcing me to perform in an impromptu manner on a day-to-day basis. My jaw dropped in confusion and amazement almost every day. Gradually I became more mindful of the life stories of the people that I saw, taking note of the courage and resilience that my patients exhibited daily in the face of poverty, physical disease, and mental illness.

My style of discovery in Zimbabwe was seat-of-the-pants, extemporaneous, curious, and disbelieving. I was forever picking the brains of the Shona psychiatric nurses who taught me about African medicine and psychiatry while acting as linguistic and cultural interpreters. As in my previous jobs, I needed an overwhelming challenge to give me enough motivation to work at all. Nowadays, still working as an emergency room psychiatrist, I remain ambivalent about my attraction to "stress-in-the-moment" jobs, which often lead to career burnout. On the upside, however, these gonzo work environments capture my attention and provide me with a platform to be garrulous and irreverent. I get to perform stream-of-consciousness stand-up comedy for my coworkers, blowing off steam, relieving the pressure of the serious work that we do.

Even before I landed in Africa, I always thought that those of us practicing psychiatry were privileged to live in the border zone between the "natural" and "unnatural" worlds. By virtue of my medical training, I had already been steeped in the "natural" world of biochemistry, physiology, and clinical medicine—a land of deductive logic and algorithms.

And I had been introduced to the power of the mind and spirituality in matters of health and healing during five years spent living and working in San Francisco. California's Bay Area remains a cultural hothouse for the study of the "unnatural" world of spirits and its influence on the practice of medicine. My interest in the relationships among mind, body, and spirit intensified during my travels in Southeast Asia. There I witnessed rituals that included the use of trance-states, repetitive chanting, interpretive dancing, self-injury, and supplication to the spirits—the participants communicating with and pleasing influential members of the

Spirit World, often demonstrating their faith on behalf of the greater community rather than themselves. These ceremonies, some of which I literally stumbled across, were intended not as spectacles for the tourist but as rituals that just happened to be conducted in public places.

Primed by my various experiences, I set foot in Zimbabwe with my mind open to the African's understanding of disease and his belief in things both seen and unseen. I hit the scene physically fit and well-rested, enjoying a relaxed state of mind, not having seen any patients for six months while experiencing a leisurely pace of travel. My cynicism and level of stress, dangerously high before my departure from America, had largely dissipated by then. At that time in my life, which was unlike any other, I was searching for a sense of meaning by way of collecting novel experiences. Although I began my work from a stance of curiosity instead of skepticism, that didn't make up for the fact that I still had a lot to learn about the influence of spirits in the practice of psychiatry.

I became fascinated with the ever-present nuances of the Spirit World on display in Zimbabwe. Not only did I want to understand the ways in which "spirits" were purported to cause illness and misfortune, but I also wanted to know how the "spirits" operated day to day in the lives of the Shona people.

At the time, I had no clue that my experience working as a psychiatrist in Zimbabwe would someday become a book. Because I didn't plan on writing a book, the work presented here is largely a product of my memory three to five years after the fact. The eleven stories told here are based on real patients whom I treated. Most of the stories are similar to the actual turn of events between psychiatrist and patient. A few of the narratives are composites of two or even three patients whom I saw. In all cases, the names and personal details of the patients have been modified to preserve their confidentiality. With one exception, these individuals have not had a chance to review these works, and, quite truthfully, I would not have a clue as to how to find most of them.

The final story is about my treatment then and friendship now with Wonder Kasimonje, a young Zimbabwean man with whom I still correspond. Wonder gave me permission to tell his story without the protection of confidentiality and had the opportunity to review my version of our doctor-patient relationship. His life story continues to unfold as I write this preface.

So, instead of going along for the ride, I embarked on a journey of my own. I worked as a psychiatrist in a foreign land, eight parts outsider to one part insider. I collected experiences, diagnosed weird diseases, helped people, absorbed pathos, explored spirituality, and learned bits of a new language and culture. But, in that world of spirits and madness, did I learn how to approach life with the attitude of an African—to "see how the day goes"?

Those readers searching for a book about African famine or war or natural disasters will need to look elsewhere. This book celebrates the triumph of the human spirit over much smaller and more personal tragedies. Some of the protagonists do well and others do not, but all of them face their problems with courage. Their steadfastness and faith in times of hardship provide an inspirational testimony to the rest of us—a gift from the people of Africa.

Paul R. Linde
San Francisco, California
February 2001

Acknowledgments

The journey that became the heart of this book started in 1993 when my wife and I took off for Southeast Asia on our way to southern Africa, where we hoped to work as doctors. We made it. In trying to thank all of the essential players along the way, I know that I am likely to forget somebody important. Notwithstanding that caution, here goes:

For jump-starting my interest in writing and restoring confidence in my abilities, I thank Paul Cohen, who helped me explore my creative writing potential with a course he taught at the University of California–Berkeley Extension in 1996. For giving me a solid foundation in writing construction and style, I thank Gladys Woolson, Carol Mattson, and David Jacobson. For providing me with insightful commentary and unflagging encouragement, I thank Adam Bluestein, Ian Wheeler-Nicholson, Mitzi-Ann Goya, and Mark Schultz, each of whom carefully read parts of my manuscript in its various stages. For helping me turn an amorphous idea into the form and structure of a book, I thank Jessica Jones, who spent hours reviewing and discussing my book proposal and early chapters. For guiding me through the literary jungle, I thank my agent, Jane Dystel, and her associate, Miriam Goderich. It was a stroke of seriously good fortune when Jane decided to represent this book. For feeding me a steady diet of news and political background about Zimbabwe, I thank a long-time friend, Jim Prose. For her hard work, thoughtfulness, and skillful steering of this book from start to finish, I thank my editor at McGraw-Hill, Amy Murphy.

I am grateful to all of my psychiatric colleagues in Zimbabwe, including Frank Chikara, Wilson Acuda, Mark Winston, Lawrence Hipshman, Iris Chagwadera, Alfred Chingono, Mohammed Sebit, Sekai Nhiwatiwa, Jane Mutambirwa, Joann Stephens, and Mohamed Suleiman. But I am particularly beholden to Vikram Patel, whose scholarship in conducting cross-cultural psychiatric research in Zimbabwe shaped my understanding of psychiatric problems among the Shona people, and whose friendship continues to be a soothing tonic to this day.

The clinical work that I did in Zimbabwe would have been overwhelming and intolerable were it not for the welcoming and always helpful attitude of the psychiatric nurses who kept the Harare Psychiatric Unit running as a mostly smooth operation, led by Matron Chengeta. Many of the key nurses, aptly called "sisters" in Zimbabwe, are mentioned along the way. Since a comprehensive listing would be impossible, I want to thank each and every nurse and student nurse with whom I worked side by side in that world of spirits and madness.

I most humbly and sincerely acknowledge each and every one of the hundreds of patients that I took care of in Zimbabwe. They reminded me that the doctor-patient relationship remains one of the most privileged partnerships in the world. I remain in debt also to their relatives and friends, who taught me about the life-spirit of Zimbabwe's people, whose courage and forbearance continue to this day in the midst of a shifting political climate and grinding poverty. I especially thank Wonder Kasimonje, my ex-patient and friend, whose story is the last one told here.

I thank my father, Lew Linde, an author, social worker, and lawyer, whose motto in life is "Straight Ahead!"

I thank my mother, Marcella Linde. May she rest in peace; I thank her for giving me gifts of faith and spiritual energy, handed to me especially as she passed from this earthly world to an everlasting one.

Finally, I thank my wife, Laurie, who has supported me emotionally and financially in writing this book. But I thank her mostly because she knew me well enough to know that I would love going to Africa. She was right!

CHAPTER ONE

"Sister, Who's Our First Patient?"

Tichaona Machewa: A Garden-Variety Manic

"Africa is mystic; it is wild; it is a sweltering inferno; a hunter's Valhalla; an escapist's Utopia. It is what you will, and it withstands all interpretations. It is the last vestige of a dead world or the cradle of a shiny new one."

—Beryl Markham
West with the Night

I couldn't have imagined a more surreal landscape than if I had landed on Mars.

Visualize a misplaced Bedlam: a dusty courtyard in Africa, its perimeter marked by a chain-link fence topped with barbed wire; its psychotic denizens milling about in institutional garb; the scene set under a canopy of blue sky and the muscular arms of a baobab tree standing guard over Dante's inferno. That was my workplace in Zimbabwe, the hospital where I worked as a psychiatrist for a year. It was a place that I got to know well, where I met a memorable manic, Tichaona Machewa, a few weeks into the job.

Approaching the gate that day, I was still taken aback by the chaos. Overmedicated and undermedicated patients wearing ill-fitting hospital pajamas and brightly striped bathrobes—some jabbering and zipping around, a few flapping and squawking, others motionless and voiceless, still others appearing completely normal—milled around the hospital's yard of patchy grass and dirt, which fronted a low-slung brick building.

Some inmates walked like Frankenstein's monster, stiff and drooling, showing the ill effects of too much chlorpromazine (Thorazine). Others virtually pranced—nimble and giddy. Talking in torrents, they greeted me over and over again in Shona, patting me on the back, following me step for step to the nurses' station. It appeared that the Thorazine, called CPZed (see-pee-ZED) in British shorthand, did nothing to harness their psychotic energy, naked before the whole world in that amphitheater of lunacy.

While the sacred world holds its holiest of Holies, my workplace in Zimbabwe cradled the craziest of crazies, who blessed me with exuberant spirits on a daily basis. They rushed me in a good-natured way with greetings as soon as I passed into the inner sanctum of madness, the courtyard of the Harare Psychiatric Unit (otherwise known as the P.U.). Making my way each workday into that scene, I had to throw the rulebook of psychiatry out the window.

"*Mangwanani, chiremba* (mahn-gwah-NAH-nee, CHA-rem-bah)," Good morning, doctor. The salutation came as I approached the front gate of the P.U.

I returned the greeting: "*Mangwanani, sekuru* (seh-KOO-roo)," I addressed the hospital's security guard as a respected elder male.

He asked: "*Mamuka sei* (mah-MOO-kah say)?" How did you wake up?

I answered: "*Tamuka mamukawo* (tah-MOO-kah mah-MOO-kah-wo)." We woke up well if you woke up well.

In Zimbabwe, and particularly in the hospital, full greetings are a cultural necessity. These salutations, called *kukwazisa* (koo-kwa-ZEE-sah) in Shona, provide a type of social glue that holds the entire community together. I learned very quickly, during the first week, in fact, that it was my social obligation to greet each of the staff individually. Every morning, it was *mangwananis* all around.

"*Tamuka*," We woke up, he replied with a smile while unlocking P.U.'s modest portal.

While the courtyard gave fresh air and sunshine, it stole privacy. Passersby, walking on a well-worn path that skirted the P.U.'s perimeter, stopped to gawk and laugh at my patients. A sign at the corner of the fence warned the public not to feed the patients, only adding to the zoolike atmosphere. If those passersby only knew—there but for the grace of spirits go they.

"You are speaking Shona, *chiremba*," continued the guard, speaking in a heavily accented English that took my dull American ears at least a month to understand. "Shona is easy."

"*Aiwa* (EYE-wha)," I said, shaking my head in the negative, laughing and wading through a gauntlet of patients who approached me, a husky jovial *marungu* (mah-ROON-goo), a white man, as if I were some incongruous modern-day prophet. A big grin on my face, I ambled down a potholed driveway, *mangwanana*-ing, chatting and shaking hands like a politician, working the crowd toward the P.U., which was a fifties'-era two-story brick edifice. Hosannas of *mangwananis* trailed me. As I walked, I felt energy, vibrancy, an undercurrent of vitality humming in that courtyard—the slow steady drumbeat of Africa, tangible even in that den of madness.

"*Mangwanani, chiremba.* Are you going to see me today?" asked Tichaona Machewa, one of my new admits, speaking in a flurry of logorrhea, his face incandescent at the front of the pack. About five-foot-seven with a medium build, Tichaona unknowingly inserted himself into my schedule's first time slot by virtue of his mania. Before I had even stepped foot onto the ward, Tichaona's "mental status examination" had begun.

"*Mangwanani.* Yes, later this morning," I replied.

"My brother is here you must see me first I want to go back to work I need to make money for my family I'm fine now there's nothing wrong with me the sisters will tell you that there is nothing the matter I am strong look at my muscles you can see *chiremba* I am ready to go to my village to . . ."

"Okay, okay, okay," I said, failing to suppress a grin at Tichaona's contagion of mania. Tichaona's smile was like quicksilver, his verbiage a tropical heat blast, his movements nimble, darting this way and that among the slower moving throng of humanity in the courtyard.

By the time I had answered Tichaona's urgent question, he had sprinted to the yard's corner, where he inspected the fence post for no good reason. I knew full well that I would be "seeing" him all morning due to his manic intrusiveness. In Shona, *tichaona* (tee-chah-OH-nah) means "we shall see."

"*Tichaona*, Tichaona." I yelled and waved to him before I walked through the industrial metal doors into the inpatient psychiatric ward, which housed between sixty and one hundred patients at any given time.

I first saw Tichaona Machewa late in April, my first month working on the unit and the month of Zimbabwe's Independence Day, April 18. Accustomed to exploring cultural rituals during our travels in Southeast Asia, my wife, Laurie, and I supplied virtually the only white faces among a crowd of tens of thousands at Harare's National Sports Stadium on Independence Day, a "bank holiday" in Zimbabwe. The populace, lured there by the promise of a free football match between two of Zimbabwe's top club teams, first heard a speech by Zimbabwe's one-and-only leader, Robert Mugabe, and witnessed displays of the country's military prowess in the form of marches and acrobatics. My wife and I drew curious stares from many of those assembled as we discovered that the annual Independence Day celebration was not a customary stop for *marungu* tourists who passed through Zimbabwe, and certainly not for the average white Zimbabwean.

Although Tichaona's case of psychotic mania appeared unusual to me at the time, I soon discovered that his presentation of illness was downright garden-variety in Zimbabwe, where patients and their relatives matter-of-factly attributed their psychotic symptoms to ancestor bewitchment.

Stopping for a moment to inhale a lung full of fresh air before I entered the indoor portion of the psychiatric ward, I noticed the landscape around the P.U.—the fertile countryside still glistening from a gentle overnight soaker, late April signaling the tail of Zimbabwe's rainy season. Mashed-potato clouds dotted a sapphire blue sky; a breeze blew in from the northwest, cool and refreshing. I could smell the wetness of the grass. I took another couple of breaths before opening the heavy metal door of the P.U.

Not wanting to stir up anyone else, I lightly padded down a dim hallway—the floor a smooth gray cement, the walls an institutional brown brick—on my way to the nurses' station. I stepped over a pail of soapy water. The patients and staff were perpetually sweeping and mopping, so the place was reasonably clean. I stuck my head into the male ward, where up to twenty men wandered about. They slept on simple metal beds furnished with barely adequate threadbare mattresses. Their sheets and robes and hospital pajamas were clean, and they were generally clothed—except for the disrobing manics, of course. I made for the nurses' station. The nurses were working in sunlight streaming through an impressive east-facing window that opened to the courtyard. Models of industriousness, they looked quite smart (or well-dressed, in the British lexicon), wearing crisp, white uniforms and hats.

"*Mangwanani*, Sister," I said, greeting that morning shift's sister-in-charge, Sister Chamoko. (In the halls of British medicine, nurses are called "sisters," a label that, in this instance, has nothing to do with the nuns of the Roman Catholic Church.) Soon to become one of my favorites, Sister Chamoko was an experienced psychiatric nurse, tall and thin with a touch of gray in her hair. Calm and levelheaded, she helped me out of many difficult clinical jams at the old P.U.

"*Mangwanani, chiremba*," she said.

Just then, Tichaona popped his head through the open window of the nurses' station. "*Chiremba* my brother is here come see him right now he's traveled all the way from Mutoko to take me home today." Then just as quickly he slipped away.

"Gee, Sister, who's our first patient today?" I said, nodding my head and flicking my eyes toward the evanescent Shona man.

"He's been like that ever since he got here yesterday," said Sister Chamoko. "He was referred from the Mutoko

District Hospital. He took 200 milligrams of CPZed by mouth with no problem, but we put him in seclusion at first because he was trying to fight with us. Dr. Chibanda admitted him. The CPZed hasn't even touched him. He only slept two or three hours. He hasn't been violent today, but restless, pacing, getting into other people's business with his foolishness."

I reviewed the general practitioner's notes from Mutoko District Hospital. Apparently, this was a first episode of disturbed behavior. The patient, Tichaona, had been in the hospital three days. No bloodwork done. No physical exam done due to violence. The patient was transferred because he assaulted another patient and couldn't be contained.

Tichaona had been treated for three days with high doses of CPZed, the sledgehammer of psychopharmacology. Dirt cheap and less than ideal because of its crippling side effects, chlorpromazine was Zimbabwe's first-line agent for psychosis. What was once a cutting-edge remedy for psychosis when introduced in the 1950s, CPZed could nowadays only be considered a bludgeon for treating psychotic patients. Multinational pharmaceutical companies were sure to price newer, more humane medications at a cost far higher than Zimbabwe's Ministry of Health could afford.

In reviewing Tichaona's scant record, my mind covered the possible causes of his illness. I considered the universal psychiatric diagnoses of schizophrenia and manic-depressive illness. I also considered medical conditions such as malaria, tuberculosis, nutritional deficiencies, drug intoxication, and AIDS as possible causes of his disturbed behavior.

Tichaona's transfer represented a fairly typical referral from the rural hospitals. The general practitioner gave him a diagnosis of schizophrenia, which was highly premature given the fact that about half of all individuals who suffer a first psychotic episode never suffer another one. By definition, schizophrenia is a chronic condition with symptoms lasting more than six months and typified by recurrent psychotic episodes. An initial psychotic episode might be the first of many more, but it might also be a one-time reaction to severe stress, the result of drug intoxication and/or withdrawal, or the result of a physical illness. This reaction should come as no surprise, because the brain is well connected to the rest of the body by blood and nerves, its communication and operation systems, if you will, sensitive to the rising and lowering of hormone levels and the on-and-off switches powered by brain chemicals called neurotransmitters.

I looked over at Tichaona, whose smiling visage again appeared in the window. He was laughing, jumping up and down, and waving at me simultaneously. He looked distracted and perplexed and I wondered if he was being bombarded with auditory hallucinations. I knew that interviewing him would yield little in the way of reliable history, so I stepped out to gather information from his brother.

Peter Machewa stood off to the side of a group of patients, distinguishing himself with his placid demeanor and lack of a brightly striped robe. He was dressed in worn but clean clothes—navy polyester pants, a white short-sleeved dress shirt, and a blue tie—the equivalent of his Sunday-go-to-meeting clothes. He no doubt had traveled three or four hours to get here via a spine-jarring bus ride, having gotten up this morning about four-thirty to do chores, take a bath, and dress up before catching the bus. He looked expectant and sheepish, probably overwhelmed by the ever-present insanity surrounding him. I approached him. He smelled clean, faintly of cheap soap, in contrast to the earthy, pungent body odor emanating from some of the surrounding patients, many of whom had forsworn basic hygiene for the time being. Peter Machewa seemed glad to see me, an oasis of relative sanity.

"*Mangwanani*. I'm Dr. Linde, I'll be seeing your brother today."

"*Mangwanani, chiremba*. A pleasure to meet you. My name is Peter."

"Peter, let's go talk in private."

We walked across the courtyard into a one-story cement-block building, shaded by yet another massive baobab tree and housing a rather large interview room. Miraculously, Tichaona did not follow us. For the moment, he was distracted by the arrival of the morning's breakfast—a maize porridge called *sadza* (SAHD-zah), Zimbabwe's staple food that looks and tastes much like hominy grits or dumplings.

We ducked into the interview room.

"How long has your brother been like this?" I began.

"It started one month ago. My father and I thought he was bewitched—by my father's brother, who died last year. We took him to a *n'anga*."

Africans view the meaning of illness from an entirely different perspective than do Europeans or Americans. The Shona, like many Africans, understand disease causation in the context of traditional spiritual beliefs, based loosely on three fundamental ideas: First, all things that exist or happen have a cause. Second, serious occurrences such as birth, puberty, natural disasters, and death are intentionally caused. Third, the cause of any occurrence can be discovered by methods of reason, memory, and divination. These methods are often employed in the context of rituals performed by Shona traditional healers, the equivalent of a shaman within Shona culture called a *n'anga* (n-AHNG-ah).

Members of the Shona culture are likely to seek the consultation of a traditional healer first when they view the cause of an illness to be from "unnatural" sources such as witchcraft and especially if they involve the soul, *mweya* (mm-WAY-yah), or less often, the mind, *pfungwa* (PFOON-gwah). If they believe the illness to arise out of the "natural" world of the external environment, then they would initially go to a clinic or hospital to seek the opinion of a Western biomedical practitioner such as a physician.

"The *n'anga* told us that Tichaona's illness was a bewitchment. He could not say who the witch was."

"Did the *n'anga* think that Tichaona was being called himself to become a *n'anga*?"

"No," said Peter, his head down. "That would make all of this easier to take."

I learned early on that symptoms of madness in the Shona culture often herald the choosing and making of a traditional healer. Bad dreams and unusual behavior can characterize an individual who has been called to be a *n'anga*, overtaken by spirits as part of the initiation ritual to become a traditional healer. It is not surprising then that so many of the individuals suffering the symptoms of a first psychotic break, and their relatives, are hoping against hope that their transcendent experiences are the commencement of a career as a respected *n'anga* rather than the onset of a chronic, disabling condition.

What I was soon to discover was that many Shona people are devout Christians who simultaneously hold traditional, culturally sanctioned beliefs in ancestor spirits and witchcraft. Not troubled by this dualism, they regularly consult traditional healers not just in times of physical illness but also to ask advice regarding family conflicts, legal disputes, marriage troubles, major decisions, and matters of faith. In analyzing physical illness, the *n'anga* is thought to be capable of discovering the "real" cause of illness and to institute a cure. Within Shona culture, disturbed behavior is generally thought to be the result of a bewitchment—customized vexing engineered by a displeased ancestor spirit or the diffuse hexing of a malevolent witch or sorcerer.

In stark contrast to the *n'anga,* I was well trained to search for psychological and physical causes of psychosis. However, I did not know how to "divine" or even adequately conceptualize what a spiritual cause of illness, let alone mental illness, might be.

"Did he offer any treatment?" I asked.

"He shaved and scarred the top of Tichaona's head and brewed a special tea, but Tichaona got worse. He told us to bring Tichaona to the hospital. He could do no more."

Psychiatric treatment from the *n'anga* (the word *n'anga* signifying both the singular and plural form of the Shona word for traditional healer) included herbal concoctions, steam baths, scarification, and throwing bones to divine the source of a bewitchment. If a specific bewitchment was discovered, then the family was given instructions to mend community rifts that might well have been caused by the misdeeds or broken taboos of someone in the afflicted person's family.

"What did you notice about his behavior at that time?" I went on.

"He was up all night, walking all over the place. Talking nonsense. Laughing to himself. He got into a couple of fights. Then he started taking off all of his clothes. We took him to the hospital after he started our neighbor's hut on fire. We didn't know what else to do."

When it comes to disturbed behavior in Zimbabwe, psychiatrists are providers of last resort. This is true partially because of a drastic undersupply of psychiatrists but also because the universal stigma of mental illness is even more vexatious in Zimbabwe than it is in Europe or the United States. In general, Africans strive to maintain a physical and emotional distance from those individuals thought to be the victims of an alleged bewitchment, for fear of possibly "catching" one themselves. By contrast, however, the members of a bewitched individual's extended family are obligated, under the traditions of Shona culture, to do whatever they can to help and support their afflicted relative.

A severely disturbed individual, in the midst of a psychotic breakdown, will eventually be brought by his relatives to a *n'anga* or medical doctor for evaluation and treatment. Not so with the less serious "problems of life" in Zimbabwe, which may very well be labeled as a pathological syndrome of "anxiety" or "depression" within European or American cultures. In Zimbabwe, an individual may just need a little extra support from his family members, a spot of counseling, or maybe a visit to a *n'anga* for these "problems of life," but he or she would feel no need to see a biomedical doctor, let alone a psychiatrist.

It's not that Africans don't understand *how* disease occurs, it's just that they are much more interested in *why* it occurs. As I noted above, from the African perspective, diseases happen for a reason, they are intentionally caused, and the source of misery can be divined. For example, an African patient suffering from a pneumococcal pneumonia fully understands the concept that bacteria have caused his illness, manifested by the symptoms of fever, cough, chest pain, shortness of breath, and fatigue. He does not dispute that notion. But the answer he cares much more about and for which he cannot get an adequate explanation from Western medicine are the questions: "Why me? Why now?"

"Has he ever acted like this before?" I asked.

"No. Nothing like this."

"What was he like as a young boy?"

"Tichaona has always been quiet. He stayed by himself. He never had very many friends. He didn't do well in school."

"Anybody else in the family—aunts, uncles, parents, grandparents, anybody—ever act like this?"

"A first cousin acted just like Tichaona. He had a fit and died after he fell in our cooking fire. Also, I have heard family stories about my great-grandmother. She was considered to have the power of prophecy but was also thought to be mad."

"*Chiremba*," Sister Chamoko interjected, "you may not know that it is a traditional belief in our culture that our deceased elders can act as 'ancestor spirits' who continue to influence the living."

"Yes, Sister," I said, "I know a little about it from my reading."

I considered this family history carefully. It generated more questions than answers: Did Tichaona's cousin suffer from epilepsy, a condition that is thought to be a conduit to the Spirit World in some cultures? Was Tichaona's great-grandmother a victim of schizophrenia three generations before? Did her powers of prophecy and witchcraft span the generations? Could it be that Tichaona inherited his great-grandmother's spiritual abilities along with her mental illness?

Sister Chamoko explained to me that Tichaona's *ambuya* (am-BOO-yah), which means either "grandmother" or "respected elder woman" in the Shona language, would be considered a likely candidate to be the source of his bewitchment, given her powers of prophecy and madness. This begged the question in my mind: Could she be hexing and vexing poor Tichaona?

"Anything really bad happen to Tichaona that might have caused this?" I asked. "You know, a death in the family, something like that?" Severe stress can cause a reactive psychosis—its hallmark being a rapid onset following a major trauma and a quick recovery, usually in less than two weeks.

"No, nothing that I can think of," answered Peter.

"Has he been physically sick? Had a hot body, tuberculosis, malaria?"

I was considering the possibility of a medical cause for his disturbed behavior. Infections such as cerebral malaria, neurosyphilis, tuberculous meningitis, human immunodeficiency virus (HIV) in the brain, and a nutritional deficiency of niacin called pellagra are all relatively common causes of psychotic illness in Zimbabwe.

"He had malaria six months ago. He drank tablets given to him by the nurse and got better. He hasn't been sick since then."

Cerebral malaria usually strikes within a few days after the initial systemic infection. Plasmodium-infected red blood cells can clog the brain's circulation of blood and cerebrospinal fluid, causing a wide range of neurological and psychiatric complications. With a good response to treatment six months earlier and no current fever, Tichaona could not have had cerebral malaria.

"Has he had a cough, a rash, excessive diarrhea, weight loss, new lumps or bumps on his body, easy bruising, hair falling out, stiff neck, recurrent headaches, complaints of blindness?" I queried, spooling out an abbreviated "Review of Symptoms," a hallowed practice in medicine—encyclopedic and entirely complete in nature only when the questioner was your average second-year medical student or the most anal-retentive of internists.

"No, none of those things," answered Peter. "I would have known. Tichaona is close to me. He relies on me to help him with a lot of things."

"Does he have sex with a lot of different women?" I asked.

"I don't know about the last year or so," Peter answered, "but he used to go to prostitutes at the *shebeen* (shah-BEAN)." *Shebeen* are relatively seedy bars scattered throughout Zimbabwe, where men and women meet for strong drink and temporary coupling.

"Did he use condoms?"

"I don't know. I don't think so."

HIV shows a particular predilection to invade the gray matter deep within the brain and also the so-called white matter buried beneath the "thinking cap" of the cerebral cortex. Coated with the basic protein myelin that enhances electrical conduction, these white matter neurons connect the cerebral cortex with deeper brain structures. It is not difficult to imagine, then, that disruption of this system could cause emotional and behavioral changes.

"Does he smoke *mbanje* (mmm-BAHN-jay)?" I continued. "You know, *dagga* (DAH-gah)?"

The churchgoing Peter faltered, his eyes drifting downward toward his shoes. "Uh, I don't know. I think he's tried it."

I took this stammering response for a "yes," and, in the interest of politeness, declined to press the matter further, knowing that a definitive toxicological screen of Tichaona's urine would be more forthcoming than his brother. "*Mbanje*" and "*dagga*" are Shona slang words for marijuana, also named cannabis in homage to the weed's psychoactive ingredients, which are called cannabinoids. Cannabis is the drug of choice in Zimbabwe because it meets the three most important criteria of a substance that can be abused—it's potent, it's cheap, and it's readily available. It appears that marijuana causes or exacerbates psychosis more frequently in Zimbabwe than in the United States. Tichaona's homeland, the Mutoko District, in the well-watered northeastern corner of Zimbabwe near Mozambique, is famous, or infamous, depending on your perspective, for the quality and quantity of its marijuana.

By now Tichaona came wandering in with Sister Chamoko close behind. She carried a stack of papers and a few pens to start morning ward rounds officially with Tichaona as our first patient. Tichaona sat down briefly at the bench, but then he popped up and began laughing to himself, mouthing words under his breath.

"Hi, Tichaona. I have just a few questions. Are you hearing voices? Are you seeing visions?"

Sister Chamoko capably translated these questions. Tichaona did not answer. He wandered over to the window. Sister repeated the questions but Tichaona just smiled and walked out the door. It didn't really matter as I had gathered plenty of information from my initial "seeing" of Tichaona, the notes from Mutoko, and particularly the information from his brother Peter. It didn't take a rocket scientist, or even a psychiatrist for that matter, to determine that Tichaona was both manic and psychotic.

Although on a later physical examination I did not find any signs of AIDS, which could have included a rash, weight loss, thinning hair, generalized swelling of the lymph nodes, or ulcers of the mouth or in the genital area, I knew that HIV-induced psychosis was still a possibility. Behavioral or emotional problems associated with HIV disease can occasionally predate the physical signs and symptoms of the illness. I ruled out any other infectious disease as the cause of

Tichaona's psychosis. I excluded the possibility of pellagra, because he looked well nourished and did not suffer the telltale rash or diarrhea.

I didn't know for sure what caused Tichaona's psychosis or what his proper diagnosis was. I didn't think it was a reactive psychosis. Although cannabis might have brought out the illness prematurely or exacerbated it, I doubted it was the sole cause of Tichaona's illness because cannabis-induced psychoses are generally brief and respond quickly to treatment. My suspicion, given a positive family history, premorbid eccentricity, and the persistence and severity of Tichaona's psychotic symptoms, was that this episode represented a first break of what would probably become a more chronic psychotic illness.

But this academic exercise of coming to a proper diagnosis did not interest me as much as the main existential question that was generated by Tichaona's case: Was Tichaona actually suffering the real effects of a bewitchment or was he just attributing the symptoms of his psychotic illness to a phenomenon much more plausible to him—namely that he was a victim of an ancestor bewitchment? Or both?

According to the tenets of conventional psychiatry, psychosis is an old but useful term, referring to a person being generally "out of contact with reality." A person with psychosis is unable to organize thoughts in a linear and logical fashion and often suffers from delusions, which are fixed false beliefs, and hallucinations, which are sensory misperceptions.

Can psychosis be caused by a bewitchment? The Western-trained psychiatrist says "no way" because he or she understands psychosis as an observed phenomenon with its basis in the malfunctioning of the brain's systems of chemical neurotransmitters and electrical pathways. The typical American psychiatrist would likely call Tichaona's belief in bewitchment a delusion or, at best, an idiosyncratic attribution.

Suddenly, Tichaona's illness was making me challenge my long-held assumptions about the nature and causes of psychosis. According to my training in traditional, middle-of-the-road psychiatry, I had always considered delusions and hallucinations to be either psychological constructions of the mind or the result of neurotransmitter malfunctioning in the brain—faulty wiring or a toppled and leaky chemistry set in the brain's limbic system. This region of the brain is a collection of neurons that run in a ring from the temporal lobes (near the ears) backward and then upward with connections to the thalamus, basal ganglia, hypothalamus, and pituitary gland. Linking the cerebral cortex to deeper brain structures, the limbic system and its physiology is still somewhat mysterious but considered crucially important in mediating the mind's experience of emotions and in determining motivation.

So, reductionistic psychiatrists would posit that "psychosis" is no more or no less than perturbations of the brain's system of neurotransmitters. Despite my biology-heavy training in psychiatry, I was beginning to question that dogma.

The P.U. turned out to be the right place and right time for me to better understand the influence of the Spirit World on those of us in the material world, the foundation having been laid by my life in San Francisco and my travels throughout Southeast Asia. Tichaona's case excited me because I had become bored with the day-to-day practice of psychiatry in America, where I sometimes felt like a Pez dispenser of medications instead of a voyager into the lives and existential realms of my patients. On an unconscious level, I already knew that I had landed on a psych ward in Zimbabwe for a reason—to see the world and help people, yes, but mostly as a seeker. I was searching for a better understanding of an exotic culture, but more than that, I was desperately seeking a greater sense of personal fulfillment from my life and my work.

Of course, I was unable to make the transition to "spiritual seeker" overnight. Since I had been indoctrinated fully into the beliefs and practices of mainstream American psychiatry, I felt a little uncomfortable, silly even, in embracing such "New Age" beliefs. I realized that the traditional approach to diagnosis and treatment would still be necessary and useful in Zimbabwe. At the same time I thought, "why not see what I can see?" by immersing myself into the Shona's belief system regarding illness and spirituality so as to learn about it and enrich my understanding of the world. Just as the Shona practice Christianity and traditional rituals simultaneously, why couldn't an American psychiatrist use the Shona's cultural beliefs to complement the best of Western medicine in treating the patients at the P.U.? I did not know the answer to that question in April.

But I did know that the tools of conventional American psychiatry—to make an accurate diagnosis and prescribe medication—would help Tichaona recover from this episode of disturbed behavior. I could apply the powers of Western "biomedicine" to Tichaona's illness, knowing that, even if it improved his outcome, it could not provide him with answers to the questions that he would consider most important, "Why me?" and "Why now?" Already, I was beginning to understand that these answers could only come from the spiritual and existential realm. For Tichaona, the meaning of his illness could exist only within his traditional culture, which, because he grew up in it, was as second nature to him as his skin or his teeth.

I ordered routine blood tests, including an HIV antibody test, and a urine toxicology screen for cannabis. The lab at Harare Central Hospital was well organized and able to supply me with nearly any type of lab test that I needed. In addition, Zimbabwe's public health-care system provided pretest and posttest counseling to those patients who agreed to an HIV antibody test. In these respects, Zimbabwe was far ahead of most third world health-care systems. I was impressed.

I stopped the CPZed and started a more potent antipsychotic medication called trifluoperazine, known as TFPZ (TEE-eff-pee-zed) in Zimbabwe and as Stelazine in the United States, to reduce his psychotic symptoms.

I "saw" Tichaona every day but I did not formally evaluate him again until a week later. He was much calmer then, although he still suffered paranoia, intermittent hallucinations, and thought disorganization. Lab tests of his kidneys, liver, thyroid, and blood system were all within normal limits. Not surprisingly, his urine tested positive for cannabis.

It was somewhat surprising to me that Tichaona's HIV test was negative, since I knew that typically about 25 percent of patients admitted to the P.U. were found to be infected with HIV. In most of Africa, the disease is endemic and spread primarily by unsafe heterosexual contact. Over the course of the year to come, the predominance of AIDS in Zimbabwe would make my job more difficult on a day-to-day basis, not the least reason being that HIV infection of the brain is considered a "great mimicker" of different psychiatric syndromes.

I decided that Tichaona was well enough to return home with his brother and scheduled a follow-up appointment in two weeks. He was instructed to take his trifluoperazine and refrain from smoking *mbanje*.

Two weeks later, Tichaona returned, accompanied by Peter. Tichaona appeared as the picture of politeness, dressed in an ill-fitting suit jacket dotted with holes. Though he was taking his medication and abstaining from smoking marijuana, he was still hearing voices and experiencing paranoia at times. This reinforced my belief that his illness would be chronic. I feared that the most accurate diagnosis was a first break of schizophrenia.

I told Tichaona and his brother Peter that it was essential for Tichaona to continue taking his medications and that he might have to be on them for several years, if not the rest of his life. I also told him that the *mbanje* would only serve to make Tichaona more paranoid and possibly hear voices. I asked him to steer clear of the recreational weed.

Peter reassured me that he and his younger sisters would keep an eye on Tichaona. I told him that it was important for Tichaona to have something to keep him occupied—in essence, that he shouldn't just be hanging around as the token village idiot. (Of course, I didn't use such language with Tichaona and his brother.) Peter said that they would keep Tichaona busy with simple chores.

"Some day you may want to come back and see me," I said to Tichaona, "maybe in three months or so, to see if we can decrease your medications. If you have any problems with your medications, you can also go see the psychiatric sister at Mutoko Hospital. I'll miss you, Tichaona. You are doing so much better than that very first day that I saw you.

"*Tichaonana* (tee-chah-oh-NAH-nah), Tichaona," I said. "We will see you later, Tichaona." I shook hands with him and also with Peter.

"*Tatenda chaizvo* (tah-TEN-dah cha-EEZ-voh), *chiremba*." Thank you very much, Doctor.

"*Titambire* (tee-tahm-BEER-ay), Peter." You're welcome. "*Fambai zvakanaka* (FAHM-bye zvah-kah-NAH-kah)." Travel well.

"*Chisarai chakanaka* (CHIZ-ah-rye chah-kah-NAH-kah)." Stay well, answered Peter, completing a ritual of leave-taking common in Zimbabwe.

Over the course of the year I would see several straightforward cases of psychosis similar to Tichaona's in which I would undertake the same systematic approach to making a diagnosis and prescribing treatment. In each case I would carefully listen for clues to the influence of spirits. Although these patients were more disturbed than others, they were the comfortable cases, analyzed within the confines of the dim, brick building that served as the inpatient psych unit where I did ward rounds every Tuesday and Friday. I saw a much wider, more bewildering potpourri of patients in the outpatient clinic, just steps away from the P.U.'s dusty courtyard of madness. It held its own special set of problems, like overcrowding and vanishing doctors and vexatious legal problems, with which I would soon be needing to come to grips.

CHAPTER TWO

"He's Not Crazy, He's Delirious!"

Joshua Mujombe: Death Doesn't Go on Strike

"That night the malaria hit. The chills came and then fever and with it the most extraordinary fever dreams. The dreams were of confusion. In a slick cocoon of sweat, I pondered visual puzzles I couldn't solve, crowded with people who didn't fit."

—Stuart Stevens
Malaria Dreams

"The first day you're on a new ward, you're lucky if you can find the bathroom." This folkloric maxim of American medical training, annually spoken each July by anxious medical students, interns, and residents toiling on the wards of America's teaching hospitals, certainly held true for me the first week that I worked in Zimbabwe. The continuation of that saying, unfortunately, is ". . . let alone get in an intravenous needle, draw blood, or heaven forbid, save the life of a dying patient."

By far the worst time to get admitted to a teaching hospital in America is in the first week of July. New students, new interns, new residents, and new attending physicians clutter the hospital, a sea of white washing over the wards. Shiny new doctors in freshly washed and ironed white coats will be sweating, palpitating, and quaking their way to your bedside to poke and prod your body and stick needles into your arm, chest, and belly. Your best hope lies with the nurses, who are going to be watching the docs like hawks and, ideally, over you, the patient, like a mother robin hovers over her pastel blue eggs.

I'll never forget my first night on call as an intern on the medicine ward at Moffitt Hospital, the primary teaching hospital of the University of California–San Francisco (UCSF) School of Medicine. It was the evening of an unseasonably hot 90-plus-degrees day in San Francisco. In the midst of admitting five new patients, I perspired a big, ugly ring through the armpit of my white dress shirt and short white coat, the one we jokingly referred to as "the ice-cream man's."

Of course, because I was a *psych* intern that July, I would have done no harm to you—too frightened to touch you, let alone jab foreign objects into your skin. I wanted to hold your hand, not spin your urine; hear your story, not stab your wrist to test your blood's oxygen supply; feel your pain, not drain your bloated belly with a 6-inch needle; probe your mind, not grope your near-nether regions in search of a hernia.

But, at least, you'd have a doctor, any doctor. Things could be worse. You could suffer the fate of a Zimbabwean patient who gets whisked into a hospital bed during a not-so-infrequent junior doctor's strike or, even more fatal, during a nurse's strike. Then you might never see a doctor before shuffling off your mortal coil, undiagnosed and untreated.

Or you could have been that Zimbabwean patient who received his care, during a doctor's strike, from a medically rusty American psychiatrist who couldn't find the bathroom, didn't know the rules of play in a foreign hospital, and hadn't seen a patient, any kind of patient, in six months.

Harare Central Hospital was normally staffed by the residents (called "registrars" in British parlance), interns (called H.O.s, short for "House Officers"), and medical students of the University of Zimbabwe School of Medicine. Attending physicians, called "consultants" in the British hierarchy, strolled onto the wards in midmorning and breezed out before noon after conducting teaching rounds in a style reminiscent of the Sermon on the Mount. They were peripherally involved, at best, but their word was the last word, no questions asked.

As an "honorary lecturer" for the medical school and a consultant psychiatrist for the Ministry of Health in Zimbabwe, I envisioned myself as a clinical teacher—on the apprenticeship model of mentoring the "baby docs," who knew essentially nothing about psychiatry. I didn't really expect to get my hands too dirty on the job. I thought that the junior doctors and students would do most of the heavy lifting, so to speak, but I found out otherwise, particularly when I started work in the midst of a nationwide doctors' strike in April of 1994.

Striking doctors? To be fair to the young physicians, it was true that their pay was low, never keeping pace with an incendiary inflation rate in the wretched economy of Zimbabwe.

Zimbabwe harbored a strong labor movement following its birth as a nation in 1980, which strengthened even further in the mid-1980s when it became an ersatz Marxist/socialist state with close ties to China, Cuba, and, to a lesser extent, Eastern Europe and Russia. However, its leader, "Comrade" Robert Mugabe, then and now, rules as something more than an equal among his fellow citizens. He has assisted in the crippling of the young country's economy by lining his pockets and those of his cronies with a healthy cut from a seemingly endless supply of international contracts, gifts, and loans to the struggling nation.

In a country with runaway inflation (30 percent in the 1990s, nowadays closer to 60 percent on an annual basis), many Zimbabwean workers routinely and regularly go on strike, mostly for higher wages. These strikes are simply symptoms of an economic system on life support. Zimbabwe's economy, always dependent on outside donors and lenders, has been rendered impotent by its government's inefficiency and insidious corruption from the top down. It took an additional blow when the World Bank and the International Monetary Fund imposed an "economic structural adjustment program" in the early 1990s, forcing the country from state-supported socialism to fledgling capitalism. (As a footnote, the World Bank and International Monetary Fund have since cut off loans to Zimbabwe because of corruption and late payments.)

So the junior doctors had plenty of good company on the picket lines. Striking bank employees would shut down the nation's banks for days at a time, bringing an already fragile economy to a standstill. Striking teachers would evict thousands of needy students from classrooms for weeks at a time. Striking railway workers and bus drivers would paralyze Zimbabwe's usually decent system of public transportation. Striking nurses and doctors were much more lethal—crippling the operation of the public hospitals and literally killing hundreds of unfortunate citizens in the process.

I didn't fully realize the gravity of the situation when I first arrived at Harare Central Hospital. If I understood then what I know now, I might have found the bathroom right away during that first day of work on the psych ward in Zimbabwe and locked myself in until teatime rolled around. Psychiatrists are not accustomed to seeing their patients die. Little did I know, when I entered the chaos of that place, that my medical inexperience and the doctors' strike would cause the needless death of one man.

"*Chiremba*, before you start your ward rounds, you'll need to see this new admission," said Matron Chengeta, the P.U.'s grand poobah of nursing. Tall and imposing in a stocky sort of way, Matron Chengeta scared me at first. I eventually came to like her very much, as she had a soft spot for our patients. She always wore a starched green uniform, sometimes with a starched white cap and sometimes without. The green color of her dress signified her position of authority in the hospital hierarchy. While she displayed a gentle manner with the patients, she could be much more assertive, shall we say, with her nursing staff if need be. She was smart enough to take it easy on me.

"What do you know about him?" I asked.

"Not much. They sent him from Casualty without calling. They wrote on his card: 'Schizophrenia. To P.U.' No vitals."

"Any family with him?"

"No."

Knowing a little about the strength and unity of the family structure in Shona society, even on my first day, I asked, "Isn't that unusual, Matron?"

"Yes it is. But these days, you never know," sighed the matron, who had been working nearly round-the-clock during the strike to keep her ward from bursting due to its ever-present entropy.

I did not understand her comment, but I didn't have time to sort it out. I had work to do. As I came around the corner, I saw my new patient, Joshua Mujombe, a Shona man in his fifties, lying on a stretcher, sweaty, his hands tremulous, eyes open but unaware of the flurry of activity around him. At least it would be a quick interview—probably none at all. I picked up the nurse's stethoscope and opened the blood pressure machine, taking refuge in the familiarity of these universal tools of medicine. I took the man's vital signs—not once, but twice.

"Shit, Sister, the blood pressure's 210 over 120. Pulse 124. Temp 39.5," I said. I often cursed lightly on the job (and still do) when under stress. "We've got to get him back to Casualty. Fever, altered mental status. Delirium. Jeez, it would help to have a little history here. Are you sure there's no relatives?"

"Not that we know of. Maybe they are still waiting over in Casualty," said a more junior sister, whose name I did not even get that first day.

"Matron, how could they mistake a guy this medically ill for a schizophrenic? I mean, sure he's confused, he's agitated, he's seeing things—but he's not crazy, he's delirious. Don't they teach that stuff in medical school over here?" I was acting a little huffy. I couldn't help it; I was that scared. "It's probably pneumonia, AIDS, alcohol withdrawal, tuberculosis, hypertensive crisis, but whatever it is, it sure as hell is not schizophrenia."

"Looks like cerebral malaria to me," said Matron Chengeta. "It could also be a poisoning by *muti* (mootee)."

"Cerebral malaria? Really? What's *muti?*"

"Traditional medicine. We don't see it much anymore, but you never know."

"Malaria? *Muti?*" I mumbled out of the side of my mouth. "Whatever he's got, we need to get him out of here and over to Medicine."

So, the nurses dragged him out to the sister-in-charge's car to take him back to Casualty, just 300 meters away. To wait for the ambulance would have taken too long.

My own heart pounded, but I figured I had done my job: medical triage, getting him to the right place to be taken care of by an internal medicine team and medical/surgical nurses. Back home, at San Francisco General Hospital, this guy would have been in good hands. I did not fully comprehend the toll that the nationwide doctor's strike was inflicting on basic health care at Harare Central Hospital.

What I didn't know was that, because of the strike, the "house" had only one doctor—and he was responsible for hundreds of seriously ill patients. What I also didn't know yet was that nary a doctor was manning the Calcutta-like Casualty (synonymous with Emergency Room, or ER, in American parlance) at Harare Central Hospital. Of course, Zimbabwe's victims of violence and accidents, pyretic AIDS patients, laboring pregnant women, and babies with diarrhea, unable to plan their medical misfortunes and urgencies, did not stop arriving in Harare's Casualty Department just because the junior doctors were out on strike.

I knew that the nurses in Zimbabwe basically ran the hospital—like in America, but to an even greater extent. Nonetheless, these starched and disciplined nurses still needed the doctors to make many of the medical management decisions, write the orders, and vanish by late morning, getting out just in time for the nurses to get the real work done. In a spasm of denial on my part, I thought and hoped that someone more medically confident and adept in the ways of African illness than I would take Mr. Mujombe's case over. I imagined that an idealized physician in a white coat (like a Lone Ranger without the white hat and white horse) would examine Mr. Mujombe in a timely fashion, diagnose the problem, and begin definitive, life-saving medical treatment. What I know now is that the chances of my fantasy wishes being granted on that day were slim to none.

Later that day, I went over to see how Mr. Mujombe was doing. He had been admitted directly to the medical ward. The scene looked okay. He was positioned in a genuine hospital bed in an open ward of twelve beds or so. A few properly starched nurses were gathered around a sturdy wooden table, its surface covered with a swirl of papers, pens, and bits of medical paraphernalia. The nurses periodically rose to check on patients or run to other wards for supplies. They certainly appeared as if they were doing their jobs.

I did not introduce myself right away. Not fully appreciating the importance of the *mangwanani* at this point, I just went up to Mr. Mujombe's bed without a word. To the nurses, a thirty-something *marungu* wearing a tie without a suit coat aroused little suspicion on the ward. White guy, no greeting, looking lost—must be a new expatriate doctor. I picked up his so-called chart, a sheaf of brown papers with no writing on them. It was late in the afternoon—six hours after we sent him back to the medical service. I looked at a clipboard with vital signs documented—still up across the board.

I stood by the side of his bed for a half-minute or more, just staring at the sight of Joshua Mujombe. A ring of perspiration encircled his form on the yellowing scratchy sheets. His breathing was rapid and shallow. About five-foot-ten, Mr. Mujombe had a chest like a barrel: he sported decent-sized muscles for a man in his fifties, suggesting that he probably made his living as a laborer. He did not possess the telltale soft belly of an upper middle-class Shona man, who, with his health insurance, would have been lying in a clean and starched bed in a private hospital, tended to by a white-coated, white-haired, possibly white-skinned, private doctor. On the other hand, he was clean-shaven, showing a tad of stubble now that he had been out of commission for a day or two. Not at all did he look like a physical specimen suffering from a serious chronic illness such as the "slim disease" of AIDS or cancer or heart disease.

Staring off into space, Mr. Mujombe showed a waxing and waning level of consciousness, sweating, blood pressure up, not so much as an intravenous line in him. I still had not lain hands on him. As a psychiatrist, I was not in the habit of performing anything close to a complete physical exam. But, as a doctor, I could certainly recognize a person flirting with death. Because I worked in an urban psychiatric emergency room before coming to Africa, I was accustomed to seeing an abundance of medical pathology. Despite the fact that it had been more than five years since I had worked as a medical intern on the wards of San Francisco General Hospital and Moffitt Hospital at UCSF, I knew that Mr. Mujombe needed aggressive medical treatment.

The majority of my patients at San Francisco General were homeless people with severe chronic mental illness who shun medical care, eat poorly, don't take their blood pressure pills or insulin or any medications properly, drink alcohol and abuse drugs, and are exposed to the nastiest of infectious diseases. I was certainly in the habit of taking vital signs, laying hands on, performing a screening neurological exam, listening to heart and lungs if need be, but as far as medically managing critically ill patients, I was definitely *not* the man for the job. I could treat chronic medical illnesses without much trouble. But if a patient was urgently ill, I needed to refer him to one of my emergency medicine colleagues. So, in San Francisco, it was really only my job to determine if a patient was sick enough to be seen by an emergency room doctor, internist, or surgeon. And if so, I would consult with an ER doc on the phone and arrange for transfer of the patient to the ER, which for me was just down the hall, for further evaluation and treatment. But there was no "just down the hall" during the doctors' strike in Zimbabwe.

I approached Mr. Mujombe, whose eyes were closed. Motionless at times, restless at others, he episodically mumbled a string of unintelligible words. His forehead was clammy. I fingered his wrist to check his pulse. Despite a heart rate of 130, which I checked and rechecked, his hands were cool to the touch, signifying that he was "clamped down"—the smaller veins and capillaries constricted to conserve his blood pressure in a reasonable range. I checked his blood pressure on the clipboard—still maintaining in a range of 110 to 140 systolic and 60 to 80 diastolic. I tried to rouse him—first speaking loudly to him and, getting no response, jamming my fist straight down on his breastbone in an attempt to gauge his level of unresponsiveness. He opened his eyes, looking but not seeing, mumbling, drifting back to his twilight of stupor.

By this time, a nurse had joined my side of the bed. "Doctor?" she asked. "Good afternoon?"

I flinched, startled, lost in my examination of poor Mr. Mujombe.

"Oh yes, sorry, good afternoon, I should have introduced myself. My name is Dr. Linde. I am the attending, I mean consultant, over at the Psychiatric Unit. I sent him back to Casualty. Obviously his problems are medical, not psychiatric." Nervous, I just kept talking, which can be a habit of mine. "I just, I just wanted to see how he is doing. And I can see, he's not doing well."

The nurse, barely in her twenties, I presumed, simply looked at me and listened.

I went on, stuttering at times. "You know, I don't know how things work around here. I just started working here. Where I'm from, you know, I would refer someone this sick to one of my colleagues."

"The house doctor has been called. Because of the strike, there is only one doctor for the whole hospital. But, don't worry, he knows about the patient, he will see him this evening," she said. Her face was a serene pool, her manner calm.

Fatigued, overwhelmed, scared, less than confident about my abilities to manage the situation, and, to a lesser extent, worried about overstepping my boundaries here in a new hospital, I was faintly reassured by her words. Part of me wanted to flee, to return to my cozy room at the Bronte Hotel, see my wife, climb back into a protective cocoon to ready myself for what could prove to be an even more stressful workday to come the next day. Another part of me wanted to tackle the problem. The condition could be a lot of things, but it sure looked like a case of a generalized infection, bacteria in the bloodstream, soon to be causing a case of "septic shock." How hard could it be to send a few blood tests, start intravenous antibiotics, give him a few liters of fluid to support his blood pressure and stave off dehydration since he was not eating or drinking anything?

Obviously, the patient was dried out, in the midst of an autonomic storm. His body was revving up the stress response—heart rate up, blood pressure up, muscles tensed, body temperature up, sweat pores wide open, pupils dilated, skin a gooseflesh. The switch for his system of "fight or flight" was stuck on overdrive. Fever, toxins, whacked-out blood chemistries, any one of a number of physical problems could have caused him to be brought to the Casualty Department for the medical illness that had caused what appeared to be a sudden onset of "brain failure." The differential diagnosis for delirium, the technical term for acute brain failure, was longer than my arm.

The young sister politely stood by me, as I myself gazed at a spot on the wall and then out the window to admire the leafy branches of an acacia in a vain attempt to free my mind, which at that point was paralyzed by ambivalence and ruminative thoughts. To confuse matters even more for me, she asked, "Will you be writing orders?" Mixed messages to my mind: First she says that another doctor would take care of the situation, but, then she says, more or less, "since you're here and interested and don't seem to be a total idiot, could you help us manage this case?"

For whatever reason, still not clear to me in hindsight, I deferred. I backed off of the case, thinking I wasn't up to the task. As I walked off the ward, I do remember justifying my behavior with thoughts of: "Are you crazy? You're a psychiatrist, let the medicine people take care of him. There's no way that you're the best medical doctor available to take care of a guy this sick."

Bone-weary from my first day on the job, I slunk off the ward and across the field to my 1982 powder blue Renault R5, purchased at auction for the equivalent of 2500 U.S. dollars (US $2500). Cars, even squirrel-powered little runts like this one, were expensive in Zimbabwe. I climbed into the driver's seat on the right side of the car, fired up the four-banger engine, and carefully drove the 8 kilometers, trying to avoid an accident, as motoring on the left side of the road was still a novelty to me, to the finely appointed Bronte Hotel. Surprisingly, I was able to put Mr. Mujombe out of my mind by the time I closed the hotel room door behind me, diving onto the hotel bed, flipping on CNN to escape a stressful, bordering on horrifying, first workday.

After working for two years as an emergency psychiatrist, I was accustomed to rapidly forgetting about the day's work when I was on my way home. Most psychiatrists, at least those who choose to retain their sanity, learn early on to compartmentalize their work from the other areas of their lives. Otherwise, they'd go crazy. Psychiatry is by far the most emotionally exhausting of the medical specialties, with oncology and AIDS work a close second, in my opinion. Third-year medical students doing their six-week clerkships routinely tell me that they cannot get their patients off of their minds even after they head home at the relatively sane hour of 6:00 p.m. from a workday on the psychiatric ward. They can't believe how tired they are after working *just* a nine-hour day with no overnight call.

So for better or worse, psychiatrists, this one included, become pretty adept at adopting an "out of sight, out of mind" attitude as a prerequisite for survival in training to become a psychiatrist. This is certainly a mixed blessing. No doubt this sort of detachment allows all doctors to do their work. But it also leads to a personal style of aloofness, arrogance, and sometimes neglect, causing many patients to feel like parts on an assembly line.

Though I hate to admit it now in retrospect, I did sleep well that night. But first thing the next morning, I returned to the Medicine ward. Mr. Mujombe's bed was filled with another patient. I asked the nurse where he was.

"Oh, he expired."

"What?" I couldn't believe it at first. "It can't be." I believed that she was lying, that he had to still be alive. I took a moment to remind myself of the sight of Joshua Mujombe just sixteen hours earlier—dehydrated, feverish, stuporous, heart racing, sweating a big ring around the bedsheet. It suddenly became quite conceivable to me that not only could he be dead, there was no way that he could still be alive.

"He's down at the morgue," said the nurse. "He died overnight."

"What happened? Did any doctor see him? Did he get a line in?"

There was no answer from the nurse, who then simply said, "I'm sorry," before turning around to go back to the nurses' station. It was evident that she was overwhelmed with a new batch of sick patients and no doctors to help. I found a chair and slumped into it. I was crushed. I'm a psychiatrist. I'm not used to patients dying on me. Should I find his family? Should I go down to the morgue and try to see him? Should I find the house doctor on call yesterday and see if he ever saw Mr. Mujombe? Should I find the medical record and see what happened? Partially out of wanting to avoid the pain of knowing what happened and partially because I already had an overflowing dance card back at Africa's slice of Bedlam, I elected to do none of the above and instead ready myself for another day.

Maybe I couldn't have saved him, but I could have at least tried. I bet that no doctor ever saw him. No line got in. No antibiotics and no sedatives were given. No laboratory tests were sent to determine the physical cause of his change in mental status. I could have at least tried: get an intravenous line in him, get some fluids going, bring his blood pressure down, make him comfortable, give him a trial of antibiotics.

But with the doctor's strike and my unfamiliarity with disease in Africa and my tentativeness, the poor man never had a chance. I vowed that if I ever had an opportunity to make up for my sin of omission in this case and possessed the wisdom to recognize such an opportunity if it came along, then I would take it on in a second. But my opportunities to practice internal medicine were never so dramatic as they were that first week working as a doctor in Zimbabwe.

My skills as a "real doctor" were often stretched over the next several months as I was called upon to treat complicated cases of epilepsy, mental retardation, nutritional deficiencies, hypertension, vascular disease, and, in particular, infectious diseases such as tuberculosis, malaria, and sexually transmitted diseases, including, of course, HIV. Many of the patients who came to the P.U. depended on psychiatrists to take care of their basic health-care needs, so I filled many prescriptions for antibiotics, vitamins, anticonvulsants, and antihypertensives. I needed to be well versed in the way in which these medical diseases could lead to a presentation of "disturbed behavior."

My education about the diseases of not just Africa, but of the tropics and of poverty, had begun. And although my timidity eventually dissipated, it was still not enough to know about and diagnose malaria, pellagra, schistosomiasis, tuberculosis, postpartum psychoses, and endemic AIDS. I still needed to know what to do and to whom to refer when one of my psychiatric patients needed urgent medical attention. What I learned over time is that many of the patients that I sent over to the medical wards would die—even long after the strike was over.

How could this be? Were the doctors less capable? I don't believe so, as I saw that the medical students trained at the University of Zimbabwe overall were quite good. Several reasons became more apparent to me during my time at Harare Central Hospital.

First, there was the brain drain. It began with South Africa's best doctors leaving for Britain or the United States, creating a medical vacuum down in that country. Zimbabwe's best doctors then left for diamond-rich Botswana or South Africa to make more money (to send home to support an extended family), leaving Zimbabwe to make do with expatriate fill-ins like myself or dubiously trained doctors from other places throughout Africa, which shall go nameless.

Second, absenteeism and a light work schedule by both house staff and attending physicians plagued the system of public hospital health care. The medical wards suffered as much as the P.U. when it came to junior doctors leaving early or not even "pitching up," the British equivalent of "showing up," for work. Furthermore, many of the medical consultants only put in a few hours a week at Harare Central Hospital, as they were also running off to run their relatively lucrative private practices. Like the junior doctors, only more so, they needed to provide for an extended family.

Third, AIDS took its on toll on Zimbabwe's hospital-based doctors, who watched helplessly as patient after patient died with no treatment available. Demoralization struck and, in my opinion, some of these doctors would give up prematurely, even on patients who did not suffer from AIDS or who would otherwise have had a decent chance for survival.

I knew for a fact that many of the medically ill patients that I sent from Psychiatry to Adult Medicine for evaluation of fever and mental confusion were never aggressively evaluated because they merely looked like they were "NS-positive." HIV tests in Zimbabwe were euphemistically called

"NS"—standing for "New Serology"—indicating what was, in actuality, a new diagnosis of being HIV positive. The internists wouldn't even bother testing many ill-appearing, confused, feverish patients for HIV despite the fact that tests were readily available and results took just a few days to come back. The use of standard antiretroviral treatment with zidovudine (commonly known as AZT) was so far out of the financial reach of their patients and the government health service it was absurd. The doctors did not routinely treat the opportunistic infections of AIDS patients. They regularly let these individuals die of bacterial infections, which were eminently treatable by intravenous antibiotics. Why?

The answer was forthcoming in the form of a rhetorical question. Why should the agony of AIDS patients be prolonged by weeks or months when bacterial pneumonia could whisk them away to the afterlife, where they might still be able to become an influential ancestor to their survivors here on this earth? The suffering inflicted by AIDS in Zimbabwe, with its promise of a relatively quick death, transcended anything physical.

Zimbabweans accept death more readily than do Americans. Death in Zimbabwe is merely considered an extension of the life cycle of "Mother Nature." The ease with which the Africans accept death reflects their faith in things natural: the rhythm of the seasons changing from cold to dry to hot to wet to warm and back to cold again; time passing in a natural progression from dawn to day to dusk to night and back to morning again. Most Zimbabweans, who believe in the traditional ways of the culture, foresee death as the beginning of a seamless journey over to the other side, the unseen Spirit World, where they can shed their cloak of earthly misery, ascending to a position of importance as an ancestor spirit.

In contrast, many Americans, living always in the material moment, possess an extraordinary fear of death, seeing it as "The End," a dive into nothingness. The process of dying in America is often prolonged by the work of overzealous physicians in intensive-care units—even though pneumonia is still called the "friend of the elderly" in the halls of American medicine, providing as it does a relatively peaceful, painless death. This aggressive staving off of death is sometimes attributed to the wishes of the patient. But a physician who orders more tests and prescribes more aggressive treatments in the face of increasingly long odds of survival is sometimes acting to avoid a lawsuit and to prevent a patient's family from viewing the physician as negligent and "not having done enough." Thankfully, this mindset is fading as hospice care becomes more accepted and available in the United States.

I was not able to fully appreciate all of these existential matters on that second day of work as I skulked across a field and down a gravel road to the P.U. to see a morning's worth of patients. The image of the seriously ill Mr. Mujombe danced across my mind's eye, tormenting me, reminding me that I failed to save a man's life when I possibly could have. I was ashamed, sick to my stomach, almost wanting to quit so that I could stay at home and drink cream teas in the morning and gin-and-tonics in the afternoon, to work on a novel that I had started on the electric typewriter that I had already purchased in Zimbabwe. What was I thinking? While my feet went one in front of the other along the dusty road, my mind wandered, coming back to reality just often enough to lay a "*Mangwanani*" and a "*Marara sei*" on a young mother carrying a baby on her back.

What could I do? I wasn't a quitter. At least, not this early in the ballgame. I stumbled into the gate of the P.U., half-heartedly *mangwana*-ing the droves of patients and handful of staff wandering about. I waved to that day's shift of nurses, working behind an open window. I tentatively pushed my way through the metal door, cringing, not fully realizing yet that I would get better at this job of working as a psychiatrist in Zimbabwe.

CHAPTER THREE

"It's Ten O'clock, Where Are My Interns?"

Doctor Gwanzura: A Big Breadwinner

"But the soul of Africa, its integrity, the slow inexorable pulse of its life, is its own and of such singular rhythm that no outsider, unless steeped from childhood in its endless, even beat, can ever hope to experience it, except only as a bystander might experience a Masai war dance knowing nothing of its music nor the meaning of its steps."

—Beryl Markham
West with the Night

Every Monday and Thursday morning around eight-thirty, I would set up shop in the largest of several interview rooms of the outpatient "clinic" adjacent to the P.U. and prepare myself to see thirty or more patients. Many of my patients on those clinic days were mostly stable—successful "graduates" from the confines of the P.U. Others suffered from less serious "nonpsychotic" conditions of anxiety, depression, and "life stress," the bread and butter of private psychiatrists in the United States.

To get to Harare Central Hospital, which stood a half-dozen or so kilometers west of downtown Harare, I drove across town, fueled by strong Zimbabwean coffee from the Eastern Highlands, and parked my Renault R5, slightly bigger than a "matchbox" car, in a rutted lot underneath mature acacia trees. Following a worldwide tradition of keeping the mentally ill cut off from the rest of the world, and out of sight if possible, the Harare Psychiatric Unit was sequestered about 300 meters away from the main hospital, an appendix to the sprawling campus of Harare Central Hospital. From the P.U.'s parking lot, I could view Zimbabwe's entire spectrum of mental health care, adorned by the riotous growth of grasses and bushes and flowering trees under the African sun.

To my right was a chain-link gate, guarded by an elderly Zimbabwean man in blue, which, when opened, led to a short driveway making its way to the nurses' station. The P.U. also functioned day and night as a de facto psychiatric emergency room, where police officers and desperate family members could roll on down the driveway to deposit their disturbed. To my left, a gravel pathway pointed its way to the ramshackle clinic, a falling-down structure, which, in a previous life, housed in style a white Rhodesian doctor of another era. Since then, pressed into action as a clinic, the house was nothing more than a well-worn cinder-block palace that catered to the "walking wounded" of Zimbabwe's system of mental health care. Nowhere else could I imagine a kitchen functioning as a dispensary, a master bedroom as a corner office and tearoom—a place where the closets and porch and even a bench outside were transformed into a doctor's examination "suite" four mornings a week.

As I walked to the old house, I offered the requisite "*mangwanani*" with a big smile to everyone in sight—pedestrians, groundskeepers, security guards, patients, nurses, and kitchen help. I waved to two psychiatric nurses, dressed in whites, too far away to hail with a "*mangwanani.*" They had just greeted each other with huge grins and a signature handshake of Shona women who know each other well. This greeting, much less formal than the somewhat stiff and conventional "*mangwanani*" greeting, involved the two women synchronizing forearm swings, their palms then meeting in a loud single clap followed by a firm lasting grasp. All the while, the women would smile broadly and laugh and vocalize in a bright Shona sing-song greeting, whose words remained unintelligible to me during my entire stay in Zimbabwe. Taking mental note of the nurses' meeting and greeting, I entered the clinic, crawling over the queue of waiting patients to take my place in a spacious, well-lit room, surrounded on two sides by the brilliant foliage of the hospital grounds.

While the actual day-to-day work was becoming more familiar and I was getting used to the place, the greeting of the two nurses reminded me that I was still an outsider. I did not comprehend the words spoken by the two women, but I did understand the bond—the warmth, a familiarity bordering on intimacy—between them and how such solidarity among women kept the country running, just as these nurses kept the hospital humming. As a man and a *marungu*, I knew that I would never be able to fully participate as an insider in their world. But my curiosity was piqued. Even if I could just skate on the edge of their world, I could learn very much about another culture and myself. I was fueled by the novelty of the place, but I knew that I would need to get my bearings straight before I would feel as comfortable settling into that culture as I did easing into that corner office.

I had been on the job a little more than a month and was gradually beginning to sort out the nuances of the mad, mad, mad, mad world of psychopathology in a culture that I barely understood. My mind may have been blinded by my experience of having lived in America for the previous thirty-three years. Unlearning cultural assumptions did not happen overnight.

My consulting room functioned as a master bedroom in its previous incarnation. On sunny days, when the windows were flung open to let in the calls of birds and the breeze, bees would often venture in from their feeding on sunflowers to check on the proceedings. On those days, the sweet scents of flowering jacaranda and honeysuckle filled the room.

My junior colleagues did not fare so well in their clinic assignments. In descending order of seniority, they interviewed patients in a cramped bedroom, a very small windowed porch, and a windowless closet. In the kitchen, psychiatric nurses bustled about in their starched whites with the business of directing patients and dispensing medications. In the spirit of self-reliance, we were our own pharmacy. It was my great good fortune to work with Sister Mada, who, though on the young side, ran the show at the clinic, supervising several student nurses and nurse's aides every day. Her body short and solid, her hair trying to bust out of her starched white nurse's cap, Sister Mada was low-key and quietly confident. She did not ruffle easily, which was important because some of the strangest things imaginable can happen when dozens of mentally ill patients from all over Zimbabwe stuff themselves into a falling-down house.

On the days that we were fully staffed with five doctors, the most junior of the physicians would sit on a bench outside the clinic, under the spreading branches of an acacia tree, practicing true "outpatient" psychiatry. I sometimes examined patients under the shade of this tree as well and occasionally would see wheelchair-bound patients (no federally mandated wheelchair access in this clinic) who had been fetched from the main hospital or driven from a rural clinic hours away.

Many Zimbabweans arrived on the clinic's doorstep with entreaties and appeals for an official letter, which had to be written on Ministry of Health letterhead and copiously rubber-stamped to obtain reduced school fees, to apply for money from the government, to receive a pension, to get free food, and so on. These petitions accurately reflected the general sense of desperation pandemic among Zimbabwe's legions of impoverished citizens. These people weren't sneaky or nasty in their requests, but they could be relentlessly persistent.

Others arrived at the Harare Psychiatric Unit to be evaluated by a government psychiatrist—a "specialist consultant" in the parlance of the Ministry of Health—for very specific purposes. Workers were sent by employers for disability evaluations; temporarily disabled police officers and soldiers were sent by commanding officers for an assessment of "fitness to return to duty"; students were sent by headmasters for school reports; perpetrators and victims of crime were sent by judges for court reports. Naturally, these solicitations, legitimate and otherwise, made me feel like a wholly inadequate and ill-prepared judge, a naked Solomon. On the other hand, not knowing what sort of inscrutable situation or bizarre case might drop into my sphere of responsibility in search of a solution on a day-to-day basis was a truly exhilarating feeling.

My most difficult cases involved the performance of court evaluations of mentally retarded girls who allegedly had been raped. My first such case was that of D.C., a twelve-year-old girl from the Midlands province, a four-hour bus ride away. She came to the clinic accompanied by her mother and the investigating police officer from around the town of Kwe Kwe. They had arrived in Harare on Tuesday and boarded at the police station until Thursday morning when I held my clinic. All that trouble to see me for twenty minutes. Once I understood their inconvenience and noted the absolute lack of complaining, I felt somewhat shamed and humbled. Entitled to no special treatment, they had to line up on the bench like everyone else—first come, first served. Knowing their situation, I acted respectfully and gave them my full, albeit brief, attention.

The Zimbabwe Republic Police (ZRP) officer knocked on the door and walked in first. He was dressed in the ZRP trademark olive green shirt, khaki shorts, and olive green socks pulled nearly up to his knees. The long-suffering mother, looking worn out, came in next. She wore a multicolored bandanna on her head, in the tradition of a rural woman, and smiled shyly, as her teeth were in poor repair. D.C., wearing a threadbare flower dress, probably her nicest piece of clothing, came in third, nearly hiding behind her mother. She was obviously neurologically impaired, walking with a stiff-legged spastic gait, her arms rigid and jack-knifed toward her body, showing a bit of drool from the corner of her mouth. She was very likely the victim of a lack of oxygen to her brain at the time of her birth. It was doubtful that she attended school. She probably stayed at home under the watchful eye of her mother and did a few simple chores under supervision. The officer and I exchanged full greetings before he handed me an envelope bearing the imprint of the provincial magistrate who was requesting my evaluation.

I was confused. On a minute-by-minute basis, I had to reinvent the wheel in Zimbabwe. I could usually figure out what people needed. But this one had me stumped. What could the courts possibly want from me? What could I do for this unfortunate girl? I read the paperwork: "In the matter of the Republic of Zimbabwe versus Mr. Criminal the court decrees that a mental evaluation be done of the alleged victim by a fully qualified specialist consultant psychiatrist no later than 1 June 1994 for the purposes of the adjudication of the aforesaid case and setting of possible penalties under the extent of the law of the Republic of Zimbabwe." The decree went on—blah, blah, blah. I remained stumped. Okay, I can tell you that the girl is retarded, but do they really need a fully qualified specialist consultant such as myself to offer up that lofty opinion? I went to seek help.

"Excuse me, officer, I will be right back." The three looked at me a little funny but said nothing as I left the room. I took the papers with me down the hallway, of course crawling over the clot of humanity patiently waiting their turn. I carted my big *marungu* self all the way to the kitchen. Sister Mada was in the midst of teaching the student nurses.

"So sorry to interrupt, Sister Mada," I said.

"*Mangwanani*, Dr. Linde."

"Do I have to *mangwanani* you again since we already *mangwanani*'d earlier?"

"No, but I thought it would be nice."

"Okay, *tamuka*."

"*Tamuka*."

"Sister, let me show you this paper. I have this mentally handicapped girl back there with her mother and a ZRP officer."

"Yes, Doctor, I saw them."

"Well, what am I supposed to do for them?"

"A mental evaluation for the court."

"Yes, yes, I figured as much, but what do they really want? Do they want me to comment on the girl's capacity to testify in court?"

"I don't know, *chiremba*. But I do know they want you to determine if she is a moron, imbecile, or idiot."

"What did you say, Sister?"

"Moron, imbecile, or an idiot."

"What? Do you still use those terms here?"

"No, we don't, but the courts do."

"Why do they need to know?"

"Well, the more mentally handicapped the girl is, then the longer the prison sentence."

"Aha! I got it. Thank you, Sister Mada."

I hustled back to my consulting room. I remembered from my reading of the history of psychiatry that the term *moron* is reserved for mild mental retardation, *imbecile* for moderate, and *idiot* for severe. I still couldn't believe that the court only wanted that information. I also assumed that they wanted some kind of opinion about whether the girl had the capacity to testify in court.

I returned to my desk and looked at the papers again. I started by asking questions of the mother to determine the girl's approximate developmental age. Since neither the mother nor the girl spoke any English, I utilized a student nurse to act as interpreter. Did she ever go to school? No. How many words can she say? Maybe fifty. Can she dress herself? Partly. Can she wash herself? No. Can she say the letters of the alphabet? No. Does she recognize all of her relatives? Yes. I also inquired about her sleep, appetite, and overall behavior to try to determine if she had developed a case of depression or post-traumatic stress disorder (PTSD) in addition to the mental handicap. The mother could not identify any major behavioral changes in her daughter, who sat quietly on a bench, sitting very close to her mother, rocking slightly.

"*Mangwanani*," I offered to the girl, giving her a smile and lowering my voice. She said nothing but did look at me with a timid smile. She began rocking a bit more and looked away. Clearly, this young girl was in the moderately retarded range, probably just a tad above the severe range. There was no way she could testify in court.

"Hi, my name is Dr. Linde. Do you know why you're here?" The questions got rapidly translated into Shona.

"*Aiwa*." No.

"It's because that bad man hurt you. Do you remember?"

"*Aiwa*," she said softly and shyly.

I asked her no further questions. "*Tatenda chaizvo*," I said with a smile. I certainly had plenty of information to report on her level of mental handicap and her ability to testify, which was none. I hoped the police had a good case to convict the assailant—with physical evidence, perhaps, or witnesses, even better.

In these cases, I found myself using situational ethics, figuring out what made the most sense, to conduct the interview, make a decision, and write a report. In my mind, because rape is detestable, rape of a minor downright execrable, and rape of a mentally retarded minor pure evil, I figured, why not help throw the book at the rapist? I would always get information from the accompanying officer (who often was the arresting and investigating police officer involved with the case) to discover just how strong the case was, either with or without the girl's testimony. So, if the case was quite strong (with some combination of a confession, reliable witnesses, and physical evidence), I would err on the side of recommending that the girl not be asked to testify so as to spare her the experience.

I turned to the ZRP officer and asked: "Were you the investigating officer on this case?"

"Yes, *chiremba*."

"When did the alleged rape occur?"

"November of 1993."

"Ouch, that's a long time ago. Do you have a good case?"

"No, *chiremba*, unfortunately not. The rape was not reported for two weeks. The mother thought the bleeding was the girl's first period."

"So, no physical evidence. Any witnesses?"

"Regrettably, *chiremba*, there were none. The state's case is very weak. But the alleged perpetrator is already behind bars for the rape of another girl that was proven in court."

I thought to myself, "What a waste of time." But at least the girl would be protected for now from the alleged perpetrator, who likely raped her. Each of these cases carried a different twist. I eventually became accustomed to jotting down a page or so of my commonsensical musings to be hand-carried back to some judge in a rural backwater. So, for the sake of the court, I would have to write something like "D.C. is a twelve-year-old girl who is an alleged victim of sexual assault who was interviewed by myself today. By history and examination, she demonstrates signs and symptoms of a moderate level of mental retardation, which, for purposes of the court, would put her in the range of an imbecile. There is no evidence of a current major depression or other mental illness. Her capacity to testify is severely diminished due to her markedly reduced level of intellectual and cognitive functioning."

I hated writing those antiquated dehumanizing terms like imbecile, but I came to enjoy the challenge of making at least a creditable assessment in fifteen or twenty minutes with the pressure of thirty people waiting behind the door. I wrote my reports longhand on a piece of cheap tablet paper and made at least two copies underneath with carbon paper. I would stamp the bejeesus out of the envelope and letter to make it look suitably official and hand it to the officer. I was never really sure if what I wrote made a shred of difference in those bizarre cases, but I was bound and determined to do what I thought was right. After sending D.C., her mother, and the polite ZRP officer back on their way to Kwe Kwe, I opened the door for my next patient.

While the work was certainly stressful, it was never boring. About two hundred patients arrived each week on the doorstep of the clinic, which probably resembled many others throughout the third world with its chaos and overcrowding. Nearly all black and mostly poor, many of the patients seen there had traveled halfway across the country by a grinding, smoke-spewing "chicken" bus—so-called because some passengers bring chickens to sell at the nearest market—only to wait several hours to meet with a psychiatrist for maybe five or ten minutes.

My mission was clearly scripted: to treat the seriously mentally ill—those unfortunate individuals with schizophrenia, manic-depressive illness, depression, and serious anxiety disorders. After expending plenty of time, money, and effort learning conventional American medicine, I needed to deprogram myself from its reliance on deductive reasoning to solve medical problems while in Zimbabwe. I needed to unlock my intuitive mind, opening it to the mysterious realms of subculture and spirituality in order to work as a psychiatrist in this new culture. I didn't have to junk those four years of medical school and another four years of psychiatric residency. I prescribed medications, performed physical examinations, and made accurate diagnoses as per the fourth edition of the American Psychiatric Association's *Diagnostic and Statistical Manual of Mental Disorders* (*DSM-IV*). But to go to Zimbabwe and simply apply *DSM-IV* and the American medical worldview would have been naive and inaccurate.

Instead, I needed to feel the pulse of the culture, its underbeats driven by a belief in the Spirit World. I felt that vibe every day at the P.U. I loved the madness and the muddle and the nearly biblical scene of the P.U. I grew up in a culture long on reserve, influenced by freezing winters and the religions of northern Europe—Catholicism and Protestantism. Minnesotans are not known for their extroversion. I felt almost addicted to the buzz of energy. On a gut level, I was beginning to feel revitalized by the vigor, both pathological and productive, that was in residence at the P.U. alongside the doctors, nurses, patients, brick, mortar, chain-link fencing, trees, weeds, and dust. I did not realize just how much I was craving new supplies of existential force when I stepped off the continent of North America several months earlier. I could especially feel the African pulse of life on clinic days as I witnessed the chaos of the hallway where patients waited and waited on the bench to see me.

First-come, first-served. No set appointment times. The earnest, the destitute, the sociopathic, the drooling, the demoralized, the euphoric—all had to wait their turn while crammed and jammed onto a hard wooden bench in a cramped hallway of the clinic.

Many of these folks carried meager belongings and wore shabby clothes while clutching ragtag medical records—

scribblings on tattered, flimsy, five-by-seven scraps of cardboard often marked by other elements of life. Stained by cooking oil. Spattered with blood—human, chicken, or otherwise. Burned on the edges by kerosene lamps or cooking fires. The cards were often disintegrating, crumbling from years of being inserted into bras, pockets, and handbags. Industrious men seeking refills of abusable substances often conveniently had "lost" or "forgotten" their cards.

The hospital notes documenting the inpatient admissions to the P.U. were not much more reliable. Saved, but not organized, the records were merely stacks of papers, many with illegible comments written on them, stuffed helter-skelter into eight-by-eleven manila envelopes. These envelopes were marked with the patients' names but were not organized by medical record numbers or dates of birth. They were filed by alphabetical means, sort of, according to a patient's surname.

The patients who came to the outpatient clinic consistently demonstrated beatific levels of patience that I have never witnessed anywhere, at any time while living or working in the United States. Nobody cut in line except for those patients who unknowingly created a ruckus fueled by their own psychosis or mania. Like the Red Sea in the time of Moses, the queue parted for such patients. These line jumpers were sanctioned by the waiting masses, most of whom had developed a keen sense of the maintenance of general tranquility. They would rather wait longer than see the house figuratively blown up by a rollicking manic patient. In ten months of working in that clinic, I never heard anyone complain, save for the deteriorating and escalating manic patients. In fact, in Zimbabwe excessive complaining is considered to be a sign of relapsing psychotic illness, whereas in America it is a normal and even valued behavior.

Strident assertiveness is considered socially inappropriate within mainstream Shona culture. Excessive civility must always be maintained. Africans are steadfast and patient, sometimes to the point of passivity and self-denigration. By contrast, "having it your way" and not getting pushed around are nearly cardinal virtues for most Americans.

Allow a few simple statistics and math to write the equation of mental health treatment in Zimbabwe—too few psychiatrists plus too many disturbed people equals insanity. Schizophrenia is thought to afflict 1 percent of the worldwide populace. With more than ten million people, then, Zimbabwe would conservatively be home to more than one hundred thousand citizens ill with schizophrenia. With just ten psychiatrists practicing in Zimbabwe, each psychiatrist is statistically responsible for taking care of more than ten thousand individuals with schizophrenia at any one time. And that's not to mention the tens of thousands suffering from other major mental illnesses in Zimbabwe, only a fraction of whom made their way to my outpatient clinic.

Major mental illness cuts across all cultures. In due time, I became more astute and efficient in practicing psychiatry in a foreign land. It was not difficult for me to quickly recognize severely disturbed behavior within my Zimbabwean patients. Amazingly enough, or maybe not, acutely psychotic people in Zimbabwe appear very similar to those in San Francisco. They look agitated, restless, and anxious; they are sometimes violent and disinhibited. They suffer from disorganized thoughts, delusions, and hallucinations. The content of the symptoms, however, is very much different in the two different cultures and reflects the day-to-day experiences of the people. For example, Zimbabweans do not report hearing auditory hallucinations of Jesus Christ, rather they report hearing those of their ancestor spirits. They are not paranoid about the FBI, rather they are paranoid about witches and sorcerers. Slowly, I became more intrigued by the importance of the Spirit World to the Shona people.

The mentally ill in Zimbabwe are seriously stigmatized, particularly because they are thought to be the victims of witchcraft and, in some ways, the Shona people see that type of spiritual illness as contagious. Most Shona people, including the vast majority of Shona medical students, keep their distance from mentally ill patients. This goes a long way toward explaining the dearth of Shona psychiatrists—at the time I worked in Zimbabwe, of the ten or so psychiatrists working there at the time, only one was Shona.

What to make of this? The answer came one day when a medical student with the surname of Mugabe delicately filled me in on the Shona medical students' aversion to psychiatry. (Of course, I couldn't resist asking him whether he was related to Zimbabwe's de facto president-for-life Robert Mugabe. He offered me an unconvincing no.) The Shona medical students concurrently believed in the traditional view (that major mental illnesses are caused by witchcraft or ancestor bewitchment) and the Western perspective (that major mental illnesses are caused by a complex interplay of biological, psychological, and social factors). Guess which perspective held sway?

These medical students grew up in households in which spiritual models of illness were not only accepted but were embraced as the most plausible. The young Mugabe told me that he and his colleagues essentially viewed psychiatry as venturing too close to witchcraft and into realms better managed by traditional healers and the clergy. So, recruiting Shona medical students into psychiatry was made nearly impossible by the same spiritual matters and beliefs that made the practice of psychiatry for me, a Westerner, so welcoming and so interesting.

I was fascinated by the fresh possibilities of the Spirit World, whose existence is not even acknowledged by the vast majority of Americans. The Shona, on the other hand, did not consider the influences of the Spirit World to be anything other than a part of their day-to-day existence. But, over time, they had no doubt observed the potent magnetism of the Spirit World, like the awakening of a sleeping giant, and might have even seen its powers used for evil, destructive purposes by suspected witches and sorcerers. Because the Shona frequently attributed their symptoms of mental illness to bewitchments, then a psychiatrist in that culture would have to expose himself to the ample dangers of the Spirit World on a daily basis. In contrast, I had no reason to fear the Spirit World because I knew virtually nothing about it.

While my clinical duties at the P.U. could be hair-raising, my teaching duties posed other challenges. As a consultant psychiatrist working for the Zimbabwe Ministry of Health and an honorary lecturer at the University of Zimbabwe School of Medicine Department of Psychiatry, I would often have four to six medical students observing me.

I also supervised rotating interns and psychiatric residents who taught me far more about Shona culture than I could ever have taught them about clinical psychiatry. The workload was crushing, and in response to that, the work ethic demonstrated by the interns and residents was totally underwhelming. They often abandoned the hospital and the care of their patients by late morning. Their apparent shirking of work and slacking off made for a very poor comparison with the nurses in Zimbabwe, who were mostly dedicated and highly disciplined in caring for patients and teaching students.

How could this be? In the United States, the interns and residents were the last to leave the hospital, motivated by a desire to learn as much as possible and to take scrupulous care of their patients. In stark contrast, the junior doctors in Zimbabwe appeared to lack the same interest and dedication. I eventually discovered, however, that the African doctors were indeed industrious and hardworking, albeit dedicated to a different cause than their American counterparts.

Nearly every clinic day, I would suffer the loss of one or more residents by midmorning teatime. It took my American mind quite a while to even become accustomed to teatime. I will never forget the first time that the deferential orderly in the blue coveralls knocked on my consulting room door with a tray of creamed tea in chipped yellow pots and clumped sugar in lime-green plastic bowls. I was absolutely flabbergasted that nurses and doctors alike would take a half-hour break while our huddled masses waited like the patron saints of the Middle Ages on the benches in the hallway, among a vapor of strong body odor.

Not knowing I was committing a bone-headed *faux pas*, I refused to take a tea break on my first clinic day. When the orderly knocked on my door offering the hot beverage at about ten o'clock, I waved him off. As far as I know, the junior doctors followed my lead on that day and worked through what normally would have been the equivalent of halftime festivities for the clinic day. I thought it was utterly ridiculous to take a refreshing pause in the midmorning. I was accustomed to pushing myself through patient after patient as I had done while working at the San Francisco General Psychiatric Emergency Service. I could slam coffee from a jumbo Styrofoam cup while on the run. I felt miffed and sanctimonious.

Of course, I broke down the second day as three thirsty and expectant junior doctors invaded my spacious consulting room in the wake of the orderly who delivered the goods. Sister came with him on that day and told me flat out that I pretty much had to take tea. I felt like a hostage to a remnant of the British occupation of the state of Southern Rhodesia. Why drink tea when the country produces some of the world's best coffee near the border with Mozambique? "I don't even like tea," I thought. "What was wrong with these people who served their tea with a heavy portion of cream and spoonfuls of sugar?" I grumbled to myself, prisoner to the culture.

Of course, it was an important part of their daily nutrition, as I later came to find out. I finally succumbed to the idea of teatime about the third week that I was there, but I still felt a tad bit guilty enjoying conversation and tea while our patients sat nearby with nothing. I learned to like tea and came to thoroughly enjoy a midmorning oasis of time away from contemplating complicated lives and acting as a repository for tales of misfortune.

One day, long after the clinic orderly had delivered the tea to the consulting room, I got out of my chair to check on the junior doctors, since none of the three assigned to be working with me that day were present. Usually, it was like clockwork, the juniors would be piling into my room for tea right away. I crept past the hordes in the hallway and checked the first room. No junior doctor. I went down to the next room, a small closet with a desk and chair. No junior doctor. I finally went to the tiny glassed-in solarium. Aha, no junior doctor. Being a deductively inclined allopathic physician, I leaped to a logical conclusion. I was seeing that day's entire batch of battered humanity—a task that might take me until next week—all by myself if I didn't succeed in finding my damn interns or calling in some reinforcements. So I went to the kitchen to find the quintessentially reliable Sister Mada and try to figure out where my house officers went.

"*Mangwanani, chiremba.*"

"*Mangwanani,*" I replied.

"*Mamuka sei?*" asked Sister Mada.

"*Tamuka mamukawo.*"

"*Tamuka,*" finished Sister, who I was pretty damn sure I had already *mangwanani*'d that morning when I arrived.

With the greetings aside, I got down to the real business: "Sister, it's ten o'clock, where are my interns?"

"Sir?" she said, looking confused.

"Oh, that's right, the British lingo," I muttered. "Sister, where are my junior doctors? They seem to have disappeared."

"I don't know," she said.

But I knew she did. "What about Dr. Ncube?"

"She called in sick. You know she's pregnant."

"Of course. How about Dr. Chingono? That skinny guy with the glasses. I don't see much of him."

"Well, he was here for an hour or so, but told me that he had to go to the bank. He didn't say when he would be back."

"Oh, no, Sister, there are at least seventy patients who still need to be seen. I can't see them all by myself. I'm already tearing my hair out." I had forgotten about Dr. Gwanzura. "Sister, what about Dr. Gwanzura? It's not like him not to show up."

Dr. Gwanzura was a large, lumbering man with owlish spectacles who didn't say much. Already in the second month of his rotation, Dr. Gwanzura had proven to me that he was intelligent and much more reliable than the average junior doctor. I was even trying to recruit him into psychiatry.

"Oh, he was here but left about ten minutes ago. Said he would be back."

"Where did he go?" I asked.

"I don't know. I'll try to call over to the ward, to see if Dr. Suleiman can come over and see a few patients."

"*Tatenda*, Sister. I'm gonna have a quick cup o' tea and get back to work." Swearing under my breath, I glumly returned to my room, brushing legs with the tired, the poor, the hungry, the certifiably insane who waited to see me, the bigshot *marungu*, the *bwana* specialist consultant who held court in the equivalent of the clinic's corner office.

Well, Dr. Suleiman, God bless him, did show up and saw about forty patients in three hours. I stumbled through the other thirty over the next four hours, not quite getting the hang of things yet. As I wrote out the last prescription, I hand-carried the card to the kitchen, where Sister Mada worked alone at this relatively late time of day.

"So, Sister, how often does that happen?" I asked. "No junior doctors? If it weren't for Suleiman, I would have been dead."

"Oh, I don't know, Dr. Linde. All I can say is that it is a problem here in Zimbabwe. The problem is not new."

"Well, I'll have to talk to those guys on Thursday—if they show up, that is. *Tichaoanana*, Sister. See you tomorrow. I'll be doing ward rounds."

"*Fambai zvakanaka, chiremba.*"

"*Chisarai.*"

So, Thursday rolled around. I figured I would have to get to these docs early in the day, before they took off, if they showed up at all. I arrived at the clinic at eight-fifteen, a little earlier than usual. There, I spied Dr. Gwanzura making his way up the dirt path to the clinic with his head down, his glasses off. He was rubbing his eyes with his right hand. He looked tired.

I caught up with him. "*Mangwanani*, Dr. Gwanzura."

"*Mangwanani*, Dr. Linde."

"*Marara sei* (mah-RAH-rah say)?" How did you sleep? I asked.

"*Tarara mararawo* (tah-RAH-rah mah-RAH-rah-wo)." We slept well if you slept well, he replied.

"*Tarara*," I said. I often skipped the formalities and plunged right in, just like a good American, I suppose. But, according to the niceties of the culture, even when you're going to give somebody a verbal whipping, you have to stumble through the mandatory greeting. Anxious to complete this task and set things right, I wasted little time then in getting to the point. "So, Dr. Gwanzura, I missed you on Monday."

"Sir?"

"Oh, come on, Dr. Gwanzura, you were gone by teatime on Monday. We still had seventy patients to see. Dr. Suleiman had to come over and pick up your slack."

"I can explain."

"Oh, I'm sure you can."

"I had an appointment at ten-thirty downtown that I had to make."

"Why didn't you tell me?" I said. Going off was not really my specialty, but this situation had made me angry.

"Because, well, because I thought you wouldn't release me."

"So, instead you just snuck off, away from here, thinking I wouldn't notice you were gone at teatime?"

"I'm sorry. You're right." Tall for a Shona man, at six-foot-one, and husky at probably 190 pounds, Dr. Gwanzura wore a white dress shirt that was a little too tight and yellowed. His shoes were coated with red dust and needed polishing. He hung his head and stood in front of me, saying nothing.

"So, what was this appointment that was so important?" I asked.

"Well, it was not really an appointment at all. I was going to work."

"But you already have a job. What do you mean, going to work?"

" I was going to work for a G.P. To make money for my family."

I knew that his house officer's salary was solid, tending towards lofty, according to Zimbabwean standards. Thinking he was referring to his wife and infant son when he mentioned his family, I tore into him pretty good. "How greedy are you? Do you want a Mercedes, like all the government ministers? You mean you can't support your wife and baby on your house officer's salary?"

"Oh, yes, Dr. Linde," said Dr. Gwanzura, his eyes looking downcast onto the dirt pathway before he raised them to look me in the eye. "But, you see, I have to pay school fees for my brothers and sisters, clothes for my nieces and nephews, and mealie meal for my cousins." (Mealie meal is ground corn, which is mixed with water and cooked to make *sadza.*)

"Oh," I said, a dim bulb igniting in my brain. "So when you say family, you really mean your extended family—uncles, aunts, siblings, nieces, nephews, cousins."

"Yes, it's more than thirty people total who count on my salary."

"Okay, I understand. You're the big breadwinner."

"Sir?"

"You have to provide for everybody," I said, explaining my American colloquialism. "I'm sorry I got mad at you." I felt guilty, falling prey to the stereotype of bemoaning those "lazy Africans," assuming initially that the Shona doctors were just avoiding work. Never a simple answer. "Well, could you at least start your moonlighting in the afternoon so you can get your work done around here? You still have an obligation to your training and to these patients."

"Yes, Dr. Linde."

"Now, get to work. If you have questions, let me know. See you at tea."

The reality, as I came to understand, is that the junior doctors were not lazy skivers at all, but rather the opposite. Dr. Gwanzura's situation was typical. Shona doctors often worked round the clock to take financial care of a large extended family. Whereas in American culture, doctors, like most people, are most likely to be working for their own or their immediate family's gain, in the Shona culture the first allegiance is to the extended family.

I did my best to enforce basic attendance until noon at both ward rounds and the clinic. Although the quality of the junior doctors' work was sometimes questionable, I could never question the quantity of it. They had often buzzed through twenty patients in the time that I took to finish six or seven. At the end of the clinic day, it was always a relief to walk out of my fabulous, well-appointed office and see that the long passage of the hall was gloriously empty. After a hectic morning, I found the silence to be a soothing tonic.

The vestiges of British colonialism, with its civilities of teatime and unfailing politeness by all parties, coupled with the average African's easygoing attitude made for a generally pleasant experience at work. Before leaving the clinic, I always checked in with the faithful Sister Mada as she dispensed the last of the day's tablets from the kitchen-cum-pharmacy, hoping that there were no catastrophes brewing. Not usually. Most days at the clinic, by the early afternoon, I was free to go visit my colleagues over at the medical school and catch up on some journal articles in the library. Or else, I could go home to write in my journal, read a book, take a snooze, go for a walk, drink a beer, eat some food—activities undertaken to recharge my emotional and intellectual batteries so that I could come again to take on the challenges of another day.

CHAPTER FOUR

"He Brought the Virus Home."

Esther Mawena: The Bride Price, a Death Sentence

"But there comes a day, there always comes a day of tears and madness."

—Saul Bellow
Henderson the Rain King

Winter had arrived in the Southern Hemisphere and the mornings were chilly, causing even this native Minnesotan to wear a light jacket to work. In June and July, I needed to keep the windows of my consulting room closed. And on the coldest mornings, Sister Mada would plug in an electric space heater for me before my arrival. Little did she know that I was an inveterate sweater who switched the heater off nearly immediately, preferring a cool draft from the poorly insulated windows. The foliage on display outside the glass was intensely green and tangled, even though the rains had ceased in April.

As I hurried to finish the paperwork from my last patient, the student nurse rose to open the door for the next one—a robust, pretty, dark-skinned young woman. She entered the room and said nothing before she performed a shallow curtsy of sorts, clapping her hands together twice, lightly, to greet me in the traditional way: "*Masikati* (ma-SCOT-tee)." Good afternoon.

The woman stood quietly over me as I scrawled a note on a piece of brown tablet paper. I did not know then that she would instruct me about three painful realities of her own life and life in general during those times in Zimbabwe. She would teach me not only about depression and suicide but also about the sorry state of affairs for the average woman in Zimbabwe, and, most tragically, about the destruction of lives and families from the AIDS virus.

I replied, "*Masikati, maswera sei* (mah-SQUARE-ah say)?" Good afternoon. How have you spent the day?

She said, "*Taswera* (tah-SQUARE-ah)." We have spent the day well.

"*Taswera*."

Upon delivering the daily greetings, the Shona people traditionally use the "we" form of personal pronoun. An individual Shona person's use of the word "we" rather than "I" during the day-to-day greetings personifies the Shona value of the community taking precedence over the individual. Within Shona culture, one person is considered next-to-nothing when compared to the family or village as a whole.

She did not look like a typical P.U. patient in that she did not suffer the characteristic drooling and stiff gait of a person hit upside the head by 600 milligrams of Thorazine each day. She wore a faded yellow dress, its hem ending demurely about midcalf, and a loose-fitting chocolate brown pullover with holes in the elbows. She wore no makeup and her hair, close-shaven without fancy braids, was covered by a blue cotton headcloth. Her attire and manner were reminiscent of a middle-aged rural woman, though she was obviously quite young.

"Come in, have a seat," I said.

She handed me her record card—a single five-by-seven piece of cardboard, which was neatly folded in half. The heading of a paragraph of writing was rubber-stamped "OBS AND GYN, HARARE CENTRAL HOSPITAL." Tight loops of blue ink, sparse but legible, told a tale in telegraphic form, likely spooling from the hand of an obstetrical registrar:

22-6-94

"Post-op check, day #4. 20 y.o. female, G3P2SAB1, s/p D and C of 12-week-by-dates fetus for fetal demise post-ingestion chloroquine #30 tabs on 7-7. Gastric lavage and charcoal in Casualty. Cleared. D and C per Dr. Madamombe on 10-7.

Hx: Spotting decreasing. No pain. Exam: Uterus soft. Internal WNL. Contraception none. Crying. Troubles at home. Refer to P.U."

The woman's name was Esther Mawena. Reading between the lines, it was safe to surmise that Esther had taken an overdose of chloroquine, antimalarial pills that were cheap and available over the counter in Zimbabwe, possibly out of desperation from dealing with "troubles at home." The overdose had induced a miscarriage of what would have been her third child. After getting her stomach pumped in the emergency room, she was sent home. She returned three days later for a dilation of her cervix and curettage of her uterus to remove parts of the dead fetus in order to prevent ongoing bleeding that may have been life threatening to her. From a physical standpoint, Esther was recovering well. Of course, she would use no contraception since Esther and her husband were planning a family of six children or more, as was the custom in the Shona culture.

The registrar astutely and wisely referred her for an evaluation of depression and suicide risk. If only I could write such brief and telegraphic notes, distilling the pathos and angst of those who passed through my consulting room.

Esther attended her appointment alone, which was strange. Who was caring for her children? Who was helping her? Did she have no sister, no aunt, no mother to escort her to finish up this unpleasant business?

"Did anyone come with you today?" I began.

"Yes, my aunt, my mother's sister, is waiting for me by the bus stop. She did not want to come here with me."

"Where are the rest of your cards?" I asked, knowing that details of her medical treatment for the overdose of chloroquine as well as the details of her two previous labors and deliveries and any other pediatric history of her own were to be found on similar cards.

She paused and stared downward into her lap, where her hands were tightly folded and pressing on her knees. "I didn't bring them." The beginning of furrowed worry lines radiated out from the corners of her eyes, which were ringed with darkened circles. They looked puffy and red from crying. "The doctor sent me here."

"Where are you from?"

"Domboshawa," said Esther sheepishly, her eyes glued to her lap. I knew the place as a popular day-trip destination for the citizens of Harare. Twenty-five kilometers northeast of Harare, the village of Domboshawa was surrounded by a landscape of rolling hillsides punctuated by boulders the size of circus tents and bigger.

The area was renowned among members of Harare's expatriate community as a pleasant place to go hiking, the exertion buying one the right to drink "sundowners" with friends—sipping chilled South African Chardonnay or knocking off a few ice-cold Zambezi beers in the twilight of a backwater Sunday evening.

However, the village of Domboshawa, with its collection of *rondavaals* (ubiquitous circular African huts made of wood, straw, and mud) and *kraals* (rickety cattle enclosures) and its harboring of traditional Shona ways, could have passed for a village in the hinterlands of Zimbabwe at the turn of the twentieth century. Valuable currency in the agrarian Shona culture, cows, called *mamombe* (mah-MOME-bay), wandered about the streets. Stick-thin vendors sold matches and cigarettes and sweet candies from cardboard boxes along the roadside. Thrown-together tin shacks alternated with proper huts. A gravel road, intersecting the village and leading out of town toward the bush, soon petered out into a rutted track.

Apropos of nothing at the time, I remembered a declaration, "there's spirits in those stones," made by a drunken African hitchhiker one Sunday evening as I drove him back to Harare from Domboshawa. The gallons of *chibuku*, Zimbabwe's commercial version of traditional beer, that he no doubt had swilled at a "beer drink" that afternoon, made his lips a little looser to share the secrets of the Shona culture with a *marungu*. He went on to tell me about the festive spirits who pound ritual drums from the afterlife that can be heard on the mountaintop nearby if one believes and listens fervently enough.

In contrast to my walk-on role as a day-tripper to Domboshawa, my daily turn as a consultant psychiatrist at the P.U. allowed me entry into the worlds of dozens of Shona people who came to the clinic for help. Prying for good reason, I needed the information and an understanding of Shona culture to perform my work. With Esther I found myself in a common on-the-job predicament. Simply put, I had a million questions for Esther and only fifteen or twenty minutes available to ask them. Nevertheless, I felt an obligation to try and steady her a bit before I plunged into the more difficult queries.

"Did you grow up there?"

"Yes, my family has always lived there—from the times of my father's father's father."

"Do you have brothers and sisters?"

"Yes."

"How many?"

"Nine."

I involuntarily said "wow" before asking, "And where do you fall in the family?"

"Eldest daughter, second oldest to my elder brother."

"Are you married?"

"Yes."

"How many children do you have?"

"Two."

"And how old are they?"

"The boy is two-and-a-half and the girl, the girl just turned one."

"What are their names?"

"The boy's name is Tafara and the girl's name is . . . " Her voice caught at this point. She collected herself. "The girl's name is Rudo." Esther closed her eyes tightly, her attempt to stanch the flow unsuccessful; her face beginning to twitch, heralding a waterfall of sadness.

Children were named in Zimbabwe with particular meaning. Tafara, which means "we are happy" in Shona, and Rudo, which means "mercy," were this family's public declaration of joy and love and optimism at receiving these children from a benevolent universe. I wondered what happened. I had only minutes to find out.

I handed Esther a rough tissue, really a piece of paper towel from the loo. "What kind of a psychiatrist didn't carry

Kleenex with him," I thought to myself. And its neurotic corollary: "What kind of a psychiatrist makes his patients cry?" The student nurse, a girl in her late teens, handed the grief-stricken woman her pressed white handkerchief.

I cleared my throat, looked down at the disheveled stack of papers on my desk, and lowered my voice before speaking, "I can see that you're feeling sad. What is it about?"

"It's, it's about my children. What if I had died? Who would have cared for them? They would have been outcasts, haunted by my family's spirits."

Though her answer generated many more questions, I needed to get to the nuts and bolts of this interview before, time permitting, I could follow up on the spiritual matters of the case. "When you took those tablets, were you intending to kill yourself?"

The tears came harder now. "Yes, yes, I am no good to my husband anymore. My father says I have brought disgrace to the family. I am nothing. At the time, I thought that my leaving this world would have been for the best. But now I know, my children need me."

"When you say you're 'no good to your husband anymore' what do you mean?"

"He says that I have brought illness into our family."

"What do you mean?" A sick feeling was forming in the pit of my stomach as I was almost sure that this was going to be a tragic scenario that I had, until now, only heard about.

"Rudo is sick. Poor girl. She has stopped gaining weight, she has diarrhea all the time, a rash and a cough that won't go away. I took her to the doctor last month and the doctor told me it might be AIDS. She wanted to test the baby. Well, I didn't really think through it at the time. I was so worried about Rudo. I told the doctor, of course, we need to know what's wrong with Rudo. The test came back positive."

I asked the next question in vain. "Did the baby ever receive a blood transfusion?"

Esther's hands clasped even more tightly as she stared at them before she answered. "No."

My worst fears were confirmed: Esther had HIV.

She went on: "I was desperate. The doctor took me aside, into a small office away from the clinic. She asked me if I knew what it meant. I did. She asked me to get tested to confirm it. What else could I do? I did it for my children. Tafara was tested also. Thank God, he came up negative."

"Does your husband know?"

"We told him that night. I told him that the doctor wanted him to get tested. He refused. He was very angry. After the children went to sleep, he rose his voice against me and threatened to beat me to teach me a lesson."

"Did he beat you?"

Looking downward once again and pausing, she said, "No, no, he did not."

What could I do but accept her answer at face value for the moment? "He accused me of having an affair with an old boyfriend of mine. Then I became angry and spoke harsh words to him, demanding that he get tested. He refused. He left to speak with my father. He did not return that night. He most likely went to sleep with one of his girlfriends." This last statement was said not with a hiss, as you might expect, but rather with a sigh of resignation.

I had heard about this type of scenario from my wife. As a consultant pediatrician on the wards and in the clinic of Harare Central Hospital, she estimated that 50 percent of the children admitted to the hospital were known or very likely to be HIV-positive. On average, five children died every day at the hospital—some from malnutrition and other infectious diseases but most of them from AIDS.

So day in and day out, she would encounter situations like Esther's.

A mother would bring in her baby and give a sickeningly familiar history: "I don't know what's wrong with him, *chiremba*." It's a history detailed with variations on a theme, none of them reassuring. "My baby won't eat; my baby has stopped gaining weight; my baby suffers constant diarrhea; my baby is always sick with a cold; my baby has lumps all over his body; my baby has a weak cry; my baby has a hot body every day; my baby breathes too fast. My baby just lies there. The life has gone out of my baby's eyes."

The pediatrician hopes against hope that the baby is suffering from some other tragic but treatable malady. What an ironic predicament it is for a physician: to hope that your patient has pneumonia, tuberculosis, malaria, malnutrition, infectious diarrhea, anemia, even leukemia, something, anything that you have a chance to forestall, to reverse, to cure.

So my wife would hope against hope. But when the examination of a baby shows signs of muscle wasting, swollen lymph nodes, fungal infection in the mouth, fast breathing, listlessness, or overwhelming rashes, oftentimes drawing the blood and sending it to the lab is just a grisly formality. The test is done to confirm a diagnosis of tragedy, the ramifications rippling destructively throughout the baby's family.

When the results come back positive, it often foretells the obliteration of a family. The baby could only have gotten the infection from one place—Mom—with the transmission of HIV occurring vertically—that is, from mother to baby either through the placenta during the pregnancy or, more likely, at the time of delivery. During the delivery, the mother's body fluids—amniotic fluid, blood, sometimes urine and feces—make contact with the baby as the baby hurtles through the birth canal and is thrown into the world. Where mama got her HIV is not much of a secret in Shona society. It nearly always means one thing—not that the mother has been out screwing around, but that papa has been out sowing his seed and then has brought home a tragic present for his wife and baby in the form of HIV.

I looked at my watch and envisioned the masses outside my door, sitting on my bench. I knew that many of them were here specifically to see me, a consultant psychiatrist, for a variety of reasons. I knew I couldn't polish off this interview in fifteen minutes. I pressed on.

"What happened next?"

"My father and mother came to my house just after sunrise the next day. My father took no note that my husband was not there. My mother started to come up to me to give me a hug, to hold my hand. My father grabbed her and said in a loud voice, 'Woman! Not now! It's my turn!' He yelled at me and told me how I had brought disgrace to the family.

"I fell to my knees, my eyes staring only at the ground. I told him, '*Ndino urombo, vasekuru* (in-DEE-no oo-ROME-boh vah-seh-KOO-roo).' I am sorry, most respected father. But he would not accept my apology. He told me how he had already paid for the services of an emergency consultation with a *n'anga* and how the *n'anga* told him that our ancestors could not rest in peace until I made amends for the trouble that I had brought to the family."

Forgetting that I was in Zimbabwe for just a moment, I asked, "But, why? Why didn't you tell him that it was your husband's affair that caused all of this? He gave you AIDS. He brought the virus home to you and Rudo."

"It doesn't work that way." Shaking her head and again clenching her hands, she looked down. Her voice lowered.

"In our families, I cannot criticize my husband to my father. My father accepted money from my husband's family. My husband's father paid a bride price to my family. He is still in debt to the moneylenders.

"I can only take the punishment," she continued. "Right away, I began to think of how I could take my life. I knew that this thought was from one of my ancestors. I considered going to a *n'anga*, but I felt the whole situation to be hopeless. *N'anga* are usually men. Why would they agree to help me?"

"So, how long had you been thinking about taking an overdose?"

"I considered other ways, but I knew that buying chloroquine would be easy and that it would probably work."

"Did you know that you were pregnant?"

"I knew. A woman knows. My periods had stopped. My milk had stopped. But I was afraid to be tested."

"Did you know that the chloroquine was likely to damage the baby?"

"I thought, I thought that I would be dead. I wanted to take the baby with me. If I knew that I would live and that I would lose the baby, I would have never taken an overdose. I would have done something more serious, like stab myself in the chest or throw myself in front of a bus."

"How do you feel about still being alive?"

"Well, things are a little better now. I am living with my aunt, my mother's eldest sister. Her children are grown. She is widowed. She lives alone on a teacher's pension. My mother's side of the family will not abandon me."

"And the children?"

"They are safe. They are with me."

I knew Esther to be lucky on this count—having a place for herself and her children. In addition to imposing a death sentence on the afflicted in Zimbabwe, HIV infection also imbues a stigma on those infected. Frequently, the infected woman's family would refuse to take her back and she would be left destitute, fending for herself on the streets, trying to make a new life for herself. And if this rejected, ostracized, and destitute woman would succumb to AIDS before her children, then the children might end up in a rudimentary orphanage. Or, worse, they could be banished to join Zimbabwe's booming number of homeless children, "street kids" who roam downtown Harare, rumored to habitually sniff spray paint or glue out of paper sacks, picking up change by begging or "guarding" parked cars. According to published studies, the estimated number of "AIDS orphans" in sub-Saharan Africa is expected to double over the next ten years if the rate of infection is left unchecked.

The disease of HIV infection in Zimbabwe, and throughout sub-Saharan Africa, is a predominantly heterosexual endemic—spread through sexual contact between adults and from mother to child in the process of labor and delivery. Because the "vertical" transmission rate from HIV-infected mother to baby is about 20 percent, four out of five AIDS orphans are free of the virus that causes AIDS and thereby sentenced to live longer than their infected siblings. Life as an AIDS orphan is, at best, extremely difficult, so a shortened life span may indeed be considered a merciful outcome.

Only recently have HIV medications, which reduce the rate of vertical transmission from mother to baby, become available to African nations. Studies—using a short course of the antiretroviral medications AZT and 3TC combined, or the medication nevirapine alone—have shown the rate of transmission to be nearly cut in half. The medications are given to a pregnant mother just prior to delivery and to the baby for a few days after birth. Unfortunately, many of those same studies have shown that the rate of HIV transmission through breast milk from mother to infant via breastfeeding is frequent enough so that, over time, the rate of HIV infection in the young children of HIV-positive mothers again approaches 20 percent.

During my time in Zimbabwe, in the mid-1990s, no effective treatment existed for AIDS. Opportunistic infections often went untreated, allowing an ill individual to pass away more quickly, theoretically putting an end to his suffering sooner. In fact, during the course of the decade, AIDS had reduced the average life expectancy in Zimbabwe from 65, one of the highest in Africa, to 39, one of the lowest. The physicians at Harare Central Hospital were getting bombarded with AIDS cases, and the fatalities piled up. AZT was too expensive and the new "triple therapies" for HIV, exceedingly expensive, were just coming out in Europe and America. Simple measures like using cheap sulfa-containing antibiotics to prevent respiratory infections were not put in place. With virtually no treatment available, the AIDS diagnosis was a death sentence soon to be inflicted on its victims by virulent infectious diseases such as tuberculosis, malaria, pneumonia, meningitis, and bacterial diarrhea. These infections would quickly overrun the depleted immune systems of those people with AIDS and, in turn, overwhelm the doctors and nurses attempting to stem the tide of disease.

Several factors may explain why Africa's rate of HIV infection is so high: Promiscuity, particularly among married men, is common. Condoms are unpopular, and, in some areas, unavailable. Up to 90 percent of prostitutes in urban Africa are infected with HIV. High rates of sexually transmitted diseases contribute to the spread of HIV because the open sores of syphilis, gonorrhea, and chancroid facilitate transmission of the virus during sexual activity. Public health infrastructures are skeletal in some African countries, many of which lack clean needles and the ability to screen banked blood for HIV. Finally, medications to treat HIV have not been available.

In addition, in Zimbabwe, certain social and cultural realities, which I observed first-hand and also heard about, contributed to a higher rate of HIV transmission. Although counterintuitive at first glance, being a married woman is a relative risk for acquiring HIV. The decline of polygamy in Zimbabwe placed young married women, like Esther Mawena, at a greater risk of infection with the virus than other women. Polygamy fell by the wayside in the 1980s and early 1990s partially because Zimbabwe's economy soured while the rate of unemployment soared. The maintenance of a polygamous lifestyle is expensive because, according to its tradition, the husband is duty-bound to financially support all of his wives and all of his children. A man has no such fiduciary responsibility to girlfriends, illegitimate children, or prostitutes. Girlfriends and prostitutes eventually replaced second and third wives as sexual partners for Shona men.

Young, single adults often have multiple sexual partners in Zimbabwe, but the bulk of promiscuity occurs between married men and girlfriends and/or prostitutes. Making matters even worse, sex is thought to be most desirable when the vagina is tight and dry, this effect often obtained by the use of one of several intravaginal herbs available on the market from your local friendly *n'anga*. Not surprisingly, a tight and dry vagina is more likely to be abraded and torn during intercourse, thereby increasing the likelihood that HIV will be transmitted during sex.

Condoms are vilified by most Zimbabwean men, contributing greatly to the infection of thousands of innocent wives and children. The prevailing line goes something like, "Who wants to eat a sweet with the wrapper on?" It would be unheard of for a married man and woman to have sex with a condom. It is also unacceptable for a married woman to use other forms of contraception, especially early in a marriage, even if these methods would prevent an HIV-infected child from being brought into the world. Zimbabwean culture puts great importance on a man siring as many children as possible, so as to have many relatives whom he can influence when, upon his death, he joins the members of the afterlife and becomes an exalted and influential ancestor spirit. Even if the wife knows of her husband's unprotected dalliances, cultural factors prohibit her from refusing to have sex with him or demanding that he wear a condom. More to the point, she may risk a thrashing.

Because of the Shona practice of paying *lobola*, a "bride price" or dowry, a husband often feels like he owns his wife. Domestic violence is commonplace, with few places for victims to turn in Zimbabwe. A husband's attitude may be that his family paid good money or donated herds of valuable cows so that he could "have" his wife and do with her as he pleases. In this way, the tradition of paying a bride price perpetuates a male-dominated society.

African countries have taken a bit of a beating in the American media for "being in denial" and ignoring the AIDS problem. To be truthful, those assertions have some merit. Throughout the 1990s, a popular theory circulating throughout Africa was that either the virus was released into Africa by malevolent Westerners or that "the white man" had made up the whole thing. Given their history of suffering at the hands of sadistic colonialists, it is not surprising that many Africans hold this view. But this does not absolve irresponsible traditional healers who tout that they had discovered a "cure" for AIDS. Nor does it exculpate those wicked types who promoted the notion that having sex with a virgin is a man's cure for AIDS.

It is true that by the mid-1990s Zimbabwe's Ministry of Health had begun condom distribution and a viable HIV education and prevention campaign. Typical of AIDS policy in Africa at the time, its emphasis was not on treatment (which was not affordable, anyway), but on prevention and education. HIV antibody testing was readily available, at least in Harare. The turnaround time for results was in the range of a week. An organization called the AIDS Counseling Trust trained putative counselors and other health-care professionals, who provided pre- and post-test counseling. Zimbabwean clinics and hospitals used clean, disposable needles, for the most part. Blood was routinely screened for HIV, at least in Harare.

But, for Esther Mawena, those preventive measures were too little, too late. They wouldn't take her HIV away and they wouldn't bring her baby back to full health. There would be no cure. Circa 1994, there would be no treatment. Through no fault of her own, Esther Mawena was in the wrong place at the wrong time with the wrong man. Her long-term fate was sealed. However, it was my job to make sure that she didn't take her short-term fate into her own hands by yet again attempting suicide.

Absorbed in hearing Esther's story to this point, I had not yet gotten to the task of fully estimating her suicide risk, which would determine whether I needed to admit her to the hospital for her own protection. With the clock ticking, I needed to move ahead.

"Have you ever tried to take your own life before this?"

"No."

"Have you ever thought about it before?"

"No, my life has always been good. Growing up, we did not have much money, but I was able to go to school and take my 'O' level examinations. We always had enough to eat. I loved my husband. I thought we had a good life."

On this note, she again started to cry. This time, she let the tears flow for a minute or more. I said, "I'm sorry you're having such a hard time." She soaked the student nurse's handkerchief. The nurse then offered Esther some toilet paper.

This was the type of situation that I hated the most while working as a psychiatrist in Zimbabwe. This woman needed more time, more counseling, a referral to a social worker, all sorts of things that I knew were unavailable to her and that, given the overriding realities of the patriarchal Shona culture and a financially overburdened Ministry of Health, she would never get.

Other than understanding this point, there wasn't much I could do. Because of the extremely high volume of patients that I saw, I really couldn't see her any more often than once a month. And because of time considerations, I could not spend forty-five minutes to an hour each week with her doing psychotherapy. And she surely could not afford to pay out of pocket to see one of the private-practice psychotherapists who had nailed up their shingles along the leafy green boulevards of Harare's affluent "low-density" suburbs.

On this day, I could only evaluate her for current suicidal risk and put the measures in place to protect her, even if that meant admitting her to the zoolike inpatient ward of the Harare Psychiatric Unit. I needed to assess her for depression and see if she could benefit from antidepressant medications. I needed to complete a semblance of a psychiatric evaluation with a whole damn bench full of people fidgeting and coughing and murmuring in the hallway outside my door, patiently waiting for their five or ten minutes of my ever-so-precious time. I also needed to chicken-scratch a note on her five-by-seven, saying enough to get the salient points across without wrecking her confidentiality, as these cards would be accessible to her husband and the rest of her family.

I sat back and only half-watched her cry, my mind wandering to the dry question of whether to call hers a case of major depression and start antidepressant medications or see it more as a reaction to severe stress, called an "adjustment disorder" in the wisdom of American psychiatric taxonomy.

Although it does not always feel authentic or morally correct, as a psychiatrist, on a moment-to-moment basis, it is my job to periscope in and out of an individual's emotions. This was one of the most difficult but useful tasks I mastered in my four years of psychiatric residency after medical school. At times, a psychiatrist needs to fully feel the emotional pain of his patients to truly understand the person. But at other times, it's more appropriate to emotionally lay back a little bit to get the job done.

This ability to surf in and out on the waves of people's feelings buffers the psychiatrist's emotions from the incredibly painful reality often on display in the interplay between psychiatrist and patient. Being there, being able to tolerate the outpouring of emotions, being able to gently dam the flood—these were important tasks, sometimes referred to as providing a "container of therapy" by psychiatric theorists. Taking the container theory a step further: If Esther Mawena's emotional suffering were allowed to fill my container completely and start spilling over the brink of my vessel, I would surely be knocked out of commission for the rest of the day. Where would that leave the members of my sardine-packed hallway queue?

She gathered herself a bit. "I'm sorry."

"No need to be. You've been through a lot. You miss your husband, I'm sure, but right now you need to be strong for yourself."

"What the hell was I saying?" I thought. That's the kind of encouragement that might fly in America, but didn't make much sense here. Or did it? I eventually learned, I think, that the self-empowerment of an individual, especially a woman in Zimbabwe's patriarchal culture, was critically essential. I regrouped. "I'm glad to hear that your aunt is supportive."

"Yes, she is. Very much so."

"Do you still think about committing suicide?"

"I'm not sure that I deserve to live, but I wouldn't do anything to hurt myself. I don't want to go through this again. And my children need me. My aunt is too old to care for them. I need to take care of myself to be there for my children, especially Rudo."

In the service of making an accurate diagnosis, which might influence my decision to prescribe or not prescribe medication, I asked Esther a number of rapid-fire questions regarding her mood, sleep, energy, appetite, hopefulness, and ability to enjoy things. I discovered that she met most of the criteria for a diagnosis of clinical depression. But, in the back of my mind, I wondered if my symptom checklist, lifted straight from the *DSM-IV*, really made any kind of sense over here in Africa. That laundry list was tested for validity and reliability in the United States, a nation with drastically different values, economic realities, traditions, cultures, and so on. Maybe what I was measuring when I asked those questions at the Harare Psychiatric Unit was only an illusion.

Maybe I should have been asking other questions, questions that I had not learned to ask as of yet in my relatively new job as a psychiatrist in Zimbabwe. Esther Mawena's symptoms may well have been transitory yet commensurate with the depth of her losses—loss of future, loss of health, loss of relationship, loss of much of her family support, and a loss of standing in her community.

I decided to hold off on the antidepressant and reassess Esther in a couple of weeks. The only antidepressants available to me at the time were amitriptyline (Elavil) and imipramine, old-fashioned medications called tricyclics that are wickedly dangerous in even a mild overdose. Ingesting just twenty-five tablets could be deadly, making chloroquine look like a sugar pill in comparison. I also decided to save her the experience of being admitted to the P.U., which, in my opinion, would have aggravated her situation even further. I didn't think she would attempt suicide again—she had more reasons to live than to die.

While I scrawled a page-and-a-half note, filling up the rest of her card, Esther and the student nurse conversed in Shona. I even heard Esther laugh softly a couple of times and I could only imagine what they were talking about. They were about the same age. But their circumstances were vastly different. Very few of the student nurses were married, since they were spending so much time studying and working on the wards. In fact, it was a bit like boot camp as the nurses lived in dormitories on the hospital grounds and were forbidden from having overnight male guests.

"So, I'd like to see you again in two weeks, to see how you are doing. I probably don't even need to tell you, since you are experiencing it, but you do have depression. However, I don't think you'll need tablets, but if your depression doesn't get better, then we might have to consider them." Because the point was important, I directed the student nurse to interpret my statement in Shona, to make sure that Esther understood. I handed her the five-by-seven.

"Thank you, *chiremba*. I'll see you in two weeks. Right here?"

"Yes, right here. Come early, to get a good seat." I laughed, motioning to the crowded hallway.

"I see," she said, managing a weak chuckle.

"*Fambai zvakanaka*," I said.

"*Chisarai chakanaka*," said Esther Mawena as she walked out the door, back into a life of unimaginable hardship for a twenty-year-old.

As my next patient, an old bearded man, manifesting the endless chewing movements of someone suffering the ill effects of years of taking antipsychotic medication, entered my room with the help of a woman half his age, I quickly asked the student nurse what she and Esther were talking about. I detected blushing on the nurse's face, as well as some hesitation.

"A lot of things, mostly about how we Shona women have to put up with so much."

"She was laughing, I saw."

"Not a laugh of joy, but a laugh of acceptance, bitter acceptance," explained the student nurse, wise beyond her years.

"Thank you, Sister." I wanted to ask more questions, but the workload beckoned. "Back to business, we've got a new one here."

Two weeks later I saw Esther Mawena again. She had heeded my words and was first in line on the bench outside my door when I arrived at eight-thirty. I had no student nurse yet. And since Esther spoke flawless English, I did not need an interpreter. I immediately invited her in. I noticed that the worry lines on her face had relaxed, her stride and manner were remarkably different, suggesting a young woman again.

"*Chiremba*, I am feeling better."

"What happened?" I had no clue that I needed to brace myself for her answer.

"I am back with my husband. The children and I are back at his home, in Mabvuku."

"What happened?" I repeated.

"My husband is a Christian man. He forgives me. He went to a *profita* who told him to take me back. The Holy Spirit commanded it, in fact."

A more recent addition to Shona culture than the *n'anga*, *profita* (pro-FEE-tah) are faith healers who are often members of the Apostolic Faith church, an evangelical Christian church popular in Zimbabwe that became more appealing to an impoverished populace as the economy slowly crumbled. *Profita* tend to be younger than the *n'anga* and their fees are lower. Just as the *n'anga* carry on the traditions of Shona culture by engaging in the practice of divination and healing, the *profita* act as faith healers and prophets on behalf of Zimbabwe's nascent movement of evangelical Christianity.

I was incredulous. "Your husband forgives you? How about admitting what he did to you? Has he agreed to be tested and take responsibility for his actions? Did he apologize to you?"

"Oh, no. He also went to a *n'anga* who told him that the virus was given to me as a bewitchment. He did tell me that he would stop seeing his girlfriends, but as far as getting tested, he simply says 'There is no need.' He believes that we will be healed by our faith."

"Hmm," I murmured. I thought about it. That man certainly had a faith of convenience. Let the traditional healer get you off the hook one way and allow the Christian holy man to unburden you another way. "And that's okay with you? What about you forgiving him?"

"I accept the situation," she said. Sidestepping the question, Esther gave me a lesson that demonstrated the effects of the dominance over Shona women by generations of patriarchy and patrilineage. "It is better for me to have a husband. He is a good man. He is a good father. My children need a father."

I was stunned. How could I argue with generations of culturally endorsed misogyny? How could I argue with her dependency, likely borne out of the culture rather than her own particular personality development? I came up against one of my foibles as a clinician; I only wanted to help people who I had a chance of helping, of influencing. Esther's denial and blind allegiance to her husband and her traditional culture were stupefying to me, particularly to my American medical twentieth-century mind. I couldn't go on some futile search-and-rescue mission here. I had people out on the bench who I could actually assist. This situation frustrated me and filled my heart with sadness.

I half-heartedly reviewed the checklist for clinical depression. Sleep, appetite, energy, spirits, hopefulness—all were better as her situation had been, if not resolved, at least clarified. Her suicidal thoughts had completely vanished. She was feeling more optimistic. In her mind, order and stability had been restored to her life. To her, it appeared that that was all that mattered. Her father had apologized to her and restored his emotional support.

"It is better that I have a husband and a home. If I am going to get sick and Rudo is going to get sick, it is better to be with a family."

"And what about your husband? You realize that he is also going to get sick and die."

"Yes, I know." For a moment, she looked saddened, staring at a point seemingly on the wall. "It is better that we are all together."

"And contraception? Are you using condoms?"

"Oh, no. It is not possible here in Zimbabwe."

I elected to let it be then. HIV roulette. Her children would have a four-in-five chance of hurtling head-first into this world without HIV along for the ride, but they would also have little chance of being raised by their biological parents. If they were fortunate, they would be raised by their extended family. If they were ostracized, they would join the legions of street kids in downtown Harare or be taken care of in an orphanage. Adoption in Shona culture is next to impossible because an adoptive family does not want to upset the ancestral spirits by incorporating the "totem" of another family into its own. The totem of a family, often symbolized by an animal, can only be passed from a father to his biological offspring. The child will always carry the totem and pass it on to his own offspring.

"Well, certainly, Esther, there is no need for you to be on tablets. You are adjusting well. I do not need to see you again. If you do become despondent or suicidal again, do not hesitate to come back and see me. I'm here on Monday and Thursday mornings, same time, same room. I wish you the best of luck."

I never saw Esther Mawena again.

CHAPTER FIVE

"Paranoid as Hell."

Happy Mufananidza: AIDS in the Brain

"Blessed are they who suffer, for the kingdom of heaven shall be theirs."

—Matthew 5:10
The Bible

One of the beauties of practicing psychiatry in Zimbabwe was that there was no way to prepare for what you might see on any given day. I liked that spontaneity, the challenge of making a reasonable decision on the spot, keeping everyone safe, getting the patient to the right place, starting treatment as soon as possible, if need be. That is why I had been drawn to the practice of emergency psychiatry in San Francisco. Like a Vegas casino, the psych ER is open twenty-four hours a day, seven days a week and takes all comers. The emergency psychiatrists there are like blackjack dealers—punch in, punch out. I am not an adrenaline junkie, but I tend to be distractible, absent-minded, and unable to plan things in advance, except with a great deal of effort. I may suffer from a bit of a disability, I guess, but my in-the-moment nature also makes me open to what the world throws at me.

Perhaps I am mostly suited to emergency room work because I am lazy. I hate to prepare. I hate to do things for which I have to prepare, because, if things do not go off swimmingly, then the perfectionist in me would have to point the finger at myself and say, "Hey buddy, you had all the time in the world to prepare and you still screwed it up!" There is no way to prepare for the rough-and-tumble of a clinical scrimmage in the psych ER, where it's always a scramble.

On many clinic days in Zimbabwe I would interview at least one person who was so disturbed and psychotic that he needed immediate admission to the inpatient ward of the P.U. Moving a floridly psychotic person—scraping past the knees of my patients waiting in the hallway, out through the kitchen, up a gravel road, across a dirt parking lot, and down a driveway into the ward's seclusion room—was no mean task. It was particularly challenging when the patient wanted to clean your clock. In the psych ER at San Francisco General, the seclusion room door was always only steps away, and experienced colleagues and institutional police officers were near at hand.

None of this was on my mind as I walked up the dirt path to the clinic one day in the winter, when I'd been just a few months on the job. I was still in a sink-or-swim period of adjustment, but I was slowly learning the ropes. Of course, I didn't know what to expect that day; but I had learned that when uniformed officers of the military or police arrived at the P.U., I might be in for a tough challenge. "Be on your toes," I thought as I spied three police officers knotted under a tree, surrounding a disheveled shell of a man dressed oddly in fatigues and a white helmet, the trademark insignia of the Red Cross emblazoned on it. Sure enough, I would soon find myself in a mental standoff and mildly physical scrap with Happy Mufananidza, a Shona man in his twenties who suffered from nearly terminal AIDS and the unfortunate complication of AIDS dementia.

Tormented by fear and hearing voices, Happy was brought to the clinic from the Harare headquarters of the Red Cross, where he had threatened his ex-boss with a small hand-ax. They had to let Happy go from his job as a security guard because he had eventually grown too confused and paranoid to perform his duties. While a little suspiciousness may be a good thing for a security guard, a passel of paranoia makes the guard's task impossible. Appropriately enough, given Happy's flagrantly psychotic symptoms, his former supervisor brought him to the hospital instead of to jail. The police were called to the Red Cross and they confiscated the ax and escorted Happy to the doorstep of my palatial office.

Happy's supervisor made his way to the head of the line while the police kept the patient fenced in underneath the tree outside. I immediately motioned for the supervisor to join me in the confines of the old master bedroom suite. I closed the door and took a seat behind a big table that served as my desk. The Red Cross supervisor, Innocent Madamombe, sat down in a chair across from me. He was dressed in a navy blue blazer, white dress shirt, and a wrinkled red-and-yellow clip-on tie. I noticed the faint smell of cheap cologne exuding from his freshly shaved face. He was drawn and pinched with worry. After exchanging the requisite salutations, he proceeded to fill me in on some of the basic facts of the situation.

"I'm afraid for my life," said Innocent. "Ever since I told him he was let go, he's been loitering around the office. He is scaring some of the people. He greeted me every day, but always with a glare. This morning, he came in screaming, carrying an ax. Somebody called the police. I know he is unwell in the mind, so we brought him here."

"So when did you first notice problems with Happy?" I asked.

"Well, we knew he was sick about six months ago when he lost 20 pounds. His hair started falling out, his face got thin, his skin always had a rash. As you know, most of us have had relatives die of AIDS," said Innocent, his eyes cast downward at the floor.

"How about his thinking?" I asked.

"Maybe three or four months ago, he became forgetful, but soon after he started accusing me of seeing a *n'anga* and putting a hex on him, engaging in sorcery. He accused me of poisoning his *sadza*, of sleeping with all of his girlfriends, of trying to get rid of him."

"And was any of that actually happening?" I asked. Since the craziest things actually do happen, we psychiatrists need to consider and exclude the real but far-fetched possibilities before labeling a belief a delusion. In my previous six years of practicing psychiatry, though, I had rarely seen a potential delusion overturned by reality.

"No, no, of course not," said Innocent. "I was trying to get help for him, but he kept insisting that nothing was wrong."

"What happened to get him fired?"

"One day, the executive director was walking into work. He noticed Happy out front and greeted him," explained Innocent. "Happy yelled, rushed him, grabbed him, and accused Doctor Chagombera of raping his sister. Happy threatened to kill him.

"Doctor Chagombera fired him then and there, saying, 'We cannot have someone who is so unwell, mentally and physically, representing us in the community,'" he continued. "We have been trying to get Happy in to see you. He has refused. But today, Happy only agreed after the police gave him the option of coming here or to prison."

"Okay," I said. "Sounds like an involuntary hold to me. But Happy must have some of his mental faculties and basic good sense left. He made the right call. Let's bring him in here."

"Well, he's waiting outside under the tree—with the police watching over him. He's quiet, but glaring at me," said Innocent.

"Paranoid as hell," I said. "He must be in the right place. Why don't you have the police bring him in and tell them to stand by."

I knew that AIDS, particularly in its later stages, can cause all sorts of different psychiatric problems, including paranoia and hallucinations, so I wasn't surprised to hear about Happy's symptoms. Given that about 25 percent of the adult population in Zimbabwe were HIV-positive, I was surprised that I didn't see *more* cases of HIV-induced psychosis and mania and dementia during my time there. I guessed that the vast majority of people with AIDS in Zimbabwe died of opportunistic infections long before the virus made its way into their brains, though I did not have any firm data to back up this assumption.

Since I had worked as a physician and psychiatrist in San Francisco from 1988 to 1993, a place and a time of tremendous learning about AIDS, I was already aware of the psychiatric complications of HIV infection by the time I arrived in Zimbabwe. AIDS dementia, a syndrome of impaired memory and various other problems of cognition, is usually a late complication of AIDS and is generally well recognized among doctors treating AIDS patients. However, HIV is an incredibly variable and resourceful virus, making AIDS an adept imitator of different psychiatric syndromes. It can cause acute symptoms of mental confusion and episodes of illness nearly indistinguishable from schizophrenia, manic-depressive illness, or major depression. The kicker is that these psychiatric problems can crop up at nearly any stage of HIV infection, not just in the later stages of illness, when AIDS dementia is most common.

How does the virus cause these psychiatric problems? There are roughly four different possibilities, any of which can occur alone or in combination. First, an individual might have been destined to suffer from one of these psychiatric problems anyway. Second, HIV is known by researchers to directly infect brain tissue, particularly parts of the brain responsible for regulation of thought, emotions, and judgment. Third, opportunistic infections associated with AIDS can affect the brain. And lastly, the overwhelming stress of discovering that one is HIV-positive can cause a psychiatric problem.

Some of these thoughts rushed through my brain as I waited for Innocent and his crew to escort Happy Mufananidza to my consulting room. As I paused, the next patient sheepishly walked in, carrying his cooking-oil stained card. I had to wave him away. "I'm sorry, you'll have to wait a bit longer. I need to see someone else first."

The elderly man said nothing, but seemed to understand as a menacing and unhappy Happy Mufananidza was led past a gauntlet of patients, like a steer brought to slaughter. The *sekuru* looked at me and nodded and took his position at the door, knowing that he might have a reasonable chance for a little eavesdropping if so inclined.

Innocent introduced Happy to me: "Doctor Linde, meet Happy Mufananidza."

I motioned Happy into my office, indicating to Innocent and the police that they should stand by outside my door.

"Welcome, Happy," I said, extending my hand to the tattered man, who refused it. "Have a seat."

Happy Mufananidza had jumped the queue, first in madness, to the head of the line. His appearance was heartbreaking. Although he had been dismissed from his job several weeks earlier, he continued to wear his security guard's outfit complete with official Red Cross headgear. He did not sit down, rather he stood there, more or less glaring at me.

Happy was a sad reminder of the particularly destructive power that AIDS has in Zimbabwe and many other African countries. Not only does it devastate families, but it is also choking off the country's lifeline to any dreams of future prosperity and economic growth. In the late 1990s, the fastest-growing rate of HIV infection in Zimbabwe was in the fifteen- to twenty-four-year-old age group. Thus the nation's young adults, who soon would have provided the heart of Zimbabwe's social infrastructure and economic power base, were instead dying from AIDS.

Happy was a prime example of that devastation. Here was a man in his twenties, who would otherwise have likely been a father by now. He had been employed within Zimbabwe's corps of essential employees, a broad spectrum of workers including security guards, clerks, teachers, engineers, government officials, accountants, doctors, bank tellers, nurses, and transportation workers. While security guards were not particularly highly paid, they did fulfill an important role for wary businesses and upper-middle-class citizens who were trying to prevent themselves from becoming the victims of burglary, a crime that was growing in prevalence as the Zimbabwean economy staggered.

Along with Happy, thousands of other men and women were also being erased from Zimbabwe's work force by the vicious power of AIDS. The obituaries of dozens of middle-aged men appeared each week in Zimbabwe's major daily newspaper, the *Harare Herald*. Under a cloak of societywide shame and denial, the cause of death was almost always conveniently excluded. Each obituary would include some variation on a theme of "Comrade X died following a lengthy illness."

It is estimated that Zimbabwe, with its rate of one-in-four adults infected with HIV will, not too surprisingly, lose about one-in-four of its able-bodied work force over the next decade, with a calamitous ripple effect. The statistics jump to life when you consider that Zimbabwe has no safety net, no kind of Social Security. The people being felled by AIDS in Zimbabwe and other African countries are the responsible adults who are often the sole supporters of the young and the elderly. Their demise puts their dependents at risk of becoming AIDS orphans and abandoned elders. Zimbabwe's fragile economy, already wracked by inflation and corruption, can scarcely absorb the loss of the best and brightest of its work force.

These morbid statistics were nowhere near my conscious mind, however, as I contemplated the flesh-and-blood challenge of Happy Mufananidza, whose face was caked with dust, his last bath a distant memory. His clothes were heavily soiled and fraying around the edges. The smell of dirt and sweat filled the room. I was glad for the open window and the breeze on this cool but sunny day in July.

Happy said nothing but sat down. He stared at me with a mixture of fear and venom and I experienced a slight chill, registering about six out of ten on my internalized barometer of potential violence—a subjective but well-honed tool that any self-respecting psychiatrist carries around with him at all times. My barometer went off fairly easily but tended to be accurate. I had so far managed to avoid getting assaulted in six years of working as a psychiatrist, including stints in the settings of emergency room, jail, and acute-care hospital.

I immediately recognized Happy Mufananidza as the most potentially dangerous patient that I'd seen in Zimbabwe in my first three months on the job. It was obvious that I would somehow have to get him over to the psychiatric ward. My heart beat a little faster. My breath grew a little short. My armpits moistened. I knew that I would have to marshal most of my experience, will, tact, and emotional reserve to accomplish the task without mishap. My task was not to reinvent the wheel with a comprehensive interview but to build just enough alliance and rapport with this incredibly paranoid man so that I wouldn't have to physically subdue him to get him into the inpatient unit.

"Welcome, Happy," I started, tentatively. "Mister Madamombe already told me a little about what happened and how you got here, but I wanted to hear from you. What happened?"

Absolute silence. Hostile gaze.

"How did you get here today?" I continued, speaking softly, avoiding direct eye contact, and taking a submissive stance in my chair, slumping with shoulders hunched, to present myself as a totally nonthreatening presence in the room. "I want to hear your side of the story."

All I got from Happy Mufananidza was a dismissive huff, a look away for a few seconds, then a return to a stare of menace.

"You look a little upset," I offered, in an attempt to offer empathy and reinforce his reality, at least my version of it.

The glare continued, then he spoke for the first time. "You would be too."

"Why is that?" I asked. I thought, "Aha, the tiniest of breakthroughs." But the silence was deafening, and my hopes were fading as the seconds ticked by and Happy continued to glare at me.

"You want to make love to my mother, too," said Happy. "You're in on it."

"In on what?"

"You know." Happy's fist started opening and closing. His breathing became more rapid and shallow, his muscles taut. I half expected him to start growling. Needless to say, my violence sensors were firing about 90 percent by now, ready to hit the red zone, which is the beginning of the end, time to abort the interview mission and get the hell out of there.

One last try: "I'm only here to help you, to find out what's going on." I tried not to show my fear, but it wasn't easy. Beads of sweat dotted my forehead.

Still silence. I took my cue. "Uh, I need to talk with the sister-in-charge about something. I'll be back in just a minute or two." I didn't have enough time to think of a better excuse. I just needed to get out and figure out how we were going to get Happy out of my office and over to the ward.

Sure enough, Innocent Madamombe and the police officers had gone out for a smoke. I fairly bounded down the hallway, leaping over the outstretched legs of my more benign customers who, unruffled, watched the spectacle. I got to the kitchen, and Sister Mada telephoned for the hospital security guards to back us up. Dressed in blue lab coats, they arrived in just a few minutes, but it felt like a few hours. I stuck my head out the door, yelling and windmilling my arms toward Mr. Madamombe, and the police officers, all of whom took the cue, stubbed out their cigarettes, and rushed into the clinic. We all went together back into the interview room.

Happy had not moved from a sinking position in the chair. Getting a second look at Happy, I observed him in a much different light. He was bone-thin, probably dehydrated and malnourished, most likely unable to leap out of the window. "What was I so afraid of?" I thought. However, my experience told me that unchecked paranoia is a fearsome motivator. I have seen frail little old ladies exact some serious damage on health-care staff. It paid to be cautious, so we presented Happy with a large and capable show of force. Three fit police officers, two seasoned hospital security guards, one burly doctor, and one experienced psychiatric nurse seemed to suffice, as far as I was concerned. We humanely left the terrified Innocent Madamombe out of our guerrilla raid.

Upon our entering, Happy shot a withering look in our direction. I'm sure he felt under attack. He continued to open and close his fists, hyperventilating, looking around the room suspiciously, eyeing the window as a possible escape route. He did, however, register some understanding of the authority figures with me, which was exactly the point. "Please don't fight with us," the entourage was supposed to say in no uncertain terms.

We stared at him briefly, then I blurted out: "Happy, you'll need to come with us. You're not well." The security guards grabbed Happy by the arms and started walking him to the door of the interview room. Happy tensed up, yelled, hissed, and spit on the floor. But thankfully he did not scrapple further. With me in tow, Happy went with the security guards and the police officers as we filed past the throng of patients, through the kitchen, up the path, across the parking lot, along the driveway, and finally down the hallway to the cement-block seclusion room in the inpatient psychiatric unit. After we got him into the room, a shot of chlorpromazine into the upper-right quadrant of the buttocks subdued him.

Standoff averted. Operating on gut instincts. Seat of the pants. Adrenaline rush. Shortener of life.

In the short run, Happy's story had a happy ending. After a few days of refusing medications and needing to stay sequestered in the seclusion room, Happy started to take trifluoperazine and diazepam (Valium) to calm himself down and control his paranoia. Within a week or so, he was much better and was able to be discharged on a low dose of medication. Although I could not, with certainty, prove that Happy's paranoia, agitation, and lack of self-care were due to HIV in his brain, a few factors were highly suggestive. One, he had no prior psychiatric history. Two, none of his extended family members suffered from any psychiatric problems. Three, he suffered the onset of his emotional problems exactly coincident with the worst of his medical illness. When it came time for treatment, the point was moot. Because he presented us with psychotic symptoms, he received antipsychotic medications and improved.

In the long run, of course, Happy's story ended tragically. He never made it as far as his follow-up appointment. A few weeks after Happy had been released, Innocent Madamombe came to inform me that Happy had died. Having frightened and alienated most of his family, he pretty much died alone. This was quite unusual in Zimbabwe, where family members assisted those unfortunate souls who were passing over the brink to the Spirit World. Things could only get better for Happy. I hope he found happiness in the hereafter.

CHAPTER SIX

"A Bewitchment?"

Constance Marondera: Catatonic, but Why?

"Although the morning was young, the hazy mirage was up. The uncertain air that magnified some things and blotted out others hung over the whole Gulf so that all sights were unreal and vision could not be trusted. . . . There was no certainty in seeing, no proof that what you saw was there or was not there."

—John Steinbeck
The Pearl

A few months into my time in Zimbabwe, my learning curve remained steep. The angle of my instruction was never more acute than when I encountered a case of postpartum catatonia. My nascent understanding of the basic tenets of traditional Shona culture, animism, and evangelical Christianity proved to be just as important to me in approaching this case as my grasp of the nuances of modern obstetrical care and clinical psychopharmacology.

A cool August dawn was burning off with the warmth of the sun as the earth meandered from a cold, clear winter to a scorching spring on the highveld of southern Africa. Low clouds of morning mist, remnants of overnight evaporation, hung over the dewy field that separated the Psychiatric Unit from the rest of Harare Central Hospital. I took note of the change of season, feeling more settled in the Southern Hemisphere. I felt grateful for the warming trend as I parked my car and ran the gauntlet to the inpatient ward where I strode through the heavy metal doors and walked down the hallway toward the nurses' station. Once inside, I immediately knew that something was amiss.

"Come quick, *chiremba*," said Sister Chimhenga, as she led me further down the cement block hallway toward the back of the ward. "Follow me."

"What? . . ." I stammered. As a psychiatrist I was not accustomed to rushing, but I followed. For her to skip the be-all and end-all "*mangwanani*" meant something serious was up.

"It's a new patient, brought in by her family to P.U. last night," she said. Rhythmic screaming, undulating in a range of high shrieks to low moans, bounced off the red brick walls. "She's in seclusion."

"Sounds like she needs it." My dull American ears still struggled at times to understand the nurses on the P.U., all of whom spoke softly in thick accents. Wearing crisp nursing whites and sensible shoes, Sister Chimhenga briskly led me past a throng of milling patients and down a drafty corridor, where the noise grew louder. The locus of wailing sailed from the cell door's judas hole, a four-by-six rectangular hole that was open to the air and situated at eye level so that nurses could check on their patients and patients could communicate, even if by yelling, with their nurses. As she turned the key and threw back the heavy metal door, Sister Chimhenga said something loudly and firmly in Shona.

Naked, crouching in the corner, her scalp shaved irregularly, Constance Marondera's eyes rolled upward and darted about the room as she rocked forward and backward on the balls of her feet, screaming just as before. Sister Chimhenga stood over her, about 6 feet away, and listened intently, nodding from time to time.

"She needs meds," I said, revealing a flair for the obvious. "But let's try to talk to her first."

"Yes, *chiremba*."

"You know, Sister," I said, "I hate to medicate first and ask questions later."

"*Chiremba*?" said Sister Chimhenga. "I do not understand."

"Oh, never mind," I said, turning my attention to the patient, who appeared as if she was in a trance, yet not exactly like anything I had ever seen in my years of practicing psychiatry stateside. "Can you make out what she is saying, Sister?"

"Yes, some of it," answered Sister Chimhenga. "*Amai* (ah-MY) is saying that her great-grandmother, *Ambuya* Zezuru, is speaking to her and possessing her. She is called by *Ambuya* to suffer for her sins."

I knew what the Shona word *ambuya* meant, and that *amai* meant mother or missus, but I did not catch all of the cultural significance of Sister's interpretation. "Sister, I'm sorry, but what does all of that mean?"

"It means that *amai* believes that she is being bewitched by her great-grandmother, who may have been a prophet in her time. An important ancestor spirit."

"A bewitchment?"

"It could be," she said, pausing. "Her family must have thought so. You can tell that she has already been to the *n'anga*, who shaved her head in spots to release *Ambuya*

Zezuru's spirit. But, if the *n'anga*'s treatment had worked, her family would not have brought her here. Psychiatry is a last resort for most of our people."

"Does she have any medical problems that we know of, Sister?" I asked.

"No. Except she delivered a baby ten days ago and had some complications. And ever since then, the family says she has not been well."

"Do you know the details of her illness?"

"She had a fever before and after the baby came, with vaginal bleeding in excess," said Sister Chimhenga. "She stayed in the hospital for three days after the delivery."

"Was she okay before all of this? Did they do labs? Do we know her hemoglobin, her white blood cell count? How much blood loss? Did they find a source for her fever? Sepsis? Endometritis? Has she been tested for HIV? Did they give her antibiotics? Did she have an altered mental status at the time?" I didn't expect Sister Chimhenga to know all these details. I merely was thinking out loud for my own benefit and also to enlist the vast medical knowledge and experience of the nursing staff. I definitely needed their help on this case, particularly since obstetrics has never been a strong suit in my medical repertoire. While I could fake a little internal medicine and neurology, I was pretty much lost in most of the other medical and surgical specialties.

From what I could gather from her cards, Constance suffered a fever as high as 39.5 degrees Celsius, corresponding to a temperature of around 103 degrees Fahrenheit. Since she also had pus coming from her vagina, in addition to blood, the diagnosis was that of a probable bacterial infection of the uterus, an uncommon but potentially deadly complication called endometritis. She received aggressive medical treatment for her infection—injections of huge doses of penicillin every twelve hours for seventy-two hours and intravenous fluids. She appeared to have made an excellent recovery, being discharged on the fourth day after delivery. The cards showed absolutely no mention of her mental status, for better or worse, during any of the illness or at the time of discharge. This did not necessarily mean that her mental state was entirely clear but that her physicians might not have detected what could have been subtle alterations of thinking or behavior.

It is more than feasible that she might have been confused and disoriented in the midst of such a severe bout of illness. Her ability to think clearly was likely clouded by fever, blood loss, changes in her body's balance of sugars and salts, and blasts of certain hormones and the disappearance of others in the neurochemical storm that occurs in a woman's body following the delivery of a baby. Since the brain must rely on the rest of the body's physiology for the steady stream of oxygen and sugar it needs to function properly, it is exquisitely sensitive to changes in the body's chemistry. In other words, severe medical illness can alter a person's thinking, emotions, and behavior.

"Sister, is her husband or any other family member here right now?"

"No, her husband, his name is Godfrey, he said he would be back this evening. He was here much of last night, though there was nothing he could do. He sat at the nurse's station for most of the time. He is praying a lot. He is a minister. He is very worried."

"Who is caring for the baby?"

"The patient's mother is."

"Is the baby all right?"

"The baby is a boy," she said. "They named him Nelson, after Nelson Mandela. He is very healthy."

"Sister," I asked, "what's this about being bewitched?"

"The husband told me that they took her to a *n'anga* about three days ago just after she got out of the hospital," said Sister, "because she was talking nonsense."

"Anything else about her behavior at the time?"

"Yes, not sleeping, on her knees praying all night, screaming."

"Any indication that she was threatening the baby?" I asked.

"Oh, no, *chiremba*."

"So what did the *n'anga* think? Did he write a card?"

"*Chiremba*?"

"It's a joke, I thought maybe the traditional healer also kept his records on those wretched little pieces of cardboard."

"Oh, no, *chiremba*. They don't keep a written record."

"Go on, Sister."

"The *n'anga* discovered a bewitchment," said Sister. "The husband wanted to take her to a *profita*. He was not at all happy about the *n'anga*'s finding. The *n'anga* was going to tell the family how to solve the bewitchment by making amends. But Godfrey told me that his wife's family was very desperate. They convinced the *n'anga* to shave and scar her scalp to release the spirit inhabiting her. The husband was very unhappy about it." Sister escorted me back to the judas hole and pointed toward the side of Constance's head, where a divot of hair had been removed and a superficial wound showed.

"What's that about releasing the spirit by shaving and cutting her scalp?" I asked Sister, puzzled.

Looking a little upset, Sister Chimhenga went on to explain to me that some traditional healers still believe in such ritual scarring. She minced no words in informing me that she didn't agree with such superstitions. "It's foolishness. The *n'anga* are still important in some matters, but in matters of mental illness like this one, they have no business." Sister Chimhenga was feisty, with a smile. Well-rounded, tending toward plump, with smooth, dark skin and a ready smile, Sister Chimhenga was only in her mid-twenties but already had five years of experience working in the psychiatric ward. I liked her. "It didn't work, so the *n'anga* suggested that they bring *amai* back to the hospital."

Anxious to get back on familiar medical turf, I asked, "Do we have any vital signs on her?"

"Here they are, *chiremba*, from last night and this morning."

I looked at the numbers and saw no evidence of fever and only a mild elevation of heart rate and blood pressure.

Constance, who had been silent for ten minutes or more as she knelt praying in the corner of the cement-block seclusion room, once again arose and started pacing around the room, mumbling in low tones an unintelligible ditty that sounded like a song.

"Sister?"

"I can't make it out."

Constance crouched again and then jumped repeatedly in the air from a squatting position, nearly touching the 8-foot-high ceiling each time. When she saw us peering through the judas hole, she screamed even more loudly and started howling in Shona, again with the crescendos and decrescendos.

"Sister?"

"She is talking again about *Ambuya* Zezuru. Asking why she sent a *marungu*, a *marungu* devil to earth to deliver such a message."

"Is she talking about me?"

"You're the only *marungu* here, aren't you?"

"Of course, Sister," I said with a laugh. "So, do you think this is a bewitchment?"

"It is," said Sister Chimhenga, "whatever she and her family think it is."

"Well, whatever you call it," I said, shaking my head, "it sure looks like madness to me."

"*Chiremba*, how much CPZed should we give her?"

"Fifty milligrams," I said. "Does that work for a bewitchment?"

"I don't know, *chiremba*. But for *this*, it will work."

By now, Constance was literally running in circles around the seclusion room. I saw no signs of leather or other restraints. In the States, in the psychiatric emergency room, we restrained patients to a bed prior to injecting them with antipsychotic medications or sedatives. Restraining an agitated, psychotic, potentially violent individual prior to administering an injection ensures the safety of both staff and patient. The staff avoids needlesticks, punches, and kicks. The patient averts orthopedic injury by not being forcibly held down by a mass of people to receive an injection. But here there were no restraints, a sign of the influence of British psychiatry, which, as a matter of philosophy and practice, does not generally allow the use of restraints.

That being said, three rather large Zimbabwean men wearing the blue coveralls designating them as hospital maintenance men-cum-security guards came to us in the hallway, after being paged on a crackly overhead speaker by Matron Chengeta. Sister Chimhenga drew up the 50 milligrams of CPZed in a syringe with a clean and disposable needle, and we all entered the room. The security guys simply grabbed the petite but thrashing woman as Sister Chimhenga skillfully and quickly stabbed the upper outer quadrant of the woman's right buttock, delivering the antipsychotic dose. Sister and I left the room first, while the blue dudes in unison let go of Constance, two of them exiting while the third blocked the doorway. Constance retreated to a far corner of her room, where she lay down in the fetal position and softly growled before falling asleep five minutes later.

For better or worse, I had ward rounds to complete before I could take another look at her. I asked Sister Chimhenga to ensure that the evening shift of nurses carefully instruct Godfrey Marondera to come back the next morning, early, so I could check in with him before starting my clinic day.

This was a complex case indeed. I needed to sort out whether this alteration in behavior was a first onset of mental illness or a recurrence of an already underlying psychotic illness. Was her psychotic break at home merely an extension of a delirium induced by medical complications during her childbirth—infection, blood loss, shifting blood chemistries, hormonal storms—any of which could potentially cause her brain to go haywire and temporarily malfunction? Or was this a full-blown case of postpartum psychosis in which the mother develops an episode of illness that may be indistinguishable from a psychotic break of schizophrenia or a manic flare of an underlying bipolar disorder, also called manic-depressive illness?

In this case, it was especially important to make the distinction, since a true postpartum psychosis can take several weeks to resolve and carries with it the potential of infanticide. Postpartum psychosis is an unusual, dramatic condition that is clearly distinguished from more common emotional problems that surface after a baby is born. One is postpartum depression, a full-blown bout of extreme, persistent sadness and other depressive symptoms that affects between one in five and one in ten women following childbirth. Another postpartum condition, more common and less serious, is the "baby blues," a condition characterized by transient sadness and tearfulness, lasting less than a week or so, that affects more than half of all women who have delivered a child.

To make matters even more complicated, it seemed to me that I had no choice but to consider the possible spiritual causes of Constance's illness. It was important that I construct a culturally sensitive differential diagnosis in this Shona woman. Was she a victim of a bewitchment, consistent with the beliefs of traditional Shona culture and Constance's parents? Was she possessed by a demon, able to be cured by the rituals and exorcisms of a Christian faith healer, consistent with the beliefs of evangelical Christianity and Constance's husband? Or was she suffering from a delirium or postpartum psychosis, consistent with the beliefs of an American psychiatrist trained on the other side of the planet?

In short, Constance had three different types of specialists operating on her behalf—a traditional healer, a faith healer, and a psychiatrist. I had a responsibility to go with what I knew best, while respecting and considering the viewpoints of the other "specialists" in the case who, as close relatives of the patient, had more than a passing interest in its outcome.

No matter what the cause of her madness, I would treat Constance's psychotic symptoms and behavioral agitation with an antipsychotic medication and, quite possibly, a sedative such as diazepam. The first, and very practical, goal would be to get her out of that cement-block seclusion room. To do so, she would have to be much more cognizant and trusting of the staff.

After I finished ward rounds that busy morning, I went to see Constance. Peering through the judas hole, I found her unmoved from her position earlier in the morning. I reflexively checked that she was breathing. In all of my years of practicing emergency psychiatry and ordering injections of sedatives and antipsychotics I have not yet pushed anyone over the brink into cardiac or respiratory suppression or death, thank heavens, and that was a string I definitely wanted to extend. I checked in with Sister Chimhenga and ordered her to change the medication to trifluoperazine, which I believed would assist Constance out of her psychotic episode in a more timely fashion than CPZed and with fewer side effects.

When I came on the wards the next morning to check in at the nurses' station, after a suitably spirited round of "*mangwananis*" with patients and staff alike, I did not notice Godfrey Marondera waiting patiently outside. It was easy to overlook someone among the hordes of people milling about the dusty courtyard, as the cast of characters changed on an hour-to-hour basis. For starters, at any time of day or night the police might arrive with a new case. In the morning, the courtyard was often filled with a flood of relatives, unfailingly humble in manner and dress, appearing from way out in the bush after a torturously jarring bus ride to visit a loved one and bring him extra food. In the afternoon, a group of Polish physicians or Canadian nurses or Pakistani counselors or Zambian health administrators might happen by.

I was often distracted by the happenings because I knew the nurses would soon hit me with a barrage of *mangwananis* followed by a hail of questions. Also, I wanted to obtain a sidelong glance at the new admits, who could very well be frolicking in the courtyard among the established patients, relatives, maintenance men, nurses, and, for all I knew, Polish physicians.

"*Mangwanani, chiremba*," said Sister Chamoko, the ever-capable sister in charge of the day shift.

"*Mangwanani, chiremba*," said Matron Chengeta, always a force in her green uniform that figuratively screamed "I'm in charge here!"

"*Mangwanani, chiremba*," said Sister Shuga, who, over time, became one of my favorite nurses because she was teaching me the finer points of the gyrating, pelvic-thrusting dance steps identified as *kwassa-kwassa*, performed to thumping Zairean rhumba music, also called *kwassa-kwassa*.

"*Mangwanani, chiremba*," chortled a chorus of student nurses, a group of six or seven young women dressed in the nursing corps' de rigeur starched white uniforms.

"*Mangwanani*," I said, nodding to all of those around me. We dispensed with the next round of greeting, seeing as how it might take fifteen minutes for everybody to complete it.

"*Chiremba*, I wanted to give you a report on Constance Marondera."

"Yes, Sister Chamoko."

"She is much better. She was able to come out of seclusion last night. She was walking all over the ward last night, talking to people, making some sense. Her husband came to visit. He thought it was a miracle. He wanted to take her home because she was cured. We had to explain to him that she had been admitted to the P.U. against her will and that she could not be released except by you or a decision of the court. He did not understand. He has been here all night. He slept out in that field there, under a tree, I think. He wants to talk to you. He is insistent on taking her home today. That is him out there, *chiremba*. He is a minister, Apostolic

Faith, I believe," said Sister Chamoko, pointing out the window to a man standing under the tree, his head bowed with eyes buried in a book, presumably a Bible, his lips soundless in their movement as he read to himself.

"Doesn't look like such a bad guy," I half-mumbled to myself. After a slight pause, I asked, "If he's an Apostolic Faith minister, Sister, then why is he not wearing white?"

"Oh, *chiremba*, I believe that's only for Sunday services."

The members of the Apostolic Faith church were known countrywide for their Sunday services. They would gather in groups of twenty or more people in fields on Sunday afternoons and sing and preach for hours at a time, occasionally breaking out into foreign tongues, products of evangelical gifts promised in the Word of the Lord. Higher education, urbanization, and the seepage of South African, British, and American culture via television and music all contributed to a very slow erosion of traditional Shona values. As economic times grew harder in Zimbabwe, and people became more desperate for something or somebody to place their faith in, membership in the Apostolic Faith church skyrocketed. Despite the popularity of evangelical Christianity, the old Shona ways did not disappear. People continue to be syncretic in their religious/spiritual attitudes and practices in Zimbabwe. That may help explain why most Shona people think nothing of going to a *n'anga* and consulting a *profita*, as well as seeing a physician steeped in biomedical principles. Both *n'anga* and *profita* practice the channeling of spirits (one, the venerated ancestor spirits and, the other, the Holy Spirit) and both employ the power of ritual in healing.

I looked again out into the courtyard. Godfrey Marondera did not stand out. He did not wear a flowing robe of white. He did not chant and cry out in tongues. He looked like any other polite and reserved relative, standing meekly with a white straw hat in his hand, dressed in a short-sleeve white polyester shirt, solid navy blue tie, gray slacks, and dusty black shoes, periodically wiping his forehead with a handkerchief. Considering that he was a man of God by trade, his reading of the Bible was not surprising.

"Hmm," I said to Sister Chamoko. "Even if Constance's illness was a brief reactive psychosis, which I don't think it is, I would want to see her well for a few more days before I would let her go home. I need to see how she is tolerating the medications."

"Yes, *chiremba*, I agree, she is not ready to go."

"And her vital signs?"

"Temp 36.5, blood pressure 130 over 80, pulse 72, respirations 14."

"Sister, let's go see her. I'll speak with her husband, after I have evaluated her for today."

We made our way to the female ward with the freshly starched student nurses following behind. Sister Chamoko cleared out the ward in a matter of seconds with a single barking order. Dozens of female patients, some dressed in the brightly striped hospital-issued robes and others outfitted in the uniform of the poor rural woman, a long rumpled cotton dress, streamed out of the ward, many of them stiff and drooling.

We entered only to find Constance Marondera on her knees with her face planted into the corner of the room, speaking rapidly, mumbling somewhat, spitting the words into the acute angle of the walls' meeting, where the sounds became muffled.

"Can you make out what she is saying?"

"She is praying, something about being delivered from the evil here." Constance continued with hands clenched, kneeling, speaking faster and faster but quieter and quieter. "I can barely hear her now, but it sounds like she is saying, 'Why? Why? Why? Why did you bring this on me?'" The young mother then broke down in tears, covering her face and sobbing. Sister Chamoko put her hand on Constance's shoulder and comforted the distraught woman as Constance slowly turned herself around. Soon Constance was sitting in the corner with her legs sprawled out in front of her. Sister asked her to get up. Nothing happened, she just sat there, staring into space. I asked Constance several questions, which Sister Chamoko translated, while Constance surveyed her surroundings blankly. I finally approached her to examine her. I instinctively took her pulse. It was a little brisk at 108. Any pulse over 100 is considered abnormal. It was my obligation to at least consider the possible medical causes of her heart racing.

I was worried about dehydration, always a concern in my evaluation of severely psychotic patients, who, because of paranoia or mental confusion, often do not eat food or drink fluids properly. Constance was definitely at risk here. Her lips were dry, but Sister Chamoko reassured me that Constance had eaten breakfast and was taking in fluids. I checked her muscle tone while she continued to gaze into nothingness, on the edge of a temporary (we hoped) existential abyss. The muscle tone of her arms was surprisingly tight. I needed to exert some effort to move them around. This exam finding was not something that I had frequently come across in my career, but neither was it unfamiliar. It was not the cogwheel type of muscle rigidity that I picked up several times a day in Zimbabwean patients suffering from Parkinson's syndrome. This sobriquet is borrowed from Parkinson's disease, a movement disorder caused by the lack of the neurotransmitter dopamine in the basal ganglia, a collection of neural structures that govern and direct the body's motor function and, to a lesser extent, coordination. All the old antipsychotic medications, including TFPZ, cause the same effects as Parkinson's disease—tremor, tight muscles characterized by "cogwheeling," a stiff gait, a reduced arm swing while walking, decreased facial expressiveness, and drooling. This was clearly a different finding. I continued to move her arms about when a lightbulb went on in my head. Ding! Waxy flexibility. A hallmark of catatonia.

For once, my mouth engaged after my brain did when I told the nurses assembled: "Waxy flexibility, Sister, catatonia. It all fits together. She was in the midst of a state of catatonic excitement or agitation yesterday and now is entering a state of catatonic stupor. The clearer mental status you saw this morning may well have been a honeymoon period in the transition from excitement to stupor. Her episodic unresponsiveness and the waxy flexibility are probably part of a postpartum psychotic mood disorder," I said, talking as much to myself now as to the sisters.

This development of catatonia was quite worrisome to me, although it helped me clarify her diagnosis, which would roughly guide my treatment. Since she showed no particular signs of being medically ill right now, I could exclude a current medical condition as the cause of her catatonia, though the nurses, other doctors, and I needed to remain vigilant in monitoring her medical status. Given the time course and the nature of the symptoms, it seemed most likely that this was a postpartum psychotic illness. And, my heart sinking, I knew that postpartum psychoses could be wickedly difficult to treat and carry high stakes, a new baby at home who needed his mother.

Catatonia is an old term of neurology and psychiatry. It is not a diagnosis per se but a syndrome of physical signs and symptoms that can occur in individuals suffering from schizophrenia, manic-depressive illness, psychotic depression, a severe reaction to medication, or a serious medical illness. Catatonia is sometimes considered a final common physiological pathway of severe psychosis. It can be inordinately difficult to treat and can last for several weeks before resolving. The syndrome of catatonia can prove fatal from self-injury, malnutrition, or dehydration. The treatment is essentially maintenance of safety during times of behavioral problems, supporting good nutrition and hydration, and a fairly nonspecific medical treatment of a combination of an antipsychotic medication and a specific type of sedative called a benzodiazepine. That a sedative could bring a person out of a catatonic stupor seems counterintuitive at first; but once you consider that sedatives are also antianxiety medications, then it is easier to understand how they might "unlock" a person in the midst of a locked-down state of mind and body.

"Well, Sister, we have our work cut out for us here," I sighed. "Check her vital signs carefully. As you know, she is at high risk for malnutrition and dehydration." I was well aware that these experienced psychiatric nurses, who had surely treated dozens of women just like Constance Marondera, also understood the challenging task ahead of them. "Let's start diazepam 5 milligrams twice a day. Either it's going to help or it's not. We'll know in a few days."

Diazepam was the only readily available benzodiazepine in Zimbabwe. Just like amitriptyline and CPZed, it didn't cost much because it's a drug that's been around for decades, meaning the big pharmaceutical companies could no longer milk a big profit margin from its manufacture and sale. The studies of benzodiazepines in the treatment of catatonia were mostly performed with another medication, lorazepam, which, of course, was unavailable in Zimbabwe due to cost. But, frankly, I was grateful just to have the diazepam. It would give me a fighting chance at reversing Constance's catatonia.

I left the ward and walked to the nurses' station where I wrote a brief progress note summarizing my findings in examining Constance. At least I had a plan for Constance's biological treatment—capable supportive nursing care, maintenance of good hydration and nutrition, a safe place where any of her behaviors could be managed, and a reasonable course of psychopharmacology with TFPZ and diazepam, which I could easily monitor.

What I could not so easily accomplish was to assuage the fears and concerns of Constance's husband. Sister Chamoko took me to meet Godfrey Marondera. On my way out to the courtyard, my mind ran through the sequence of events. I wasn't sure that I could make him understand my biomedical perspective on his wife's illness and change in behavior. I had no clue about his belief system of evangelical Christianity. In fact, I knew precious little of how Godfrey Marondera viewed the world. Here I was, in the middle of southern Africa without a roadmap, entrusted with the responsibility and duty to try and do something for this unfortunate woman. What else could I do but apply my worldview, knowledge, and experience to the care of this woman? Could I, in good conscience, suddenly adopt a new way of looking at the world—to, in essence, start experimenting with her care?

Sister Chamoko and I approached Godfrey under the spreading arms of a thorn tree. For the moment, there was no one else around. As we got closer, I couldn't help but notice that Godfrey looked a little rough around the edges. He was unshaven; bags hung prominently around his eyes; his once-white dress shirt showed gray smudges—as if someone had shaded parts of it with a big piece of charcoal chalk. I was surprised at how bad he looked. Considering that his wife was psychotic in the hospital and his newborn baby was being cared for at home by his mother-in-law while he was sleeping underneath a tree in a field, maybe I shouldn't have been surprised. In Godfrey Marondera's galaxy, the stars and planets were most certainly out of alignment.

Sister Chamoko interrupted Godfrey's biblical reverie with what sounded like a quick-and-dirty greeting. He looked up, appearing puzzled, lost in thought. After the mandatory pleasantries, Godfrey Marondera came right out and said what was on his mind: "She's possessed and needs to see a *profita*. It can wait no longer. To do so would endanger her life." It appeared that Godfrey had formulated a diagnosis, treatment plan, and even a prognosis, according to his beliefs, experience, and training.

In his early thirties, Godfrey was a stocky, handsome man with close-cropped hair. His eyes were bloodshot but fierce. His speech was rapid fire, his gaze just this side of hostile. I thought to myself, "Is this guy coming undone, going crazy himself?" I ticked off the weak evidence for such a case—he's certainly under a tremendous amount of stress, he's hyperreligious, he's disheveled, his manner and speech may suggest a bout of irritable mania. I thought again: "Nah, come on, give the guy a break. He's just under a lot of stress, not processing things well." Sometimes, we psychiatrists can suffer our own brand of what Zimbabweans call *kufungisisa* (koo-foon-ghee-SEE-sah), thinking too much.

These types of situations in any culture are always tricky. Godfrey had known his wife on a day-to-day basis for nearly five years. He knew her idiosyncracies, her manner of speech, her smell, her smile, her hopes, her dreams, her blemishes, her failings. They were husband and wife. What did I know? I had "known" Constance for a half a day, spending a grand total of half an hour with her. Who was I but an outsider *marungu* doctor with authority?

In the States, I was accustomed to being questioned by family, by colleagues, by nurses, by insurance companies, by nearly everybody but the janitor while practicing psychiatry. But, in Zimbabwe, I had rarely been confronted with much questioning by any patient or the friends and relatives of any patient.

The reasons for this were complicated: Many of the black Zimbabweans unconsciously continued in a colonial mindset, having grown accustomed to complying with whatever a white authority figure told them to do. In addition, British-style medicine is much more hierarchical than American medicine; the chief consultant has the last word and cannot be questioned. Thus, patients in a British-based system like Zimbabwe's are much more likely to be compliant. Finally, Zimbabweans are generally a much more respectful people than are Americans or Europeans. Why? Shona individuals are raised in the context of an extended family and the structure of a village, with a greater awareness of other people. They also grow up in patriarchal families in which the authority of father is indeed final and immutable.

But Godfrey Marondera was a man of deep convictions. His Christian beliefs took precedence over any of these other generalities of the culture. "I want to take her home, *chiremba*. I need her. Nelson needs her. Her family needs her." He looked me straight in the eye, just this side of menacing. He said these words with the quiet passion of a preacher—surprisingly slow and soft now, speaking precise English with a heavy Shona accent.

I was feeling the heat, just a little. I was perched on the brink of talking too much, like a rookie politician at his first big news conference. "I understand your position. You hate to see your wife here in the hospital. I realize it's not a very nice place. You miss her. You have a small baby at home who needs his mother. I understand all of that. It's just that he should have a mother and you should have a wife who is well, who is able to fully be a mother and a wife. The nurses and I agree that she needs to stay here for more treatment. Your wife has a very serious psychiatric illness called a postpartum psychosis. She is likely hearing voices, she's paranoid, she is not eating or drinking well. I have started medications that can treat these things, but it may be a few weeks before she is back to her normal self."

My speech went nowhere. "With all due respect, *chiremba*, you don't have the authority to keep her here. You are just a doctor, just a man. It should be God's decision."

I involuntarily broke into the smallest of ironic grins. "Well, there is a problem. Your wife is here because the Casualty doctor placed her on a legal hold for psychiatric treatment under the Mental Health Section of the laws governing public health in Zimbabwe. It is what we call 'being sectioned.' Theoretically, a judge can release her. But, practically speaking, only I can drop that hold and let her go and, in good conscience, I do not feel that she is anywhere near well enough to go home."

Godfrey's insistence on taking Constance home and his apparent inability to hear anything that I had to say made me feel frustrated and a little bit miffed at him. In some ways, he was obstructing his wife's care. My well-laid plans to get all of that careful collateral history regarding Constance's medical treatment and her previous psychiatric history were going to be relegated to the ashcan this morning while I talked to Godfrey Marondera about this pressing matter. If she were indeed going to be in the hospital for several more days, if not weeks, then I would have plenty of time to fill in the blanks.

On the spot, I mentally scrambled to conjure up a creative solution to this problem. I am always open to trying anything and everything to help a patient as long as it does no harm. "Aha," I thought. "I've got it!" "Mr. Marondera, what about bringing a *profita* here to the P.U. to see your wife? I don't have a problem with that. If the sisters feel like it's okay, then . . . "

"That cannot be," said Godfrey, his voice rising, his stance hardening. "This is not a place of God. The healing needs to occur in a place of faith."

Distracted by the discussion and mildly annoyed at Godfrey's stubbornness, I had forgotten a key question, which I hastened to ask, mostly to confirm what to me was only secondhand information. "If you believe so strongly that a *profita* could solve your wife's problem, then why did you not seek out the opinion and treatment of one before bringing her back to the hospital?" I didn't fully grasp the provocative nature of my question at the time. But, to be honest, Godfrey and I were locking horns in a brewing battle. I carried with me the authority of Western biomedicine and the government of Zimbabwe while Godfrey shouldered the shield of none other than God.

Polite, respectful, articulate Godfrey Marondera made a little snorting sound and blew a prolonged stream of breath out of his tightly clenched teeth, a show of emotion out of character for a Shona man dealing with an authority figure that he had never met before. "Oh, that." Godfrey shuffled his feet and smoothed his hands along the front of his pants before he spoke further. "By the time her parents had finished the *n'anga*'s treatment, Constance had grown too ill. I had no choice but to bring her here. That *n'anga*'s treatment was barbaric. I disagreed, but my father-in-law insisted."

"But you paid *lobola*, didn't you?" I said, knowing that his family's payment of bride price gave him societal ownership of sorts over his young wife.

"Yes, but my family is still paying it off, so it is complicated," he said. "I was obligated to consult her father, which I would have done anyway."

"Of course," I followed along.

"And her father, he, he was adamant. He grew up in the *musha* and for him, the traditional way is the only way. I don't believe in such witchcraft. I grew up with it, I understand it, but I don't agree with it. I only agreed to bring Constance to the hospital because I was afraid that she was physically unwell. Mentally and emotionally, she is fine. It is a spiritual affliction that she is suffering under."

He continued, "What I do believe in is the Word of our Lord Jesus Christ and his ability to heal my wife of her affliction, which is of the Devil. Now, please let me take my wife home so I can take her to a *profita*."

"Listen," I said, growing a little impatient. "I don't think you realize yet just how sick your wife is."

"I saw her last night and early this morning. She is much better."

Just then, Sister Chamoko, who had been at my side, listening with half an ear to this conversation as she directed patients in the courtyard away from us, began a conversation with Godfrey in Shona. He listened intently for half a minute while the sister spoke. He then replied with animation and what I may have even detected for a touch of sarcasm, if those verbal nuances can be culturally translated. Sister Chamoko gave a long answer as Godfrey nodded and periodically said "*Eh-he* (ay-HAY)," yes, in Shona.

Sister Chamoko turned and spoke to me in English, "*Chiremba*, I was just explaining to him that she was much sicker just now, that she has a serious illness, and that you know what you are doing and that we have faith in your treatment."

Godfrey turned to me: "Can I visit my wife now?"

"Yes," I said. "We can discuss this later."

"Thank you, *chiremba*," he said and walked away, accompanied by a student nurse who took him to the female ward for a brief visit.

I hated this kind of confrontation, although the tone was polite, and I went looking for reassurance from Sister Chamoko, a nurse with at least fifteen years of experience who had pretty much done and seen it all in Zimbabwean psychiatry.

"Sister, what do you think? Am I doing the right thing?"

"Yes, *chiremba*. She is nowhere near ready to go home. They would be bringing her back within a few days. She is quite ill. He is confused because he is heartbroken. He is not thinking clearly and is jumping to what he knows best. We need to remain firm. We need to keep her safe and give the medications a chance to work. After he sees how sick she is this morning, I'm sure he'll change his mind about taking her home."

"I hope so, Sister, I hate to fight with the guy," I said. "*Chisarai chakanaka*, Sister."

"*Tichaonana, chiremba*."

As I parted the multicolored sea of madness in the courtyard, plying the gravel and dirt pathways on my way to the cinder-block palace, I was adrift in thought, muttering half-hearted "*mangwanani*s" and "*tamuka*s" out of the side of my mouth as I walked. I was beginning to appreciate the high degree of difficulty presented by Constance Marondera. If this case were an Olympic dive, then it would be the equivalent of a three-and-half reverse tuck with a twist off the 10-meter board. Not only was Constance extremely sick with a newborn baby at home and a contentious husband, but those of us responsible for helping Constance viewed the situation from three widely variant perspectives as to just what might be the cause of Constance's disturbed behavior. And the fourth view, quite plausible, was that all three hypotheses were cockeyed and false and that really we were all operating in an abyss of darkness, stumbling and fumbling and hoping for the best.

If one were to believe the Shona traditional view, Constance was suffering from a savage intractable bewitchment by an aggrieved ancestor spirit. Just because the traditional treatment didn't work doesn't mean that this hypothesis can be ruled out. At the risk of being obvious, plenty of conventional medical treatments are ineffective for certain conditions in which there is little doubt that the cause is a biomedical one.

If one were to believe the evangelical Christian's view, held by Godfrey Marondera, his wife was possibly possessed by the Devil (the one and only uppercase one). Borrowing from a strongly held philosophy of the world being a battleground for the ultimate war of Good versus Evil, this type of demonic possession is made valid by historical evidence of such states occurring.

If one were to believe the Western biomedical view, held by her doctors and nurses, Constance was suffering from a postpartum psychotic illness, possibly related to a flurry of postdelivery hormones and perturbations of the brain's neurotransmitters. As to a consideration of the traditional African's questions of "Why Constance?" and "Why now?," Western biomedicine, for better or worse, frankly doesn't give a damn. As I've mentioned before, Euro-American medicine does not trouble itself with such questions but wants to live in a world of empiricism and pragmatism to answer the questions of "What caused this?" and, more importantly, "How can we fix this?" In Constance's case, I could wax rhapsodic about hormones and infections and neurotransmitters and the traditions of psychiatric phenomenology and antipsychotics and benzodiazepines and intravenous hydration—all to build a case for the psychiatric perspective, which is my bias. But, as a wise and venerable psychiatry professor once said during an inscrutable lecture on psychodynamic theory: "Let me back up before I begin."

Let me back up to review the dominant behaviors of Constance Marondera: fasting, praying, not sleeping, not responding to others in a meaningful way despite being awake and alert, careering around restlessly at times, retreating into a torpor at other times, verbally reeling out snippets of supernatural experiences. Who am I to say that these behaviors do not closely resemble a demonic possession in the cosmology of Christianity or a bewitchment by an ancestor spirit in the phenomenology of traditional Shona beliefs? Why couldn't the behavior of Constance Marondera simply be consistent with a religious conversion or a dissociative state or a spirit-possession state or trance state—all of which have been documented and described by centuries of priests, philosophers, shamans, anthropologists, and physicians?

How does one distinguish the transient state of mind of a catatonic psychiatric patient from those who enter a state of transcendence as a routine part of their day-to-day lives? How might Constance's state of mind differ from one of many other characters who utilize trance states and dissociation in both sacred and not-so-sacred ceremonies? These might include a Christian zealot, speaking in tongues, filled with the Holy Spirit while experiencing a sign from God; a Shona *n'anga* putting himself into a trance state to be transformed into a spirit-medium to channel a deceased ancestor spirit; a Haitian voodoo practitioner casting spells; a New Age spirit-medium channeling her client's past lives via regression; a Navajo medicine man on a peyote-assisted vision quest; a Hindu mystic deep in a meditative trance; an Aztec shaman who follows the path of the jaguar with or without psychedelics; a 1960s' hippie tripping on acid. Constance, then, like many other "mental patients," was experiencing an alternate reality and transcendence that those of us literally stuck in the concrete world of mundane day to-day existence will never know. This is one of the ironic awes of insanity, which can never make up for its infliction of pain and suffering on those afflicted.

Would this awareness change the way that I treated Constance Marondera? I descended from the clouds of these lofty thoughts, landing with a thud as I passed through the kitchen-cum-pharmacy for a round of "*mangwananis*" and then on to the half-walk, half-crawl through the tangled legs of my patient patients clustered on the hard bench in the hallway. Time for work on the front lines, on the hard dirt ground far beneath the academic denizens of the Ivory Tower. It had been my choice to live in the real world of clinical psychiatry and, to drive home the point, there were my two dozen "real-world" patients waiting for me. Not being a priest or a philosopher or a shaman but rather an earthbound clinical psychiatrist, I could only treat Constance Marondera with the tools readily available to me in my repertoire. And those included such mundane things as solid nursing care, a safe environment, medical monitoring, medications of trifluoperazine and diazepam, and ongoing education of the family. But just because I had a plan didn't mean things would go the way I had envisioned.

When I returned to see Constance on ward rounds on Friday morning, the place was eerily quiet. According to Sister Shuga, that day's sister-in-charge, Constance Marondera was not doing well. She remained in a catatonic stupor and had eaten nothing for three days. She drank only small amounts of tea and water with maximal assistance from the nursing staff. Her vital signs were worsening, with her pulse spiking up into the 130s and her blood pressure tanking to about 90 over 60, consistent with dehydration. She had been taking the medications as prescribed.

Ward rounds were a bit of a misnomer since I generally did not go around at all but set up shop in a small treatment room with a wooden table and a handful of chairs, surrounded by the clutter of books, medical records, bandages, resuscitation equipment, and gowns. The sister-in-charge would bring in a pile of disheveled charts stuffed with mismatched tags and slips of brownish paper and we'd just start with the top of our stack and work our way down. I would try to see the new admissions first, as it might have been three or four days between their time of arrival and an examination by the attending psychiatrist. A student nurse would be commandeered to run and fetch the patient in question, who would be led to the treatment room for an interview. I would get some sort of report from the charge nurse on the patient's progress—eating, sleeping, behavior, hygiene—plus a report on the symptoms that we were following as well as medication compliance and side effects.

But, from time to time, when patients were too medically ill or catatonic to walk to the interview room, I would mobilize with the sister-in-charge and a couple of student nurses to perform old-fashioned ward rounds. We did our best to see the nonambulatory severely medically ill or catatonic patients first, since they were often the sickest. If we were going to engineer a transfer to Medicine, it was best done early in the day before the internal-medicine residents and attendings had vanished from the workplace to go "moonlight" for extra pay. We weren't in the habit of "dumping" our sick patients in the Casualty Department; instead we did things the proper way and arranged a formal transfer of the patient from the psychiatry service to the medicine service.

Sister Shuga went on ahead, clearing the female ward for our modest entourage. Because I hadn't seen Constance in a few days, I was shocked by her appearance. Her skin was dry, her eyes were sunken, her empty gaze peered into the void, her lower legs jutted from the bottom hem of her rough-cut blue dress like sticks from a matchbox. She did not move, she said nothing. Her breathing was even, not too fast, not too slow.

"When did she last pee?" I asked.

"Sorry?" said Sister Shuga. "I do not understand."

Not in the mildly profane landscape of American medicine anymore, I rephrased my question: "Sorry, Sister, when did she last urinate?"

One of the student nurses piped in: "We cleaned her this morning. She had been incontinent overnight. It was a large amount of urine, *chiremba*."

"Thank you," I said. "Do we have orthostatic vital signs, Sister?" A measure of blood pressure and pulse taken in both the supine and standing positions, the orthostatic vital signs were a reliable indicator of a patient's level of dehydration, reflecting the amount of fluid circulating within the bloodstream.

"No, *chiremba*."

"Let's get a set. I'll do it, if you'll help me."

Borrowing a stethoscope from one of the student nurses, I took the pulse of a recumbent Constance. Rapid and thumping, "hyperdynamic" in medical parlance, her pulse was 124 at rest. Her blood pressure was not as bad as I expected at 110 over 70. With great difficulty we stood her up. She mumbled something unintelligible in Shona as we waited three minutes, giving her body a chance to equilibrate before I rechecked.

When the time was right, I fingered her pulse. Even more bounding, her pulse now measured an alarming 140, her blood pressure dropping to 90 over 60. These changes were consistent with at least a moderate level of dehydration. The drop in blood pressure reflected a relative dearth of blood circulating within a closed system. The increase in pulse signaled the body's attempt to compensate for this drop in pressure: the body essentially saying "since there's less of it, let's move it faster" in an attempt to capture and deliver more oxygen and sugars to far-flung body tissues.

"Sister, you know how I feel about your physicians here," I said, still smarting from the death of Joshua Mujombe.

"She needs intravenous fluids, but I hate to send her to Medicine. I'm afraid we'll never get her back. Can we start an intravenous line in her and give her a solution of 5 percent dextrose with normal saline and potassium?"

"Normally," said Sister Shuga, "we don't do IV's over here, but in this case, *chiremba*, we can make an exception."

"Thank you. Let's give her two or three liters and see where we're at. I'd like to increase her dose of trifluoperazine and diazepam to 5 milligrams three times a day for each of them—see if we can get a handle on her catatonia. I'll personally speak to whomever is on call tonight."

"Dr. Stephens, *chiremba*."

"Excellent," I said, knowing that Dr. Stephens was one of our most conscientious house officers. "I am pretty worried about her."

"Yes, *chiremba*."

"Have you seen her husband?"

"Yes, *chiremba*, that is another problem. He still wants to take her home."

"Is he here now?"

"No, but he said he would be coming back later this morning."

I saw about fifteen patients that day, each one presenting a unique challenge. The new admissions were always the most interesting and difficult because they were still pretty unstable, often demonstrating flagrant psychopathology that most medical students will only read about in a textbook. I also had to deal with a lack of information in many cases, depending on which house officer had performed the initial history and physical examination. If it were one of the experienced psychiatric residents, I often had a plenitude of solid information about the patient. If it were done by a disinterested or dispirited junior house officer fresh out of medical school, only doing the psychiatry rotation as a mandatory requirement of internship, then I might know essentially nothing. The nurses, many with ten or more years of experience working with psychiatric patients, were routinely full of accurate and pertinent information. To say that I relied on their clinical judgment to sort out the psychiatric problems of my patients in Zimbabwe was a serious understatement. I would regularly consult and collaborate with the more experienced ones. It was a satisfying working relationship. Even with little information, I enjoyed the scramble.

After seeing the last patient on ward rounds, I walked down the hallway to the nurses' station, which was centrally located with a prime view of the courtyard and its usual collection of players. As I stepped out into the courtyard momentarily, I nearly bumped into Godfrey Marondera. We exchanged the afternoon greetings before commencing with the real business at hand.

"I'm glad we're getting a chance to talk," I started. "I'm very worried about your wife. Because of her psychiatric illness, she is not eating or drinking very well and is getting into a state of . . ."

"*Chiremba*, I want to take her home," interrupted Godfrey. "Your treatment is making her worse. I want to take her home before your treatments kill her."

"Mr. Marondera, I'm not sure you understand. We're giving your wife fluids to make sure that . . . "

"No, she needs to be healed by a *profita*," he interrupted again, without raising his voice.

"Godfrey, she is too sick to leave the hospital. I cannot in good conscience let her go. She might die at this point without medical and psychiatric treatment."

"No, I must take her to a *profita*," he said once again, emphatically.

"Listen, Mr. Marondera, can you just slow it down for five or ten minutes here?" I'm sure the slightest bit of irritation sounded in my tone of voice. "Every time I see you, I get a barrage of your demands."

"Yes . . . yes . . . yes, yes, yes, yes," said Godfrey rhythmically, not sarcastically, nodding his head as if a lightbulb had ignited over it. "You are right," he said. "I am sorry. It's just that I am so worried."

"Of course you are. I am, too. We can agree on that. I want you to know that I will do the best I can to get her home as soon as possible," I said. "We can try to work something out. At this point, you and I are both worried about your wife, but we strongly disagree on what's best to treat her. I would like to work something out, but first, I'd like to get some basic background information that would help me make a decision about her care. I haven't even had a chance to get some of the basics that I know that only you can provide about your wife."

"Sure, anything."

I noticed that Godfrey seemed calmer today. He was clean-shaven and wore fresh-scrubbed clothes. He looked tired, but, although he was insistent and persuasive in stating his case, he did not demonstrate that borderline maniacal style and hint of menace that I had witnessed just three days earlier. In spite of his wife being sicker than on Tuesday, Godfrey seemed to have calmed down. I fantasized, "Maybe, just maybe, he is coming around to understanding our perspective on his wife's situation."

"So, if I could, I'd like to ask a few questions. First, has Constance ever had any problems like this before?"

"No."

"Any periods of persistent sadness, thoughts of wanting to kill herself, not eating, not sleeping, not feeling any hope for the future, anything like that?"

"No, she has always been upbeat, the one who would lift my spirits, calm me when I was upset. She has been a very strong person."

"Okay," I said. "Has anybody in her family suffered similar problems—anybody—sisters, brothers, uncles, aunts, parents, cousins?"

"No," said Godfrey. "But, wait a minute, she did have an uncle, her father's brother, who did have a similar problem. It lasted only a day or so. It turned out that he was being called to be a *n'anga*. That was more than ten years ago. He is now fine, a well-respected *n'anga* in his community."

"I can see then why her family is so keen about the use of a *n'anga* to address her current problem."

"Right, yes that's right, *chiremba*." Godfrey nodded as he answered.

I went on with the history-taking: "Does Constance drink alcohol or use drugs, like *mbanje*?"

"No, of course not. We are Christians."

"Other than these problems with her childbirth, does Constance have any major medical problems?"

"No."

"Has she been drinking any tablets or herbal medications?"

"No."

"What was Constance like as a young girl?" I continued. "Did she have a lot of friends, did she get along okay with her brothers and sisters?"

"Oh, she has always been very cheerful, outgoing, one of the most popular girls in her school." As Godfrey said this, he smiled, no doubt remembering the beautiful young woman that he had married two years earlier.

"And did she do well in her schoolwork?"

"Yes, always near the top of her class."

As I listened to Godfrey's answers, my mind eased a bit. "Okay, Godfrey, thank you, all of that information is very helpful to me in figuring out what to do." Her healthy premorbid functioning—with an outgoing personality, good performance at school, and popularity—and lack of any significant personal or family psychiatric history indicated a more favorable long-term prognosis than I had first thought.

"So, *chiremba*, please, please, can I take her home, to see a *profita*?"

"Godfrey, let's see if we can make a deal. This is the best deal that I can offer at this time. I absolutely cannot let Constance go home now. Maybe Monday, but right now her vital signs are unstable. She is dehydrated, barely eating, barely drinking, barely able to take care of her basic needs. Give me the weekend to stabilize her. I will simplify her medication regimen and hope for the best. I know we already talked about this, but what about bringing a *profita* here?"

"*Chiremba*, with all due respect, the answer is the same. This is not a place of God."

"I don't understand, Godfrey, I don't understand, why not?"

"*Chiremba*, I have an idea. Maybe, just maybe, it is something that will work."

"Yes, Godrey, what is it?"

"I do not feel comfortable having a *profita* come here directly to do his work. But my church, the members of my church, we can worship in the field just outside the fence of the courtyard here this coming Sunday afternoon. I can invite the best *profita* of my church to join in my Sunday services in the field right here. Constance can stand right here," he said, pointing to the corner of the courtyard, "to be near our services at least. There is no church law against worshiping in that field out there." He motioned me to a balding patch of scruffy, dying, tall, yellow weeds outside the P.U.'s boundary, shaded by one small thorn tree and bisected by a dirt path running from the main hospital of Harare Central Hospital to the shops and post office of the industrial suburb of Southerton.

"Hey, Godfrey, that's a great idea," I said, with genuine enthusiasm for his plans. "Okay, on my side of things, I will do all I can to get Constance better by Monday. I will meet you here early on Monday morning, eight o'clock, make it eight-fifteen, and we'll meet and decide what to do. I have a good feeling about this."

"Thank you, *chiremba*. So do I."

I walked away, hating to rely on dumb luck and chance. But all of us were banking on the faith of Constance, the faith of Godfrey Marondera, the faith of Godfrey's outdoor congregation, and, at the risk of sounding hyperbolic, the very power of God. My flimsy status as a retired Catholic with a lukewarm Christian faith and a mere religious vitae of a shaky set of good works as a doctor, did not inspire me on that Friday in August to think that Constance would be much better by Monday. My cold, calculating, quasiscientific perspective as a psychiatrist told me that Constance would be no better by Monday. Then my tentative promise to Godfrey, to seriously consider Constance's discharge, would be rendered meaningless because I would have no choice but to continue to incarcerate Constance behind the barbed-wire fence and chain-link gate of the P.U. Having arrived at that thought, I was still hoping to be surprised.

When Monday came, I was running a little late. Godfrey was already there, in the courtyard, talking to his wife as they both sat under a tree. I flung my "*mangwanani*s" in their direction, telling them I needed to review her chart and speak with the nurses before I examined Constance and talked to Godfrey. They both nodded their assent and I entered the P.U. Constance looked a little flat, a little stiff, but in the best shape that I had seen her.

Sister Chamoko was again the sister-in-charge. "She is doing better," she said. "She still mumbles to herself at times and is praying most of the time, but she is at least drinking fluids better."

"Sister, did Godfrey's Apostolic Faith congregation hold services outside the fence yesterday?"

"*Chiremba*, that I do not know. I was not here. Let me ask Sister Mugongo. She was here yesterday." Sister Chamoko called to a younger nurse speaking with a patient down the hallway. They held a brief but spirited discussion in Shona. "*Aiwa*, sorry, *chiremba*, no, there was no Apostolic Faith service outside the fence yesterday."

"Are you sure, Sister?" I asked. "Because Godfrey told me that he would bring his church here to help Constance."

"One moment, *chiremba*, let me ask someone else." Sister Chamoko then walked away and came back a few minutes later. "*Chiremba*, no, I have asked four different people who worked here yesterday and they all say the same thing. No Apostolic Faith service outside the fence. It was a quiet Sunday around here."

"Hmm, that's interesting," I said. "I'll have to ask Godfrey about that." I briefly turned to Constance's records, a growing pile of thin, mustard-colored sheets of paper with scrawls and hieroglyphics on them, my own included. I turned again to the note that I had written on Friday. I had ordered a rapid taper of her diazepam and she was now only on a modest dose of TFPZ, 5 milligrams twice a day. The weekend notes were sparse, but they all seemed to indicate that Constance enjoyed a low-key weekend without any outrageous behavioral outbursts.

I wandered out to see Godfrey and Constance. Sister Chamoko walked with me. We had another round of "*mangwanani*s" between the four of us, like a Marx Brothers routine with a lot of bowing and mumbling but with no funny glasses or moustaches.

I proceeded to ask several direct questions of Constance. She gave me direct, brief, accurate answers. I examined her muscle tone and found a bit of telltale ratcheting, consistent with the side effects of TFPZ, but none of the waxy flexibility of catatonia.

"Godfrey, she is much better. I think she is good enough for you to take her home."

"Thank you, *chiremba*. I agree."

"But Godfrey, let me ask you a question. Did you or did you not bring your church here, with your *profita*, to hold services in that field out there?"

"Uh, well, *chiremba*, we meant to, but there were quite a set of problems moving the service from Highfield, problems of transport for many of my church members, and my *profita*'s wife fell ill herself."

"I hope not with the same kind of problem as Constance has?"

"Oh, no, *chiremba*, no, she has an infection of the lungs. She is actually admitted as a patient over in the main hospital."

"Sorry to hear that," I said. "Hey, Godfrey, that's okay that you didn't make it. I'm just glad to see that your wife is so much better. How do you account for it?"

"We, my whole church, prayed with our whole souls and spirits on Sunday for Constance to get better. I still see it as the healing power of God, no offense intended, *chiremba*."

"None taken, Godfrey, none taken. So you can take Constance home. I want her to continue taking the tablets twice a day. I believe that she is going to make a full recovery. Come back exactly one week from today in the late morning, and I will see her. I hope that we can discontinue her tablets at that time. If she exhibits any bizarre or violent behavior, do not hesitate to bring her back. Do you understand? Sister will help pack up her belongings." I turned to Constance, who had lost 20 pounds and aged ten years during her ten days on the P.U. "*Fambai zvakanaka*, Constance," I said, clapping my hands, nearly genuflecting, in the deferential stance and manner of the subservient son-in-law in Shona culture.

"*Chisarai chakanaka, chiremba*," said Constance, managing a weak smile, her facial muscles tightened by TFPZ.

"Thank you again, *chiremba*," said Godfrey. "Sorry I made it so hard on you. Even though God did the healing, *chiremba*, you acted as an instrument of His peace and healing power."

"Thank you, Godfrey. That's kind of you to say," I said. "One last question, Godfrey, before you go, if you don't mind?"

"Sure, anything, *chiremba*." He smiled broadly, the pall of worry having been cast off by his wife's improvement.

"Are you still going to take her to see a *profita*?" I asked.

"No," answered Godfrey without hesitation. "No, *chiremba*. Now there is no need." With that, he and Constance and Sister Chamoko went inside to prepare Constance for her discharge.

Meanwhile, I veered toward the chain-link gate to leave the courtyard of the P.U., to start my day at the clinic. "Wonder what he meant by that?" I pondered, sprinkling "*mangwanani*s" around me as I trudged the dirt path to the clinic. I suppose I could have asked him, but there are just some things I don't mind keeping locked up in the land of uncertainty and mystery, embracing the unknown. Godfrey and Constance never returned to see me the next week. I can only hope that she continued to get better, because I have no idea.

CHAPTER SEVEN

"You What? You Need to Rest Your Mind?"

Sister Pagomo: A Case of *Kufungisisa*

"Of course, in an age of madness, to expect to be untouched by madness is a form of madness. But the pursuit of sanity can be a form of madness, too."

—Saul Bellow
Henderson the Rain King

Matron Chengeta caught me after ward rounds one day. I was tired, I was a little grumpy; I didn't feel like doing any extra work. It sounds crazy, but if I had to stay past about one o'clock in the afternoon, I would feel overworked. After powering through twenty to thirty patients in a morning, I often felt as if I needed to rest my own mind, at least for the afternoon.

Matron Chengeta found me chatting with the nurses on the ward. I knew well enough not to hang around too long, because inevitably some unfortunate psychotic soul would be unloaded from the back of a pickup truck following a three- or four-hour ride from some outlying district hospital. Although the nurses were more than capable of tucking the patient in before the on-call house officer would come and perform an initial history, physical exam, and mental status exam, I would often feel compelled to go see the new arrival myself.

Or else some patient, who missed the morning clinic, would come by, hat and medical record card in hand, looking for a refill of medications. Most of these people were on the level and sincerely sought help. They always put me in a dilemma. If I took the time to see them and order a refill of medications, I would feel just the slightest bit of resentment at having to stay longer at a workplace, where, truth be told, the duties never ended, the flow of patients never stopped. If I politely told them to come back on the next clinic day, then I would feel a twinge of guilt for not helping a poor soul in need. Matron Chengeta, attired in the green color of her authority, head crowned in starched white, entered the nurses' station and caught me unawares. The nurses toned down their laughter, but without cowering. For their boss they felt respect, leavened with just the right touch of fear.

Matron Chengeta was always nice to me, always trying to make my life easier, perpetually trying to convince me to stay on in Zimbabwe. I always joked with her that I would be happy to stay if she could come up with about US $80,000, the amount that my wife and I still owed on our medical school loans, the interest racking up while we spoke. Matron always chortled at this figure, equivalent to more than 600,000 Zimbabwean dollars (ZW$600,000), a king's ransom, almost, in that country.

Matron Chengeta was nice to me because she needed me, not because I was such a superstar but because I was not a total idiot. I showed up. I demonstrated an interest. I did the basic work. She depended on me to provide clinical leadership on the tough cases, which I usually could do. But she also wanted me to be a leader. I was (and still am) one of the world's worst, and least interested, administrators. Seeing a difficult patient, lecturing to a room full of students, discussing a knotty case with colleagues—those tasks interest me because they engage me. In my mind, when I perform those activities I am actually *doing* something useful, in the moment. But don't put me in a polyester navy blue sports jacket and plop me down in meeting after meeting, deciding on policy changes, planning disciplinary action of employees, obsessing about the regulators and the revenuers. Just shoot me first.

Matron Chengeta liked me in spite of my disinterest in things bureaucratic. And the feeling was mutual. I always figured that it was better for her to throw her administrative weight around than for me to try to run things. She was Shona, she was very experienced, she was a natural leader respected by the hospital's higher-ups, and she was also a helluva lot more headstrong than I was. She was destined to be a much stronger advocate for the care of the mentally ill than I could ever be. While the fact that she was a woman might hamper her effectiveness in the higher reaches of the male-dominated Ministry of Health, Matron Chengeta was a powerful figure in the circles of nursing administration at Harare Central Hospital. And as I have already stated, the nurses pretty much run the place.

I had not seen the matron yet that day. "*Masikati*, Matron Chengeta," I said, clapping three times with the proper technique, momentarily genuflecting in the pose of the son-in-law beseeching a powerful mother-in-law. We were the pooh-bahs of the P.U. and needed to set a good example with our greeting. I demonstrated this with a flourish, in front of the nurses, for maximal comic effect.

"*Maswera sei, chiremba.*" She clapped in return, nodding her head once, like Queen Elizabeth.

"*Taswera maswerawo.*" I continued with the light hand clapping of a compliant son-in-law.

"*Taswera,*" she finished with a laugh. "You can stop the clapping now." Then she got down to brass tacks.

"Doctor Linde, I have a favor to ask," she said sheepishly. The corners of her lips drooped downward. She folded her hands and looked meekly at the floor, a stance of supplication.

That was not a good sign. "It must be a big favor," I thought. Just then, I noticed a woman standing behind the matron, almost hiding behind her in a submissive posture, her eyes glumly glued to the floor. In a flash I sized her up. She was as wide as the matron but much shorter, a touch of gray at her temples. She frowned severely, like she had just eaten a lemon or possibly bitten the head off a live chicken.

"Yes, Matron, what is it?" I said, cautiously, glancing quickly back at the matron and then at my watch, a quarter-to-two. I wanted to get out of there.

"Can we discuss it in my office?" she asked.

With a sinking heart, I dutifully followed the matron and the forlorn woman wordlessly down the hallway, slowly up a stairwell, and out into another passage that led straight to Matron Chengeta's office. "Great, just great," I thought.

Matron said something quickly to the woman in Shona, then turned to me. "Come in, *chiremba.*" The sourpuss woman stayed put, staring out a narrow window into the P.U. courtyard, which was nearly deserted in the heat of late September, the mild winter having turned abruptly into a hot spring day. Many of the patients were no doubt enjoying an afternoon siesta courtesy of CPZed and Valium, sprawled on their thin mattresses in the relative cool of the cement-block ward.

Matron Chengeta's office was on the small side, but she had a window facing the courtyard and another one looking toward the clinic. It was a cramped corner office, cluttered with papers and dusty memorabilia, dominated by an industrial-sized metal desk befitting a person of Matron Chengeta's position in the leadership pyramid. A big, black dial phone, circa 1965, rested on the corner of her desk. A minuscule fan lazily blew moist, warm air toward Matron Chengeta and then back over to me. I pulled out a handkerchief and wiped my brow before leaning my face forward into the tiniest of jet streams flowing from the fan. Despite the heat, Matron Chengeta unscrewed the lid off a big Thermos of creamed tea and poured herself a tall mug of steaming, caramel-colored fluid.

"I know I'm not supposed to use so much milk. My diabetes," she said to no one in particular. I wasn't there to be her health conscience. "Do you want some, *chiremba*?" she offered.

"*Aiwa, tatenda*," I said. "So what's up? I take it that this favor has something to do with the woman outside your door."

"Yes." Matron Chengeta drew a heavy sigh before speaking further. " I want you to see her."

I just sat there, listening for the other shoe to drop, beads of sweat lining up again on my brow only to be knocked off by a swipe of my damp handkerchief.

"Her name is Sister Pagomo. She is a nurse's aide on the surgical ward. She is struggling. She is not doing her job. She is on probation. Missing work on some days, pitching up late on others. She forgets to do her chores. She leaves early."

"So, how does that make it a psychiatric problem?" I interrupted. "Sounds like a personnel problem to me," I said, my limited sympathy waning in the heat and the relative lateness of the day.

Matron Chengeta sidestepped my bait and continued with the story. "They almost let her go before they consulted me. Her immediate supervisor, Matron Mukaranga, has spoken to her many, many times. She has tried to be firm, she has tried to be nice. Nothing has worked. At first, Matron Mukaranga thought that Sister Pagomo was merely stubborn, insubordinate. But she has changed her mind. After dealing with her for some time, she now thinks that Sister Pagomo is depressed, maybe even psychotic. She referred Sister Pagomo to me."

"And you're then referring Sister Pagomo over to me," I said, nodding my head up and down, trying hard to stay even-tempered.

"Yes. I need your help. You are the main consultant psychiatrist here at P.U. I need your expert opinion about the matter."

"But, Matron, how can this be fair to Sister Pagomo? She should be able to see a psychiatrist independently. I'm an employee of the Ministry of Health and this hospital. How can I be objective in evaluating her?" I asked, my face flushing. "This would never happen in the States. There we have what's called an employee assistance program. She should see an independent person, one who could advocate for her, on her behalf."

Matron Chengeta looked at me peculiarly, half-puzzled, half-wounded. Obviously, we weren't in the States here. Obviously, there were only a half-dozen psychiatrists for the nearly two million people in the greater Harare area. "We do not have those resources here. There is no one else to see her. She can't afford to go see a private doctor. You must help me. You can be objective.

"I am under some pressure here. The matter has gone all the way to the matron-in-charge. There are some who say she should be terminated outright, who don't want her to get a psychiatric evaluation. Others are sticking up for her. The matron-in-charge would like for her to be seen. I already told her that you would see her."

I believed that it was ridiculous to have a shrink in your own institution evaluate you for ability to work. I thought, "What about confidentiality? What about boundaries?" But I was too tired to fight about it.

"I don't like it," I finally said, "but I'll do it."

"Thank you, *chiremba*," said Matron Chengeta, breathing a sigh of what appeared to be relief.

"But," I interjected with my own set of rules. "I want to see her first thing in the clinic tomorrow morning, at eight-fifteen. I don't want to see her now. I'm too pooped, I'm too hot. Tell her to come to the clinic at eight-fifteen tomorrow morning. I will find her and bring her into my office to be seen first, ahead of all the other patients. Tell her to bring all of her medical cards. Tell her to be on time, because if she's late by more than a few minutes, I won't be able to see her."

"That's fine. Thank you, *chiremba*," said Matron Chengeta. "I'll tell her. I'm sure she'll be there. I will also report to the matron-in-charge."

I thought, "Wonderful, every move in this case was going to be reported to the powers-that-be around here." I wasn't afraid of them, but I didn't think it was really any of their business what was wrong with Sister Pagomo. On the other hand, some of them were trying to give her a fair shake. In spite of my best efforts to escape, I was entangled in a cultural mismatch.

The next morning I made sure I was punctual, heading into the parking lot at eight-fifteen sharp. Pregnant black clouds hung in the western sky. After a steady downpour last night, it had stopped raining, but now it looked like we might be in for a morning thundershower. A cool southwesterly wind blew in, but I was ready for a dog day afternoon.

Several patients were already lined up on the bench when I poked my head into the hallway of the clinic. But there was no sign of Sister Pagomo. I wound my way back to see Sister Mada in the kitchen. No, she had not seen anyone matching the forlorn woman's description asking for me. Since I had a few spare minutes, I went over to the inpatient ward with the usual "*mangwananis*" up, down, here, there, everywhere on my way over. I made a beeline for the matron's office. She was not there. So I poked around the nurses' station, male ward, and female ward in search of her. I finally found the matron.

"Any sign of Sister Pagomo?" I asked—after the morning greeting, of course.

"Isn't she at the clinic?" asked Matron Chengeta.

"No, that's why I was looking for her over here," I said, my face calm, my insides churning, thinking, "Now, Matron Chengeta, if I had seen her over there, would I be looking for her over here?"

"I haven't seen her this morning." She murmured something briefly in Shona to the nurses assembled around her before again speaking to me. "None of the sisters have seen her, either."

"*Tatenda*, Matron. I will head back over to the clinic. I hope I see her." I really hoped I didn't see her—ever. Sure enough, she was not there when I returned to the clinic about eight-twenty-five. Time to get going, I thought. No-shows to the clinic were always a mixed blessing. A missed appointment freed up precious time, but it could also mean that something had gone terribly wrong with your patient or that he'd show up later at a totally inopportune time and need to be seen. For the moment, I was relieved.

The patient load on that rainy morning was in the average range: Two police officers from the hinterlands with mentally retarded girls; a soldier wanting to return to duty after a psychotic break; one suicide attempt; four letters written for a request to waive school fees; three cases of serious depression; two epileptics needing refills of their phenobarbital; a whole lineup of schizophrenic patients arriving for their monthly injections of long-acting depot, slow-releasing antipsychotic medications; no admissions from the clinic to the inpatient ward. The count of 106 patients seen that morning by a total of four doctors, only one of whom bailed out before eleven o'clock with a lame excuse that I reluctantly accepted.

At twelve-thirty, I was in the process of gathering up my materials for an early exit home, eagerly looking forward to lunch and a pleasant afternoon spent listening to the radio, writing letters, making a quick trip to the market, or even taking a nap. In my mind, I was already there, sprawled out on my government-issued genuine vinyl couch.

Then, a knock on the door. "*Chiremba*" came the voice loudly. It was only Sister Mada, probably with a prescription to sign. "Yes? *Pindai!* (pin-DIE), Come in," I yelled, with a chuckle, showing off the little bit of Shona that I had learned in a night class.

The door opened. I saw the familiar face of Sister Mada, but behind her, I saw the dreaded Sister Pagomo, with the same astringent look on her face as the day before. My afternoon plans evaporated in the heavy air.

I turned to Sister Pagomo, who appeared before me, in body and manner, as a chastised Buddha. "Why was it so easy to beat up on the masochistic?" I asked myself, a notion that I had entertained many times before in situations like these. "Why is it that the masochistic are so talented at bringing out the sadist in me?" I'm sure I came across as a bit peeved to Sister Pagomo. She got me.

"Didn't Matron Chengeta tell you to be here at eight-fifteen this morning?"

Castigated Buddha just stood there looking totally lost in her nurse's aide uniform. On every ward, all over Harare Central Hospital, the women working as nurse's aides wore frumpy dark blue dresses, falling below their knees, with maroon aprons to protect them from all the dirty work that they had to do. Whether the job involved washing dishes or wiping butts, the nurse's aides were sure to be at great risk to get soiled on the job. Sister Pagomo stared at the floor, her face appearing more acidic with the passing of each moment. I stared blankly at her, trying to decide whether to dismiss her or submit to the will of the process and see her now.

Finally, she said, "Yes. Yes, she told me to be here at eight-fifteen. But I couldn't get out of bed in time. I missed my bus." Speaking slowly, Sister Pagomo's voice, with a nasal tone, sounded low-pitched and flat, trampled, as if she had to exert tremendous effort to push the air between her sour, pursed lips. The effect on the listener was either soporific or enraging.

"I see," I said. As I looked at her, a feeling of pity began to well up inside of me, tempering my anger. Here she was: getting older, clearly unhappy with her lot, unattractive, maybe in poor health, unmarried as far as I could tell, unable to handle what should have been a relatively easy job. She went through life with a big "KICK ME" sign on her back. That's probably why she rankled me so much. I felt a little ashamed of myself for being so selfish, so angry. Who was I, anyway? Would it really kill me to burn an hour this afternoon? My rage dissipated, washed away by a wave of sublimation mixed with a dash of martyrdom. Maybe I could help her.

"Please come in. I'll see you now," I told her, motioning to the chair opposite my consulting table. I closed the door and then opened a window. A pelting morning shower, complete with rolls of thunder and lightning, had given way to a steamy rise of heat from the wet ground. The springtime sun of the Southern Hemisphere had found its way out from behind a curtain of clouds. The afternoon was heating up.

I found my way to my chair, sat down, and plucked a black pen from my shirt pocket. As usual, I would start the interview with a brief introduction of purpose and then a series of open-ended questions, theoretically, at least, to discover just what issue was uppermost in the patient's mind. Not only was this likely to be important psychological information, it also would help with the patient's long-term compliance. If I could address a patient's primary concern, then the individual would be more likely to comply with the entire treatment plan. A well-recognized trick from the practitioners of the "art" of medicine, this approach seemed to work as well in Zimbabwe as it did in San Francisco.

"Matron Chengeta told me about your troubles at work and how Matron Mukaranga and the matron-in-charge were trying to help you," I started. "They asked me to perform a psychiatric evaluation on you to see if I could help you and also to see how they could help you. My name is Dr. Linde. I am the consultant psychiatrist here at P.U. I will ask you several questions today and then we'll make at least one more appointment for follow-up. I will try to come up with a plan today to try and help you. Do you understand?"

"Yes, *chiremba*. Thank you."

"Okay, then. Let's get started. What kind of problems were you having over there on the surgical ward?"

"Oh, none," was all she said, sitting there impassively.

I didn't wait long. "That's not what Matron Chengeta said. She said you're off work, suspended."

"Yes, I'm using up my vacation time. I'm due to run out at the end of this week."

"What kind of problems was the matron referring to?"

"The other sisters," she stopped. I could hear my watch's second hand moving. I waited at least ten seconds.

"The other sisters what?" I asked.

"The other sisters complained about me." I waited another ten seconds or so, wanting more.

"What did they complain about?"

"I don't know." More silence.

I was getting nowhere fast with the open-ended approach. It wasn't clear to me why it wasn't working with Sister Pagomo. The open-ended approach could fizzle for a variety of reasons: The patient might not trust you because of paranoia. The patient might be too confused from either delirium or dementia. The patient might be too poorly motivated due to depression to give you much of anything in the interview. The patient could be too concrete in his thinking patterns, not even being able to cogitate in abstract enough terms to "tell you his story." Or the patient, because of a personality style of dependency or passive-aggressiveness, might simply not offer much, wanting you, the health-care professional, to do the heavy lifting, failing to see the interview as the collaborative effort that it truly should be. I didn't know yet whether Sister Pagomo was paranoid, depressed, demented, or suffering from a personality disorder, or some combination of the above. That's what the initial investigation would be about. To get there, I would have to take more of a Perry Mason approach.

"Well, according to Matron Chengeta, there were several problems from Matron Mukaranga's perspective. One was missing work. Is that true?'

"Yes, I haven't gone to work at all this week."

"How about last week?"

"I missed three days."

"And the week before?"

"Let me think. Yes, I missed some work. Two days, I believe."

"What about coming late on the other days? Is that true?"

"On the other days. Let me see. I'm usually late by an hour or more."

"Why are you late?"

"I oversleep. I'm tired." She continued to frown throughout the interview, pushing the air with all her might from her lungs, through her vocal cords, and past her tightened lips to make a sort of toneless, guttural speech.

"Is it true that, when you do come to work, that you don't always get your assigned work done?"

"Yes."

"And why is that?"

"My mind."

"What, what about your mind?"

"My mind is full of things."

I got to thinking. Could that mean that she's psychotic, hearing terrible auditory hallucinations, or that she's obsessed with repetitive thoughts, or manic, with her thoughts racing, unable to keep up with them? I pictured tiny spiders cavorting on giant cobwebs and dusty bookshelves in the recesses of her mind. I viewed her mind uncharitably as cavernous and moldy.

"Do you ever hear the voice of another person talking to you even when you are all alone, like an imaginary voice?"

"No. It's my mind. It doesn't stop. It is full of too many things. I think too much."

"Uh-huh. And what's that like?"

"It hurts. I need to rest my mind." She spoke in a thick British/Shona accent, saying the phrase "rest my mind" slowly, distinctly, clearly, sharply, rolling the *r* in *rest* and accenting the "eye" sound in the words *my* and *mind*.

I had never heard any patient at any time use this type of description before and the phrase reverberated through my head—"I need to rest my mind." "You what?" I asked. "You need to rest your mind?"

"I need to rest my mind." Again, the rolling *r* and the exaggerated "eyes."

"I can't go back to work," she continued. "Can you write me a medical excuse to miss work? They will pay me for two weeks' sick leave. Can I be out for two weeks? You see, I need to rest my mind."

If I had been in a clinical setting almost anywhere back in the United States, I would have been chuckling to myself, observing such an amateurish display of malingering. Because I have worked in jails and disability clinics where doctors are commonly manipulated for all sorts of goodies, I have a lot of experience at being "jammed" for stuff by some of the best and some of the worst. The first step to getting on disability, legitimate or otherwise, starts with a request for a doctor's note to miss work, which in some cases is merely a prelude to a stress disability claim or a workers' compensation case.

What stopped me short with Sister Pagomo is that in my previous six months of practice in Zimbabwe, I had seen only a handful of lying or malingering patients. And all of those were men trying to get a greater supply of a medication called Benzhexol, also known as trihexiphenidyl (try-hex-ee-FEN-ah-dill), which offsets the muscle stiffness and tremors that are side effects of antipsychotic medications. Benzhexol acts as a mild stimulant, giving patients a quick little buzz.

"We'll get to that question in just a bit," I said, "about taking time off from work. What is it that you're thinking about all the time?"

"All of my problems," she started. "I live alone. I'm lonely. My brother won't help me. I have high blood pressure. My back hurts. My heart is heavy, my chest hurts, I can't breathe." As Sister Pagomo cited this litany of ills, her lower lip drew downward, her frown grew until her entire face became a giant upside-down smile.

"Don't you ever feel like crying?"

"All the time."

"Do you cry sometimes?"

"I can't. No matter how bad I feel." A double burden: to be depressed and unable to cry. Crying helps to unload the emotional and physical tension that builds when a person holds himself or herself in a suspended state of depression.

I took note of her physical complaints. She told me that she had been diagnosed with high blood pressure, high cholesterol, and arthritis. I could see by her cards that her doctor was worried about her having heart disease. He had done an electrocardiogram, which was normal. He believed that her chest pain resulted directly from depression, although he hadn't completely excluded other potential medical causes.

Only in her mid-thirties, Sister Pagomo, with her slumped shoulders, frown, and gray hair, fraying around the edges, appeared fifteen or twenty years older. I noted that her blood pressure pills included Aldomet and hydrochlorothiazide. These were a couple of older medications for hypertension, with Aldomet being notorious for potentially causing depression in about 10 percent of patients who took it. "Aha," I thought, "now I have a small toehold." I would start by asking her primary doctor to switch her to different pills for her high blood pressure.

"Sister, did you suffer any losses recently—you know, a friend or relative dying, a breakup of a relationship?"

"Yes, my mother died."

"When?" I asked, my interest piqued, trying to get a line on something to address in this woman's life.

"Five years ago."

I was not surprised. It was nearly universal that patients described their parents as dying "recently" if it was any time in the last ten years.

"How did your mother die?"

"A heart attack."

"Did she ever feel like she needed to 'rest her mind'?"

"Yes, she had many worries before she died. The worries killed her. She was young, only forty-nine. She was still raising the youngest of my seven brothers and sisters. She could not rest. She had to clean and cook and tend the garden and watch my cousins."

"So you think the worrying contributed to her having a heart attack and dying?"

"Yes, *chiremba*. I need to rest my mind."

This piece of information was very telling. It indicated that Sister Pagomo was a somewhat suggestible individual who, unconsciously, may regress to the role of being sick to avoid emotional pain or responsibility. She saw her mother as something that we call a "symptom model" in psychiatry. Her mother suffered similar medical symptoms and emotional problems as Sister Pagomo was now experiencing. This can be considered as a strong identification with her mother, occurring entirely on an unconscious level.

This similarity of symptoms between Sister Pagomo and her dead mother was an ominous sign as far as I was concerned. It meant to me that Sister Pagomo's depression and recent regression were pretty well socked in. It also meant that her recovery would take a fair amount of hard work and possibly the aggressive use of medications to lift the veil of fog that hung over her mind, body, and spirit.

"Do you feel as if you're bewitched? By her? Or anyone else?"

"No, my mother is trying to help me. She has not abandoned me. I do not feel bewitched by her."

"Have you been to a *n'anga*?"

"No, I do not believe in them. I am a Christian."

"Well, then, have you been to a *profita*?"

"No, I am studying to be a nurse. I believe in modern things, not the old ways of our elders or the new ways of the missionaries."

I realized that in an odd sort of a way, her "rational" attitude might make her more difficult to treat. I often found it helpful to refer patients to their *n'anga* or *profita* of choice so they could benefit from a combination of traditional cultural treatment and conventional Western medical treatment.

I wanted to believe that benevolent spirits, much like guardian angels, could facilitate the healing process in my patients by virtue of the individual's faith in those spirits. I did not necessarily believe that the *n'anga* could induce improvement in my patients via the direct intercession of spirits and ancestors, but I was wholeheartedly banking on a variation of the placebo effect, which too many people inappropriately brush off as skullduggery. The power of the patient's expectation of getting better with the help of a doctor or a minister is a genuine phenomenon and its effect alone contributes to the improvement of an amazing one-in-three patients. As a clinician, I welcome anything that can improve my chances of being effective as long as that treatment "does no harm." Among practitioners of the "art" of medicine, the placebo effect, because it works as often as it does, is a powerful and welcome tool in the clinical armamentarium.

Within Shona culture, not only are beliefs in the Spirit World common, but they are also held deeply, without question. That is precisely why Shona patients prefer to initially consult with *n'anga* and *profita*, seeking help from these "traditional medical providers" with a confidence and an expectation that their treatments will help. Social psychologists might call this a serendipitous "expectancy set" while theologians would simply classify it as "faith." For me, the point was moot. Among my Shona patients, I could not distinguish the placebo effect from the effect of faith in benevolent spirits. The debatable, unanswerable question becomes: "Does the magnitude of an individual's faith correspond with the efficacy of the placebo effect within that individual?" The answer from a clinician who's not a metaphysician: "I don't know and I don't care as long as that faith does no harm and the patient gets better." And in the case of Sister Pagomo, as challenging as it was appearing already, I wanted to marshal any type of help that I could find.

"You mentioned being alone. Are you divorced, widowed, never married?"

"Never married. I had a boyfriend once, when I was twenty-two, I was pretty then, I wasn't fat, but he never proposed to me and then he married someone else."

"Have you dated since then?"

"No."

"What's the problem with your brother?"

"He lives nearby, with his wife and four children. He never visits me. He says that I am crazy. He doesn't want me to be around his children, he says."

"What's he afraid of?"

"He says I am a bad influence because I am unhappy, fat, lazy. He even called me 'slovenly' the other day."

"Can't you just ignore him?"

"I can, but he is the only family that I have left. The rest have either died or moved to South Africa. Like I said, I am alone."

I eventually moved on to questions regarding the symptoms of depression. These were largely pro forma, given the fact that Sister Pagomo appeared as a "poster child" for depression—thoughts slowed, experiencing sadness, sleeping too much, feeling sluggish and lonely, not functioning at work. She had gained 15 pounds in the last month. She admitted to taking only one bath per week, down from every other day, and said that her housekeeping had deteriorated significantly. She denied active plans to attempt suicide.

It seemed quite obvious to me that she was suffering from a clinical depression. As for this condition of thinking too much, it was reminiscent of several cases of depression with obsessive-compulsive features that I had seen both in the clinic in Zimbabwe and also among several patients that I had had in San Francisco. These people often responded well to a trial of an antidepressant medication and a bit of therapy. Sister Pagomo's case seemed more complicated than many cases of depression that I had come across in Zimbabwe because of the psychological complications of her unconscious identification with her mother and the possibility that she was exaggerating her symptoms to avoid going back to work. I also considered a concurrent diagnosis of a personality disorder—maybe dependent, maybe schizoid, maybe avoidant—or else a touch of psychotic thinking, any of which would make her depression more difficult to treat.

I thought it made sense to start her on imipramine, a tricyclic antidepressant. I noted her normal electrocardiogram. This record was important because imipramine can alter the heart's system of electrical conduction. I also noted that it did not have any dangerous interactions with her other medications. I started her on 25 milligrams at night until we would meet again next Monday, in just four days, to continue the evaluation. If she were tolerating that dose of medication, then I would increase it to 50 milligrams and on upward to a target dose of 150 milligrams or so.

I wrote a cryptic note on her flimsy medical card, assuming that the matrons of the hospital would get their information some other way. I still felt weird about having to report my clinical findings to Sister Pagomo's supervisors, in a separate meeting, thereby breaking her confidentiality, but the rules of play were obviously different here in Zimbabwe. I made a conscious decision to play along. I also wrote a letter to Matron Mukaranga, requesting a two-week leave of absence from work for Sister Pagomo because of her illness of depression. In retrospect, granting such a long sick leave to Sister Pagomo might have been a mistake.

Sister Pagomo's mantra of "I need to rest my mind" reverberated around my head for the next week. I found myself repeating it over and over again, delivering the phrase in a tight-lipped, low-pitched, monotone style. I did not fully realize it at the time, but her mantra was a valuable clue to what she thought she was suffering from. It was then that I learned about the uniquely Shona illness of *kufungisisa* (koo-foon-ghee-SEE-sah) from my colleagues, Vikram Patel and Mark Winston, in the Department of Psychiatry.

Saying that she needed to "rest her mind" told me that Sister Pagomo believed that she was afflicted with the condition of *kufungisisa*, literally "to think too much" in Shona. As I came to find out, *kufungisisa* was a word and an affliction understood by many Shona people. The fact that the Shona even have a specific one-word verb for something that takes three words for us to say in English tells you something about how well-established this condition is among the Shona.

Shona health-care professionals believed that day-to-day stress and "life problems" were the most common cause of anxiety and depression in their patients. However, most patients suffering from *kufungisisa* often believed in supernatural factors as potential causes of their anxiety and depression. According to research by Dr. Patel, more than half of patients seen at a primary-care clinic and identified as suffering from the Western equivalent of anxiety or mild to moderate depression attributed their symptoms to the condition of *kufungisisa*. In general, they felt that *kufungisisa* was an illness of the *pfungwa* and *mweya*, the mind and the soul, and considered the possibility that supernatural factors caused their illness.

While some of these individuals consulted *n'anga* for their problems, many others responded to simple measures of support and counseling. A few patients with *kufungisisa* suffered from the equivalent of a major depression or anxiety disorder, however, and required medication and follow-up. Unwilling to see a *n'anga* and unmoved by counseling, Sister Pagomo presented a particularly tough case of *kufungisisa*.

Sister Pagomo didn't show up on Monday. I was a little bit frustrated and a little bit relieved because I didn't relish having to try to dynamite that woman out of her depression. I remember clearly telling her that I wanted to see her four days hence and writing her appointment time and date on her card. I visualized her now-perpetual scowl and remembered her mouthing "yes, *chiremba*" while clutching her valuable talisman of my letter, signed, stamped, sealed, to be hand-delivered by Sister Pagomo that Thursday afternoon to her supervisor, Matron Mukaranga.

Finishing up the last of my work, delivering a "*chisarai chakanaka*" to Sister Mada, I decided to amble over to pay Matron Chengeta a visit. I knew that my "gift" of a carte-blanche two-week sick leave to Sister Pagomo might have deprived her of the motivation to come back and see me. She might have thought, "Hey, I need to rest my mind [r-r-r-rest m-EYE m-EYE-nd] and here this nice *marungu* consultant psychiatrist kindly gives me two weeks to r-r-r-rest m-EYE m-EYE-nd. Can't beat that."

I entered the chain-link gate. No throngs then, as they were still occupied by lunch—morning, noon, and night it was *sadza*, *sadza*, and more *sadza,* sometimes mixed with a few greens or chunks of gristle in a thin soup. I made my way directly for Matron Chengeta's office. She sat at her desk, head bent over the typewriter, doing God knows what. Her door was open. I stuck my head in.

"*Masikati*, Matron Chengeta."

"Oh, *chiremba, masikati, maswera sei*?"

"*Taswera*. So, I came by to tell you that Sister Pagomo did not make her appointment for today."

"Oh."

"I saw her last Thursday, she said she'd come and see me today, and . . ."

"We need to go out and do a home visit," interrupted the matron.

"What?"

"A home visit. We need to go out and see her. I spoke with the matron-in-charge Friday and she told me she is very worried about her."

This was getting a little too deep for me. I knew that British psychiatrists often went to their patients' homes, but, still, I thought that making a home visit to see Sister Pagomo was overkill. Just because the matron-in-charge was worried, the whole system was getting overheated. I could think of dozens of patients that I had seen in the weeks before who were more in need of a home visit than Sister Pagomo. I thought about arguing with the matron, but I relented, understanding her rationale and her lack of choice, really, in deciding whether we should go out to see Sister Pagomo.

Early the next day I found Matron Chengeta and her second-in-command, Sister Zvomuya, waiting by the matron's slightly battered, high-mileage, late 1970s Datsun. No Mercedes for the matron, only for the government ministers. *Mangwanani*s were exchanged and off we went. Sister Pagomo lived just south of Harare's downtown, on the way to the airport southeast of the city center, in a suburb called Hatfield.

The suburbs of Harare are generally divided into two distinct types: the "low-density" suburbs, home to mostly whites and the most affluent blacks, with big homes and lots, lush gardens, high fences, and nighttime security guards; and the "high-density" suburbs, site of densely packed apartments and small homes crammed together on small lots, where the unemployed and working poor lived.

Somewhere between the two extremes, Hatfield was a medium-density suburb, home primarily to black people with decent jobs and some financial backing.

We pulled up to Sister Pagomo's home, a smallish wooden structure situated toward the back of a wooded, decent-sized lot. Her yard was a shambles of junk thrown all around, the vines and bushes overgrown, the sprawl guarded by a fair-sized German shepherd mix who barked loudly at our arrival at the front of the gate. There was no other sign of life. The fence was topped with barbed wire, looking something like the security system at the P.U. The matron pushed the door buzzer over and over again, but there was no answer and no visible movement from the house. The dog approached us, woofing at us with teeth bared, then it quickly backed off and just looked up at us as a curiosity. Matron Chengeta then pushed her car horn; the tooting getting softer and softer as it drained the juice on the battery. The dog started howling again. The matron stopped her hooting.

We just stood there, surveying the padlocked gate. It wouldn't have been impossible to scale the fence, but we all decided to hold off. None of us was the nimble sort and the thought of wrestling with a German shepherd mix gave me pause. We were still standing there, like the three amigos of African mental hygiene, discussing our options, when a hulking but timid figure emerged from the side door of the house. Wearing a faded yellow housedress with black smudgy handprints along her sides, Sister Pagomo methodically waddled to the gate. Her hair was uncombed and unwashed. Her frown was more pronounced than ever. She had nothing to say.

Matron Chengeta took charge. "We are worried about you. How are you looking after yourself?"

Sister Pagomo stood there, looking dumbfounded.

"When did you last take a bath? How are you cooking for yourself? Have you had any visitors?"

Matron Chengeta might as well have been speaking to someone who was blind, deaf, and dumb.

"When are you coming to work? When are you going to see Dr. Linde again? Do you have clean water? Do you have any food in the house? Who is doing your yard work these days?"

Finally, Matron Chengeta got down to brass tacks. "We're coming in! Let us in!" Her tone a strange brew of pleading and anger, she implored, "You can't live like this!"

"No!" said Sister Pagomo loudly. "Leave me alone!"

"Let us in! We came to see how you are taking care of yourself. We came to do a home visit!"

"No!" said Sister Pagomo again. "Leave me alone. I need to rest my mind." She then tottered back toward her house.

Matron Chengeta yelled after her: "If you don't come to see me by ten o'clock tomorrow morning, I will have the police come and get you, I'll have you sectioned, and you'll be admitted to the P.U. Do you understand?"

By this time, Sister Pagomo had reached the door, silently opened it, and walked inside. Matron Chengeta was now more than a little miffed. She essentially gave a direct order to an underling, only to find it rebuffed. This was like a buck private ignoring the order of a decorated captain. I was glad to share my responsibility and frustration with Matron Chengeta in the matter of Sister Pagomo's precarious mental health.

The next morning Sister Pagomo showed up at Matron Chengeta's office at two minutes to ten. She was dressed in her shapeless nurse's aide uniform, apron and all. Smelling strongly of body odor, her hair still a tangle, Sister Pagomo sadly reminded me of Happy Mufananidza in his soiled Red Cross uniform, hanging on to a shred of self-esteem by the thinnest of tethers. Matron Chengeta took one look at her and marched her over to Harare Central's Casualty Department to have her "sectioned" by the Casualty doctor. As the matron and two blue-coated security guards tried to escort Sister Pagomo back to the P.U., the nurse's aide cried hysterically, rolling around on the ground, trying to run away across the fields. The guards gently restrained her, and she eventually calmed down enough to walk back to the P.U.

I was working away that day in the outpatient clinic, blissfully unaware of all these goings-on. As usual, my mind was fully occupied by the various plights of the stream of patients who came to see me. Tragedy and misfortune and need never go out of style. Fortunately, I had a good crew of junior doctors on duty that day. They stayed on task and we saw 135 patients in five hours. I swung by the inpatient ward after clinic and was surprised to see Sister Pagomo decked out in hospital pajamas and a striped bathrobe. She sat glumly on a log over in the corner of the courtyard, unprotected from a blazing afternoon sun on a still day in which the temperature flirted with the 40-degree centigrade mark (more than 100 degrees Fahrenheit). Her clothes were filthy with dust, her forehead glistened with sweat, and her frown threatened to pull her nose beneath her chin, a subjugated and dusty Buddha.

Sister Pagomo took no notice of me as I walked past her, on my way to the nurses' station. I waved meekly in her direction, appearing ridiculous I'm sure, flashing her the bared teeth of a sliver of a grin. Matron Chengeta presided over the goings-on at the nurses' station. After a perfunctory greeting, she took me aside, into the dimly lit interview room, to explain to me the events of the morning. She began to talk feverishly to me about the treatment plan for Sister Pagomo when I caught her off guard by reminding her that I was scheduled for a week's vacation, due to depart in just two days. That meant that my colleague, Dr. Mark Winston, a Welsh psychiatrist in the midst of a two-year stint as an academic psychiatrist at the University of Zimbabwe Medical School and a fellow laborer as a consultant psychiatrist at the P.U., would assume Sister Pagomo's care for the next week.

"No problem, Matron," I said. "I will catch up with Dr. Winston tomorrow and fill him in on the case. "Let's increase her imipramine to 100 milligrams, that is, if she's even taking it. Get a full set of labs. Dr. Nhiwatiwa will be admitting her. She'll be in good hands."

Before I left, I informed Dr. Winston of the situation, trying to forewarn him of Sister Pagomo's definite intransigence, possible psychosis, and probable personality disorder. He took the information in stride.

When I returned from my holiday, I heard Dr. Winston singing a decidedly different tune. Normally reserved and always politic, he did not mince words in referring to Sister Pagomo.

"Now, I see what you were talking about," said Dr. Winston, clapping me on the back, chipper, thin, energetic, bespectacled, wearing a white shirt and a conservative striped red tie, speaking loudly in his clipped British accent. A nervous laugh danced around the corners of his mouth. "At first, I thought your protests were overblown, but she is a stubborn one. She remains invested in a continuation of the sick role. She has gone on a hunger strike and," with a chuckle and a wink, he said "given her girth, it might take more than a year to do her in. In spite of this hunger strike, her weight has not changed. She is probably sneaking leftovers after the others have eaten. I don't know who she's torturing more—Matron Chengeta, herself, the nursing staff, me, or soon to be you. That's the bad news. The good news is that, objectively, she is looking less depressed—her affect is brighter, her hygiene has improved, she is getting up in the morning. I even caught her smiling once. She is now on a solid dose of imipramine, 150 milligrams, and I also put her on a low dose of trifluoperazine, just 5 milligrams. She seems to be tolerating her medications just fine. Now, I'm ready to turn the case back over to my esteemed colleague from the United States of America, back from his holiday, fresh and ready for a new challenge."

"Thanks again, Mark."

"Right! Cheers!" said Dr. Winston in a deep tone of voice.

"Cheers!" I yelled to him as he briskly walked to his bicycle, which was parked just outside the gate. The hypermetabolic Dr. Winston preferred to cycle the several kilometers from the medical school to the hospital and back again, while his slothful colleagues, myself included, always drove or took a taxi or bus.

I saw Sister Pagomo the next morning on ward rounds. Her hair was clean, done up in a bun on top of her head. She wore fresh clothes. She was still wet from a shower that morning. She did not know that I had spied her in the hallway earlier that morning before rounds, smiling and talking to a fellow patient. But when she sat before me on my morning ward rounds, her frown once again distorted her face, eyes down, nothing to say.

"How is your mood?" I started.

"No better."

"Are you eating?"

"No, I have eaten nothing. I am on a hunger strike."

"I see. Then why does Matron Chengeta tell me that she thinks you are doing so much better?"

"I don't know. *Chiremba*, my two weeks is coming to an end. I need more time. I need to r-r-r-r-est m-EYE m-EYE-nd."

"Is your *kufungisisa* getting any better?"

"Ah, you are speaking Shona," said Sister Pagomo, her face involuntarily breeching into a brief grin. I had to restrain myself from yelling "Hah, caught ya lookin' happy." She reverted to her frown immediately. "No, I am still suffering from it."

"Do the medicines help at all?"

"Yes, they are helping. My chest is less heavy. My headaches went away. Thank you for your help. I need a letter. I need to r-r-r-r-est m-EYE m-EYE-nd."

"Well, Sister Pagomo, I think you need to think about going back to work. I'm worried that the longer that you are away from work, the harder it will be for you to go back. I'm afraid that writing a letter for you may make things worse."

"Oh, no, *chiremba*, no, I still need to r-r-r-r-est m-EYE m-EYE-nd."

"Well, we still have until next week. I will be back here on Friday. We'll see how you feel then and we'll talk more about it then."

I felt good about the case. Not that I could take very much credit for what had transpired, but I felt good about moving Sister Pagomo along in life, getting her back to work. I was so pleased with this development that I nearly skipped out of the unit that day, happy to have Sister Pagomo one more step toward being out of my life.

What Matron Chengeta was to tell me on Friday knocked me for a loop.

"I spoke to Matron Mukaranga about Sister Pagomo. She is glad that she is better, but she does not want her back. She has already filled her position with someone else."

"But, but, what does the matron-in-charge say? Isn't it her decision?"

"Oh, the matron-in-charge agrees with Matron Mukaranga. She has assigned Sister Pagomo to work on the P.U."

"What?" The thought of working around Sister Pagomo's walking frown on a day-to-day basis terrified me.

"The matron-in-charge says it will be a good part of her recovery. Matron tells me that she is relieved that you and I can keep a close eye on Sister Pagomo in case the sister again becomes unwell."

"And what did you say to that?" I implored, my anger rising. "That's a dump! It's a crazy idea if I ever heard one. Dump your personnel problems over on psych? How convenient."

"What could I say?" said Matron Chengeta, drawing a heavy sigh. "I have to obey her order. The hospital is not a democracy. If the matron-in-charge says that's the way it will be, then it will be that way. It's just the way things work here in Zimbabwe."

"Does Sister Pagomo know about the plan?"

"I told her. She doesn't like it, but she will accept it."

"Okay," I said, sighing an exhalation of resignation. "If she is better on Friday, then I will discharge her and she can start work on Monday."

Friday ward rounds rolled around. My fears of Sister Pagomo regressing into a shell of catatonia or breaking out into a contagion of mania were unfounded. Although she presented me with yet another version of an upside-down smile, she continued to take care of basic hygiene and improve on her sleep. She grudgingly acknowledged that her spirits were a little bit better.

After exchanging greetings that morning, Sister Pagomo started our conversation. "Matron told me. I am to start work here next week. I can't. Don't you see, *chiremba*? I still need to rest my mind."

I thought about throwing a wrench into the proceedings and writing her another two-week sick leave, giving me a respite from her. But, if she deteriorated, then she would be back here as a patient on the psychiatric ward. That wouldn't do anybody any favors. I knew that, from an ethical standpoint, the matter had nothing to do with how the situation affected me but what was best for the patient, in this case Sister Pagomo. I realized that her returning to work gave her the best chance of overcoming her depression, regaining her confidence, and returning to independence.

I'm sure Sister Pagomo saw me as both a sucker and savior. In her mind, I could rescue her with another miraculous two-week leave. Rather than getting angry with her, however, I decided to steal a page from the book of psychodynamic theory and attempt a psychological interpretation on her. Maybe I was selling her a little too short by thinking she wasn't worth the trouble. Maybe I had been a little too condescending and impatient, causing me to think unkindly of her.

"Sister, do you remember telling me that your mother died of heart problems."

"Yes."

"If I remember correctly, she was in her late forties when she died. She had too many worries. She needed to rest her mind, but never got a chance to because of all her responsibilities at home."

"That's right, *chiremba*."

"I think I know why you are so frightened."

"Yes?"

"You are terrified that you are going to die like your mother, of heart problems. You think that her worries killed her. That's why you are so desperate to 'rest your mind.' You think the only way to prevent your death is to do nothing for the next several years, to rest at home and do nothing."

Sister Pagomo looked downward, the frown rippling the corners of her mouth. Slowly, miraculously, a tear rolled out of her right eye and down her cheek. A single solitary tear. She made no attempt to dab it. "You are right, *chiremba*," she said.

"Sister, you need to be around people," I said. "Or else you will wither up and die. Since you do not have seven children and a husband to take care of, you can rest your mind every evening after you get home from work. But you need to come to work, to be around people, to combat loneliness. You may even make some friends, to help you with your loneliness. I think that your depression drove your brother away and kept many others at a distance. Your depression is much better, in my opinion, and you should make a full recovery over time. I think you're okay to be discharged today. Keep drinking your tablets. I will give you a two-week prescription for now."

Sister Pagomo went home that day. The next week she showed up punctually for work. I can only imagine that those patients who knew her as a peer had to be dumbfounded by her reappearance in a nurse's aide uniform. Whenever I passed her, after the greeting, she would look down and frown. But at other times, I would see her chatting in Shona. At first, she did well in her duties, but by Thursday, Sister Pagomo arrived an hour late and was listless in performing her work.

By Friday, she did not show up for work at all. Back to the drawing board. After ward rounds, around noon, I set off for Matron Chengeta's office to commiserate and to sketch out a blueprint of attack. What was once the surgical ward's problem and responsibility was now ours. Maybe Sister Pagomo's vigorous positive response to my slick interpretation was just too good to be true.

I knocked on Matron Chengeta's door. She had kept a low profile that morning, sequestered in her office, doing paperwork and returning telephone calls. I knew that she was also getting frustrated with Sister Pagomo's disappearance and seeming obstinacy. Matron Chengeta opened the door, saying nothing, seemingly not surprised to see me. She looked spent, like the blood had been drained from her face. I slumped in a chair and hung my head. I didn't feel like crying, just like throwing up. I gathered my wits.

"So, Matron, now what?" I asked. "Can we just transfer her back? What should we do?"

"She's ours, *chiremba,*" said Matron Chengeta. "I thought she was getting better. She was doing a good job through Wednesday. I don't know what happened."

"Oh, Matron, I hate to say this, but I think that there is more than a trace of malingering and personality disorder in Sister Pagomo's case."

"Yes, I'm afraid you're right, *chiremba*. It is not something that we see much of around here."

"So, can you tell the matron-in-charge," I asked, "and have her fired?" A gleam of a wicked smile passed my lips.

"As much as I would like to, I think we need to try harder," said Matron Chengeta.

"Ugh, don't say that," I winced.

"And here's what we need to do next."

"Yes?" I said, swallowing hard.

Matron Chengeta paused. "We need to do another home visit."

"No, no, no, please!" I yelped. I lay my sweaty forehead down on the palms of my hands, which were resting in front of me on the matron's desk. Slowly I began hyperventilating. The sweat dripped off my forehead. "I can't do it. My head hurts, Matron. I can't breathe. My mind, I need to rest my mind."

"Oh, no," said the matron. "Not you, too."

CHAPTER EIGHT

"There Are No Guarantees."

Mister Dube: Nearly Scared to Death

"Broken bodies, broken bones,
Broken voices on broken phones.
Take a deep breath, feel like you're chokin'
Everything is broken."

-Bob Dylan
Everything Is Broken

I thought I had made a full and rapid recovery from my Sister Pagomo episode when Thomas Dube came to see me with his mother on a busy clinic day. It was a blazing morning, overexposed by a whiteout of hot yellow sunshine, the kind that makes one blink repeatedly even while wearing sunglasses. The month was October, which the natives in Zimbabwe call "the suicide month" because the heat and humidity can be staggering: southern Africa reaches an agonizing crescendo of dust, glare, and wind building up to the first rains of the year. There is a persistent worry that drought will cause pockets of starvation in the country. Allegedly, the suicide rate peaks in October.

The timing of Mr. Dube's visit had little to do with this seasonal cycle of the earth, however. He was, rather, a victim of a man-made cycle—specifically a seven-year period of incarceration at Mlondolozi, an infamous forensic mental hospital near Zimbabwe's "Second City," Bulawayo, in the country's parched southwestern corner. I refer to Thomas Dube as Mr. Dube and not by his first name out of respect for him, borne out of my horror at imagining the level of his suffering at the hands of his guards. I did not have direct evidence of his torture, but I could reasonably surmise from the mental wreckage he presented that Mr. Dube was literally nearly scared to death while he was an inmate at Mlondolozi.

Although he was only in his late twenties, Mr. Dube was psychologically a very old man, living on an emotional deathbed. My task, to resuscitate him emotionally, was a daunting one with long odds. Medications were unlikely to undo the damage that had been done. His condition, either an especially severe case of post-traumatic stress disorder or a treatment-resistant psychotic depression, rendered Mr. Dube emotionally withered, drawn inward, hardened like the spore of a plant trying to survive the harshness of drought. I speculate that he shut himself down during his time at Mlondolozi in order to save himself.

Mr. Dube was accompanied, on his first visit to me, by his mother, an unassuming rural woman in her fifties, who should have been relieved of such monumentally difficult mothering duties at her age. She should have been enjoying a well-deserved rest, basking in the status of being a respected elder female within her tight community, visiting friends and family, leisurely tending to her garden, drinking ceremonial beer, and occasionally babysitting her grandchildren. She had raised Thomas and his four siblings as a single mother, all of whom except Thomas had grown up to live lives of independence and modest success. But now Grace Dube was saddled with the care of her damaged youngest son, who needed constant supervision and occasional assistance with simple activities of daily living such as feeding, dressing, and washing.

While my treatment of Thomas Dube would push me up against my limitations as a psychiatrist, the experience also taught me a valuable lesson. Grace and Thomas Dube unintentionally reminded me of the stigma that demonizes mentally ill people everywhere and instructed me on the unique twists of that discrimination in Zimbabwe. They also alerted me to the brutal reality that is the forensic mental health system in their country. I never thought I would be in the position of defending America's seriously flawed system of care for mentally ill criminal offenders, but, I have to admit, Zimbabwe's forensic psychiatric hospitals made America's look downright cheery.

A short, thin woman with lightly muscled forearms and calves entered the room. She curtsied lightly and grinned just long enough for me to note that her teeth were in poor repair. Gray hair sprouted from underneath a blue-and-white gingham kerchief. She wore a clean, threadbare, blue dress and certain bright yellow plastic sandals that were often advertised before movies at Harare's cinemas, with Oliver M'tukudzi, one of Zimbabwe's celebrity musicians, singing the praises of the shoe—"Sandak, it's the right direction." This would be Grace Dube's only nod to fashion. As she made a shallow bow and clapped her hands in the traditional way, she greeted me: "*Mangwanani, chiremba.*"

"*Mangwanani, ambuya,*" I offered, referring to her as a respected elder female, simultaneously performing a deferential "son-in-law" clap of the hands. She probably got a kick out of the *marungu* male doctor deferring to *her*, a simple peasant woman. But I believed that her status as an elder demanded that she be respected.

We completed a formal version of the morning greeting before she handed me her son's cards. But there was no sign of the son. I looked at the card on top of a stack of half a dozen or so and saw the name of Thomas Dube. I quickly glanced down—a few visits out in the district clinic for medication refills on his trifluoperazine and amitriptyline. Little other information was there.

"My name is Dr. Linde," I said. "A pleasure to meet you. Who is Thomas Dube? How can I help you?"

"Pleased to meet you. My name is Grace Dube. Thomas is my son. He is outside the door, waiting. I wanted to speak with you first. I also have a letter for you."

She handed me an officially stamped and sealed manila brown business-sized envelope. I ripped it open and pulled out a handwritten note, printed carefully in blue ink on a flimsy lined piece of paper, from the psychiatric nurse who ministered at the Dubes' local clinic near Shurugwi. Of course, both the letter and envelope had been copiously stamped.

It read, in brief: "Thomas is a 27-year-old man with a diagnosis of schizophrenia who is on TFPZ and AMT [short for the antidepressant amitriptyline]. He is not improving with these medications. He speaks little, doesn't always respond to questions, and appears to hear voices. His sleep, eating, hygiene are okay and his mother says he follows directions and does not cry. He sits alone in his room much of the day, staring at the walls and looking out the window. He was an inmate at Mlondolozi for several years. Could this be a factor in his current mental status? I refer him to you for an evaluation and possible treatment. We are happy to follow him here and prescribe his medications, but I wait for your input. Yours sincerely, Sister S. Guvamombe, psychiatric sister."

I was always happy to get a referral from the psychiatric nurses out in the bush. They were dedicated and possessed a much greater knowledge of mental health and illness than the general practitioners on the front lines of health care in Zimbabwe. They were some of the very same sisters, who, in the past, might have worked at the Harare Psychiatric Unit. Reading between the lines of the letter and observing the worry lines on Grace Dube's face, I could see that this was going to be an uphill case—certainly not one in which a small medication change would make much of a difference.

"*Chiremba*, he just sits there, staring off into space. It seems to be getting worse. He doesn't do anything unless I tell him to."

I could tell that Grace Dube would be easy to work with. She did not take on the aggrieved whine of a hysterical mother. Nor did she shy away from the challenging task of caring for her son. She was obviously a caring, observant, intelligent, and plainspoken woman.

"I need to tell you a few things before he comes in the room," said Grace as she clasped her hands and exhaled, about to tell a story that she had likely held secret except from her immediate family and the psychiatric sister back in Shurugwi. Not only did she feel shame at these events, but she also knew that, being Ndebele, it would be hard to find a sympathetic ear in the heart of Shona country. Since I was both a professional and a supposedly neutral visitor to Zimbabwe, I imagined that she had few qualms about telling me all the details.

"When Thomas was eighteen, he chased a man down the road with a machete. When Thomas caught up with him, he hit the man several times on the head. And then for some reason, he stopped. The man survived but was never the same. He was a Shona man with a large family. It was a great tragedy for his family. We have tried to pay restitution, but our finances are tight. I live on a small pension from my husband's military service.

"People in the village called the police, who came to arrest Thomas. They took away his weapon. He did not offer resistance. They took him into custody at the police station, where I have reason to believe he was chained to a chair and beaten. At trial, the judge found him insane and committed him to Mlondolozi. He served out the maximum sentence for attempted murder—seven years. He just got out a year or so ago and he has been living with me in the *musha* ever since.

"*Chiremba*, something happened there in Mlondolozi. He has never been the same since." Pointing to the letter in my hands, she said: "Sister has been very kind. She sent us here to see if there is anything else that can be done. I don't know."

"Is it okay for him to come in now?" I asked Grace, knowing that this would be a complex evaluation and that I had many more questions for her, but that I also needed to get a look at Thomas and move things ahead.

"Yes. I'll get him."

In many ways, Mr. Dube looked unremarkable. He was short, about five-foot-seven, and somewhat stocky, with a receding hairline camouflaged by a short buzz-cut. He was dressed in long khaki shorts and a white dress shirt. A somewhat lighter complexion than the average Shona man, along with certain facial features, suggested his Ndebele lineage.

"*Mangwanani*, Mr. Dube," I said, looking him in the eyes, nodding and smiling in his direction. "Please have a seat." He sat down and acknowledged me with a brief glance into my eyes. His face showed no emotion. His arms hung stiffly at his sides and he stared off into space. He was wide-awake, almost hyperalert. He occasionally peered in my direction, but never for long enough to make eye contact. He did not seem to be fearful and lacked the telltale vigilance and scanning of the surroundings that characterized the many paranoid patients that I evaluated in Zimbabwe.

At first glance, he appeared to be overmedicated. But his manner and motor behavior could also have been that of one who suffers the permanent effects of a brain injury or catatonia or who is experiencing the psychological aftermath of severe trauma.

"Your mother was just telling me a little bit about your situation," I said to Mr. Dube. "She seems to be pretty concerned about you."

"Oh, *chiremba*, I forgot to tell you. His English is poor. He can't understand you."

"Does he speak Shona?" I asked, nearly positive that I didn't have an Ndebele-speaking nurse to work with me on that day.

"His Shona is okay, but not very good. I can translate for you into Ndebele."

"I would prefer a nurse to do that for us, but for today that would be okay."

Grace Dube spoke to Thomas in Ndebele for about twenty seconds. "I just told him what you said." Mr. Dube remained motionless, sitting bolt-upright in the wooden chair. I thought to myself, "Was he lost in thought? Lost in space? Lost to the universe?" Whatever he was, he looked like a forlorn little boy, waiting patiently for his mother to return from the store. He almost looked like he was stuck in childhood at about six or seven years old.

Not knowing that Mr. Dube's near muteness was seemingly permanent, I proceeded to ask him a series of open-ended questions, each of which were translated into Ndebele by his mother. Questions such as "How are you feeling?" and "How is your mood?" and "How is your concentration?" were met with blank stares and an occasional tiny smile of politeness and possibly embarrassment. I asked Grace whether he understood.

"These are questions that I'm sure he understands."

I wasn't so sure. How could she be so sure? Yes, he is her son and has been her son for nearly three decades. She should know him well. But, how would I know whether or not he had suffered a small stroke in his brain that was affecting his ability to comprehend, repeat, and speak not just his language, but any language at all? I did some quick thinking. He had virtually no speech output so, if this were a language disorder, it would likely be what neurologists call a nonfluent aphasia in which an individual can comprehend, but not speak, language. If he had had a stroke or tumor in that area of the brain, I would have expected some facial drooping or arm or leg weakness. There was no obvious evidence of problems with motor coordination or strength.

A reasonable opinion from a seasoned internal medicine doctor or neurologist would have been helpful in this case, as in many others. The country supported absolutely no neurologists and just a handful of internal medicine specialists who knew more neurology than the average psychiatrist, which isn't saying much. This was troublesome for me. My skills and knowledge in neurology were fairly limited and, of course, the resources for sophisticated neurological investigations were scanty. I could perform a reasonable neurological exam and identify abnormal findings on exam, but I often was unable to put the history and findings into a coherent whole to identify the problem. An individual essentially needed health insurance or to pay out of pocket to get a computed tomography, or CT, scan of the head. A CT machine, which would have provided a detailed cross-sectional view of the brain, was not available at Harare Central Hospital. I evaluated several patients during my stint in Zimbabwe who very much needed to see a fully qualified neurologist and have access to modern tests.

Similarly, how could I know whether or not he suffered long-term ill effects from having been beaten about the head—rendered bloodied and unconscious by recalcitrant prison guards? Chronic subdural hematomas, collections of bruised soft tissue and old blood underneath the dura, the rubbery covering between the skull and the brain's "thinking cap" of gray matter, could cause confusion and motor slowness. I instinctively looked for scars on his close-shaven head and saw a doozy of a jagged one along his hairline behind the left temple, one that I would have to ask his mother about.

Yet again, how could I know whether Thomas Dube would not have become such a befuddled young man even without spending seven years of his life locked up behind bars at such a brutal prison? In other words, his violent behavior, eight years prior, may have been perpetrated in the midst of an initial psychotic breakdown at an age, in the late teens, when schizophrenia often strikes its victims for the first time. Mr. Dube's attack could very well have been driven from a feeling of paranoia toward the man that he struck. He might have felt a need, at the time, to defend himself against imagined dangers and demons.

Police officers, both in Zimbabwe and in the United States, possess the discretion to escort mentally disturbed individuals, even if they have perpetrated minor crimes, to a hospital for a crisis psychiatric evaluation. But even so, mentally ill people often end up going straight to jail for committing even trifling crimes. Given the seriousness of Mr. Dube's alleged attack on his fellow citizen, I was not surprised that the police had taken him into their own custody.

The local officials in the small village near Shurugwi very likely chose to view the attack as racially motivated, between African brother and African brother—a warlike Ndebele tribesman taking matters into his own hands against his superior, the Shona tribesman. According to some Shona people, Mr. Dube would have harbored numerous reasons to harm his Shona brother—a likely motivation being that of jealousy. In the late 1980s the dominant Shona clearly possessed greater political and economic power than the Ndebele people, a minority comprising about 15 percent of the population. Shona officials near Shurugwi might have then concluded that Mr. Dube viciously assaulted the Shona man because he could never have the things that the Shona man possessed, short of killing him for it.

The conflict between the Shona and Ndebele people has deep historical roots. The Shona say the Ndebele are aggressive, disrespectful, liars, cheats, and thieves. The Ndebele say that the Shona men covet their women and lord their political superiority over the Ndebele. This bad blood between Shona and Ndebele could have meant that Mr. Dube suffered an inordinate amount of mistreatment at the hands of his guards, most certainly Shona, in Mlondolozi.

At times, after Grace Dube had translated another of my futile questions for her apparently mute son, Thomas would break out into an inappropriately bright smile and stare off toward the yellow-painted walls or out the window, where dry, lifeless bushes and small trees stood guard during the hot season. He did not mouth any words to himself; rather he sat there with a goofy fool's grin, staring as if into the void, or down the abyss.

Not a single whiff of wind ruffled the flowery curtains that decorated the windows of my consulting room. I followed Mr. Dube's gaze far out the window over to a field, where I observed a patient of mine, Abraham Mubaranika, the hospital's groundskeeper and a father of six children, swinging a scythe through a tangle of yellowed grass hard up against a wooden fence. Once again I was a shy first-grader on my first day of elementary school, staring out the classroom window toward a sun-scorched field on an unmercifully hot August day in Minnesota, wondering how could I ever survive in the world that I was just then entering. Now, the problems of Mr. Dube made me feel powerless, like a beginner despite my years of experience, like a schoolchild knowing that he can never go back again, never return to the safety and peace of the womb.

"*Chiremba?*" asked Grace Dube, "*Chiremba*, are you okay?"

"Oh, yes," I said. "Thank you. I was just thinking about something else there for a minute."

"I thought perhaps you were unwell, the heat and everything."

"No, no, I'm fine. *Tatenda*."

The thought of treating Mr. Dube unnerved me to the point of distraction, bordering on dissociation. I decided to veer away from the obviously disturbed man before me to get more background from his mother; to painlessly gather pieces of the psychiatric puzzle that I would need if I were ever going to get this situation all sorted out.

"What was Thomas like as a child?" I asked, daring an open-ended question, which seemed like a reasonable gamble given Grace Dube's obvious intelligence and eagerness to help her son.

"He was a happy, normal little boy," she said. "He was the youngest of five children. He was a favorite of my eldest daughter. She took him everywhere for many years."

"Did he socialize with other people?"

"I do remember that he was fairly quiet, his big eyes always watching, watching, watching, trying to figure things out. He was more of a follower than a leader."

"What do you mean? Can you give me an example?"

"He could be easily influenced to do bad things. Like stealing small things, doing what some bad boys would do."

"Did he ever get into any fights, was he aggressive with other children?"

"No, if anything, he was always getting picked on."

"How did he do in school?"

"He was an average student. He completed Form Six. Then our money ran out. He went to work at a commercial farm nearby."

"How old was he then?"

"Maybe twelve."

"And was he a good worker?"

"The bosses liked him because he was strong and quiet. He did not complain. He did not ask for anything other than what they gave him—*sadza*, water, and one short lunch break."

"Does anybody in your family suffer from psychiatric problems?"

"No, nothing like this."

"And how about that scar? The one over his left ear? Did he get that at Mlondolozi?"

"No, oh, no. When he was seven he was hit by a rock playing games with the older boys."

"Was he knocked out? Unconscious?"

"No, but you should have heard him cry." She laughed and looked at her son who sat there, unresponsive to his mother's amazingly persistent delight in him. He appeared as nothing more than a statue with a silly smile plastered across his face as he stared into space. Her own smile waned. "He bled a lot."

"Do you believe that Thomas is being called to be an ancestor spirit? Or has the power of prophecy?"

"No, those are more the ways of the Shona. The Ndebele have a different tradition. But the old ways are dying out, even out in the *musha*. Both the white man and the Shona kill our spirits, kill our traditions."

I looked more closely at Mr. Dube's medical cards and exhaled deeply. There are days that I love a challenge and, for some reason, the first day that I evaluated Mr. Dube was one of them. My interest was piqued, my heartstrings plucked. I was propelled by a complex blend of motivations inherent in the psyche and souls of many caretaker types: one part dry academic interest, one part hot flash of codependency (complete with rescue fantasies), and one part macho challenge. It forced me to dream the impossible dream of fixing someone so irretrievably broken, to make a promise of forevermore in the heat of the moment, just like the unintentional lies of a young lover during a moment of passion. Instead of the ridiculous absolute of "I'll love you forever" it was more like "I can fix this problem once and for all." I wanted to see Mr. Dube several more times, to try and figure out just what ticked inside that masklike demeanor.

"You know, Mrs. Dube, your son's situation is very complicated and my time today is short. I would like to spend more time performing an evaluation and possibly trying some therapy as well. Can you come back next week and for several weeks thereafter so I can get this sorted out?"

"Oh, yes," she said, her face brightening. "We are staying with my father's sister's son's family out in Highfield for as long as it takes."

I noted her face lighting up and the phrase "for as long as it takes" and felt a little sick in my stomach. I did not want to offer false hope. My hot ember of codependency suddenly turned to ash. The chances that I could reverse even a tiny bit of this socked-in psychiatric disturbance, several years in the making, with several weeks of psychopharmacologic tinkering, good intentions, and a smattering of psychotherapy was far-fetched. Nonetheless, I would give it a shot and felt responsible to lay it on the line for her.

"I will see Thomas several times. We'll try different things with the medications. I will do my best to help you and Thomas," I said, before pausing. "But there are no guarantees. Thomas is very sick. I'll do what I can."

I knew that even this statement meant a lot to Grace Dube. Caring for a chronically ill relative is a grinding burden beyond description. The promise of any kind of help is a tremendous relief. One cannot downplay the importance of a competent professional just being there, showing an interest, and attempting different interventions to improve matters and reduce suffering. That being said, many forms of pathology, be they emotional or physical, never respond to the best efforts of well-intentioned doctors and nurses. Her culture and her years of suffering would not allow Grace Dube to be optimistic. But her smile was one of relief, a temporary respite, a slim sliver of hope for her son.

"Next Thursday, come to see me about twelve-thirty. I'll see Thomas last, then we won't be rushed for time. For today, though, I need to stop." I nodded toward the door, where I could envision the usual clinic day mob.

A week passed quickly and I once again found myself at the clinic on a Thursday morning, tending to the usual mental, physical, spiritual, economic, social, and moral problems that presented themselves to me in the form of a whole lineup of patients. The October heat was still with us. Waterfalls of sweat fell from my forehead, back, armpits, and chest. Of course, by the time twelve-thirty came around I was thinking only of making a beeline to my cool cement-block apartment for a pitcher of iced tea and an afternoon siesta on the couch. By twelve-forty-five, as I chicken-scratched the last of my prescriptions and then an official letter, finished off with a flurry of loud and vigorous stamping, I had totally forgotten about my pact with Grace and Thomas Dube.

Visions of a menthol cigarette and a cold soda danced in my head. I nearly sprinted out of the kitchen-cum-pharmacy, bidding a cheery "*Chisarai chakanaka!*" to the ever-faithful and competent Sister Mada when up the gravel path walked the Dubes, huffing and sweating and gleaming, no doubt relieved that they had caught the *marungu* doctor before he left for the day. "Oh, shit," I thought to myself, looking at my watch—ten to one.

"*Chiremba*!" said Grace, "So sorry that we are late. It's my fault. I know you said twelve-thirty and we got on the wrong emergency taxi." The only emergency of the so-called "emergency" taxis, the adjective a vestige of some long-ago transportation crisis in Zimbabwe, is that a flat tire or an exploding engine might kill off one of these sputtering, ancient Peugot station wagons, a popular commuting option in and around Harare. To get from point A to point B, riders get stacked like firewood, nine to a vehicle, for a few Zim dollars apiece, to move across town quickly, on the cheap.

I took one look at this breathless old woman and her hapless son, with his eyes fixed like a fawn in the headlights of an oncoming car, and waved them into my consulting room. They had probably spent nearly ZW$15 and an hour-and-a-half getting here, having had to change emergency taxis at least once, at the Mbare market. How could I just turn them away? Was my quest for immediate personal comfort, in general, and a modest daily nicotine fix, in particular, more important than the needs of these two souls who had been whipsawed by God or the fates or whomever one believes in these days? On some days in Zimbabwe, I made the decision that my needs came first, but on this occasion I could not justify gallivanting off in my luxurious minicompact car after enjoying a furtive smoke and bottle of lemonade in the dusty parking lot in front of the main hospital.

After we settled in my office, I couldn't help but notice the pungent sweetness of ripening sweat in the room, emanating from their bodies, leavened with a hint of woodsmoke. Mr. Dube's tee-shirt was smudged. It appeared as if the relatives had put him to work, hauling wood and working in their small vegetable garden. The smell, of perspiration with hints of wood-smoke, was commonplace among the Zimbabweans that I saw, particularly among the rural and poorer people and especially on the hottest days of the year. I was accustomed to it and, after living in-country for eight months, I had accepted the smell and almost welcomed the fragrance while passing through crowded public places or while in close proximity—such as in this room with the door closed on a sweltering day.

"*Chiremba*, thank you for seeing us. I know you are a busy man."

"If she only knew my slacker agenda for the rest of the day," I thought to myself before I said: "Well, today, one of the things I want to do is sort out your son's medications and still try to get at what his diagnosis may really be."

"Yes, *chiremba*. I brought all the cards."

She handed me a stack of cards nearly 2 inches thick. "Ouch," I thought to myself, "am I really gonna look at all of those cards?" I took up the cards from Grace Dube and peered at the top few. I noticed, in the careful printing of Shurugwi's psychiatric sister, the prescription for last month's medications. The card, dated three weeks earlier, read: "TFPZ 5 mg bds × 1 month [twice a day for one month], AMT 25 mg nocte × 1 month [at bedtime for one month]." I noticed that he had been on the same dosages for several months.

"Has he been taking them?"

"Yes, I always make sure he gets them."

"Do they seem to help at all, as far as you can tell?" I almost always asked this question in Zimbabwe. On rushed days of too many patients and too little time, it was one of the most helpful questions, followed up with "How do they help? In what way?"

"No, I don't think so. He is always just the same."

Following the most basic premise of clinical psychopharmacology (and all of clinical medicine, for that matter)—"Maximize benefit! Minimize harm!"—I continued with my inquiry.

"Well, do the meds give him any problems—stiff arms or legs, trouble swallowing, drooling, shakiness?"

"Not really."

"He looks a little stiff to me. Does he ever get 'locked up' like when he can't move his mouth or his neck or his arms?"

"No. He has always been tight in his joints and his muscles, ever since he got back from Mlondolozi. Like he's on guard or something. But now at home, he has nothing to fear. He doesn't go out. He helps out with chores at home, but everything is taken care of for him."

"Any other side effects that you notice from the medication? Dizziness, dry mouth, double vision, constipation, trouble urinating?"

"No, maybe a little dry mouth," she said. "I'll ask him these questions myself." She turned to him and smiled before starting. His little Cheshire cat grin broadened slightly while she asked him the laundry list of symptoms in the Ndebele language, with its sharp clicks and staccato syncopation. Mr. Dube just looked at his mother blankly after she finished speaking. I thought to myself, cynically, "Yeah, sure, we're gonna get a lot from him."

I proceeded to ask Grace Dube about several different "target symptoms" that psychiatrists attempt to reduce or abolish with psychiatric medications. These are symptoms that the patient has identified as bothersome, ones that can be realistically identified and monitored over time. Such symptoms fall into several broad categories—psychotic, manic, depressed, confused (from dementia or a medical problem), and anxious. Now this next point might seem obvious, but our goal in psychiatry is to use a certain agent to reduce specific symptoms. Antipsychotics target hallucinations and delusions; antidepressants put the symptoms of clinical depression in their sights; anti-anxiety agents ameliorate nervousness; mood stabilizers prevent people's emotions from careening too high or crashing too low. While it is tempting to do so, one shouldn't assume that the medication being prescribed by another doctor is an indicator of the most accurate psychiatric diagnosis. Ideally, a clinical psychiatrist tries to sort out the right diagnosis first before jumping off into prescribing new medications or changing the old ones willy-nilly.

The single best way to make an accurate diagnosis is to obtain as much history as possible, matching the time of onset, course of illness, types and severity of symptoms with a standardized taxonomy of psychiatric diagnoses. A mental illness is often chronic with multiple relapses. Understanding the sequence and context of stressors, symptoms, and treatments within an individual's personal history often allows the doctor to solve these diagnostic puzzles.

I was lucky to have Grace Dube as a historian. Getting the story from a reliable source was critical to making the right call, especially in Zimbabwe, where medical records were not always available, having been lost, burned, stained, shredded, besotted, or otherwise mutilated. Of course, Grace Dube could not tell me much about Mr. Dube's time at Mlondolozi.

The second most important piece of information in making an accurate diagnosis comes from the performance of a current mental status examination of the patient. Unlike in general medicine, where the basic skills of history-taking and performing a physical examination have been usurped by the introduction of high-tech gee-whiz scans and lab tests, the practice of psychiatry has remained remarkably low-tech. In psychiatry, the history and mental status examination are indispensable for making a reasonable diagnosis. The psychiatrist must observe the patient closely and document his appearance, speech, behavior, movements, affect (the facial mask that we present to the world), mood, thought process, perceptions (including abnormal ones like hallucinations), thought content (including false beliefs, preoccupations, suicidal or homicidal thoughts), cognitive abilities, insight, and judgment.

With the invaluable help of Grace Dube, I discovered that Mr. Dube did seem confused and that he did, at times, talk to himself, but he did not voice delusions of paranoia or grandeur. He did not mention suicide. He did not clearly state a mood, but did not seem particularly elevated, euphoric, depressed, or anxious. He seemed mostly blah.

It appeared that Mr. Dube had been in the midst of a prolonged psychotic breakdown around the time he assaulted a prominent member of the Shona community. Because, as Grace Dube tells it (and I had no reason to doubt her veracity), Thomas Dube had been acting strangely for weeks prior to his commission of the assault and subsequent arrest. At the time, Thomas Dube repetitively muttered to himself, stopped washing, referred to his neighbors as "Shona devils," and slept less and less, eventually staying up all night, becoming more hyperactive. In fact, she had taken him to a traditional healer who recommended that she take her son to a medical doctor since the healer could not sort out a spiritual cause of the young man's behavioral disturbance. The day before the assault, Thomas Dube had seen a general practitioner, who had performed a physical examination and sent off for several blood tests, searching for a medical cause for the young man's strange behavior. A referral to a psychiatrist or psychiatric nurse was sure to follow. But it would be too late for Mr. Dube.

So, one could quite safely assume that Mr. Dube was psychotic at the time. We call this severely disturbed behavior "crazy as hell" among ourselves in the business. I am not necessarily proud of this brand of professional irreverence, gallows humor, if you will, but it is the truth. I further probed Grace to find out whether she had ever observed a recurrence of this behavior. She clearly stated "no" and reiterated that her son had been this reclusive, confused, nearly mute self since he had gotten out of Mlondolozi.

As I've mentioned before, one episode of grossly disturbed behavior does not necessarily mean that a patient will go on to become chronically psychotic. About half of all individuals who suffer a psychotic episode will never suffer another one. Many of these people are afflicted with an acute medical illness that causes "brain failure" or they become psychotic in response to overwhelming psychosocial stress or intoxication on drugs or alcohol.

"Mrs. Dube, is it possible that Thomas was abusing *mbanje* at the time of his breakdown?"

"Yes," she stammered. "Yes, I'm afraid he might have been. It was a good growing season and all of the plants were high that spring. I know the older boys grew it. They tried to hide it from me, but a mother always knows these things."

"Well, if he was using it, I'm sure it didn't help, but given how long Thomas was unwell, there must have been more to it than just that." Cannabis-induced psychoses are usually fairly brief.

Given that the time of onset and the quality of his symptoms back then were consistent with a psychotic disorder or possibly an adolescent onset of manic-depressive illness, I thought it was plausible that he might have suffered from schizophrenia or bipolar disorder. His current mental status exam suggested either someone who was psychotic—thoughts slowed, nearly mute, affect blunted, talking to himself at home, smiling inappropriately—or possibly depressed, although I doubted this, given his bland and blah mood state. Thomas Dube seemed idiotically unaware of his predicament, wearing a peaceful, almost blissed-out smile—his pilot light was on, but the flame of emotionality had been permanently extinguished. Although the potentates of American psychiatric taxonomy find this observation unscientific, those of us working on the front lines of clinical psychiatry would say that this lack of awareness and lack of ability to relate to other people more likely indicated a psychotic disorder rather than a disorder of mood. So my best guess is that Mr. Dube probably would have been saddled with a chronic, relapsing, psychotic illness even under the best of circumstances.

On top of all this, I needed to factor in the trauma that he no doubt experienced while an inmate in Mlondolozi. I had to consider it, his visage and manner were exactly consistent with a textbook case of "shellshock"—what the wizards of *DSM-IV* refer to as an acute stress disorder, the precursor to the chronic illness called post-traumatic stress disorder. His state of emotional shutdown might very well have been in response to his trauma—as a way to protect his core self from the onslaught of danger and suffering at the hands of his captors. But my investigation of that would have to wait until the next visit.

With some sort of handle on his diagnosis, I turned next to a consideration of his medications. The rationale for his current regimen was obscure to me on several fronts. The doses were modest. Did that mean they were just for maintenance? Or was it because no one thought to change them over the years? Was someone trying to treat schizophrenia? Or psychotic depression? Or PTSD? Was the TFPZ causing more harm than good by inducing neurological side effects? Was that piddling dose of amitriptyline meant to treat insomnia? Or was someone inadequately dosing him for depression? Were these medications doing anything useful for him? Would he be much worse off without them? Would any medications really do a thing for his severe emotional freeze-out?

The amitriptyline mystified me the most. The dosage of 25 milligrams would do absolutely nothing for depression, which requires dosages of 100 milligrams, at a minimum, up to 250 milligrams or so, to be effective for the treatment of a major depressive episode. It might help his sleep, so I inquired about that and discovered that, if anything, Mr. Dube slept a little too much, up to twelve hours a night, and was groggy in the morning, as if he had a hangover. I was convinced that Mr. Dube's prominent problems were related to some combination of a psychotic disorder and post-traumatic stress disorder and that the AMT was causing his morning grogginess. Therefore I advised Grace to stop the amitriptyline and explained my rationale. She agreed.

Now on to the TFPZ. Given that Mr. Dube probably suffered from some form of a psychotic disorder, it was quite reasonable to prescribe an antipsychotic medication. However, I suspected that his dose was not right. I checked him further for neurological side effects.

"I want to do a little bit of a physical on him," I said to Grace. "Stand up," I said to Thomas Dube. Grace quickly translated. Mr. Dube just sat there, dumbfounded. "Okay, okay," I said. "No problem." I got up and stood in front of Mr. Dube. I picked up both of his forearms with my hands and held them out in front of him. I noticed no tremor. I slowly flexed and then extended his forearms at the elbow joints, in a passive range of motion, trying to detect any muscle tightness or rigidity. His biceps tendon ratcheted and vibrated somewhat as I performed this exercise. Some tightness there, what we call "cogwheel rigidity," a ratcheting telltale type of tightness found in those suffering from Parkinson's. The presence of this finding and his overall stiffness suggested that the TFPZ was causing this side effect, so, on that side of the ledger, I needed to consider decreasing his dose or changing to another medication in an attempt to unlock him physically.

Of course, in Zimbabwe, I did not have access to modern medicine's most recent advances in the realm of psychopharmacology. My only choices were CPZed and TFPZ. CPZed would be too sedating and not provide enough antipsychotic "punch" for his illness, so I considered a decrease in his dose of TFPZ. However, on the other hand, he suffered chronic thought slowing, probable hallucinations and other stigmata of psychotic illness that, theoretically at least, should be reduced by antipsychotic medications; so I couldn't drop his dose too low. To complicate matters further, it was possible that the TFPZ was not just slowing his muscles down, it might have significantly contributed to his thought slowing, the cause of his mental dullness. So, all in all, I decided to reduce his TFPZ, to cut it in half to only a nighttime dose of 5 milligrams. This type of rationalizing and balancing was done in a matter of a few minutes, a typical act of mental gymnastics inherent in the practice of clinical psychopharmacology that psychiatrists perform dozens of times a day.

"So, Grace, I'd like to reduce his antipsychotic medication. I see that it is causing him to lock up, slow down. It may be doing more harm than good," I offered. "There are a few things for you to look out for in the next week. I am hoping that his face and arms and legs will loosen up a little bit. I do want you to monitor him for a worsening of his talking to himself or becoming more withdrawn. So stop the yellow ones completely. And cut out the morning brown ones. Just have him take those at night.

"At our next visit, we'll reassess the medications. We might start something different. I also want to talk to you more about therapy that either I or someone else can do with your son."

Shades of America here, I surreptitiously peered down at my watch and noted that it was nearly 1:20. Just like a psychotherapy hour, in my head and in reality I would be meeting with Mr. Dube from 12:30 to 1:20 every Thursday, the proverbial fifty-minute hour, which was virtually unheard of in the clinic and psychiatric ward of the old P.U.

I penned a brief note on the bottom of his final card, mostly to remind me of my rationale for stopping his amitriptyline and reducing his TFPZ. I finished my note with a prescription and return appointment: "D/C AMT. Decrease TFPZ 5 mg nocte #30. RTC 1 week," the shorthand saying discontinue amitriptyline, decrease trifluoperazine to 5 milligrams taken at bedtime, give the patient thirty tablets to take home, return to the clinic in a week.

I bid the Dubes goodbye, confirming their appointment for next Thursday, instructing them to wait just then on the cool bench under a shade tree outside the clinic. I reminded them that Sister Mada was soon to return from lunch and that she would dispense the medication to them. The nurses kept a huge stash of psychiatric medications under lock and key in the kitchen of the old cinder-block palace that we used as the outpatient psychiatric clinic. When Sister Mada returned from lunch, she would take the card and fill up a little white plastic Ziploc bag with thirty TFPZ tablets. With a blue ink pen, she would write the instructions, in Shona or Ndebele, if need be, on the little white bag and seal it up for the road. The nurses also did a fair amount of education regarding the medications. There were no prescription pads or private pharmacies for the poor people who frequented Harare Central Hospital. The patients would simply take their cards to Sister Mada in the kitchen.

I returned to my consulting room to gather my thoughts on the case for a few minutes. My hunger for nicotine and sugar had temporarily abated while my mind labored over this brain-teaser of a case—a sublimation of my wicked desires for legal mood-altering chemicals. Physicians strive to attain the principle of parsimony in making a diagnosis. If one can attribute all of a patient's signs and symptoms to just one disorder, then one makes that call. But, in the real world, and the psych ward in Zimbabwe was as real as it gets, patients do not follow the textbook example and may be unfortunate enough to be suffering from two different afflictions. In this case, my working hypothesis was that Mr. Dube would have inevitably suffered a chronic mental illness such as schizophrenia or a recurring mood disorder, but, in my opinion, his course was complicated by his experience of serious trauma while he was incarcerated. In other words, a likely diagnosis of post-traumatic stress disorder caused him even more suffering. The treatment of his psychotic illness rested much more on the prescription of psychotropic medications and the maintenance of social stability and support rather than on psychotherapy. Sure, I could tinker around with the medications and suggest that he keep himself more occupied during the day, but it was quite unlikely that I was going to make a significant dent in his psychotic illness.

Then, I thought about what it would take for me to treat his PTSD. In the early 1990s, the individual psychotherapy treatment of choice for PTSD was to have the patient gradually re-experience bits and pieces of the traumatic event without becoming flooded and overwhelmed, thereby learning a sense of mastery over the memories and the actual experience itself. As you can imagine, this is pretty delicate work. If the therapist overdoes it, then the patient collapses in a flood of traumatic memories. If the therapist soft-pedals the matter, then the patient muddles and wallows and doesn't make any progress at all. So I thought, "What the hell does Mr. Dube have to lose?" and decided that at the next visit I would begin to explore the traumatic events. Now, given that Mr. Dube spoke about as much as a potted plant, I anticipated that this exploration might be decidedly one-sided. I planned to ask a series of open-ended and then closed questions about his experience at Mlondolozi.

Sitting there, lost in thought, I felt a nascent afternoon breeze blowing through the window and noticed that some cloud cover was finally coming in to cool things off. My brain hurt. I looked at my watch. It was quarter-to-two. An uneasy meditation. Psychotherapy was not my strong suit in psychiatry and I was undoubtedly a stranger in a strange land here in Zimbabwe. I shivered a tad before I got up to go for my solitary vice of a menthol cigarette, still looking forward to a brief afternoon siesta.

My psychodynamic musings about Mr. Dube's diagnosis and treatment were long forgotten by the time next Thursday rolled around, a day on which I would perceive his case as a hopeless dead end. At 12:35, as I sat in my consulting room finishing up a letter, a gentle knock came on the door. Seeing the well-groomed Mr. Dube with his tireless elderly mother pulled at my heartstrings. I would try to do what I could, within reason, to try and pull Mr. Dube out of his virtual nonentity of a life.

"*Masikati, chiremba*," said Grace.

"*Masikati, ambuya,*" I replied.

"*Maswera sei?*"

"*Taswera maswerawo.*" Here we were, the two of us greeting each other in what was a nonnative tongue for each of us; performed in knee-jerk homage to the dominant Shona culture.

"*Taswera,*" she replied.

"So, how are things going?" I asked.

"A little better."

"Really? How so?" I felt the smallest glimmer of hope.

"He is eating more. I see him smiling some. He is not so stiff, he is moving around the house more."

"And, is he communicating more with you?"

"Oh, no. He still says very little."

"Does he still talk to himself? Any more than before?"

"That is about the same. He is calm, takes care of basic things—like eating, dressing, taking a bath every other day."

I looked over at Mr. Dube and found the same Mona Lisa smirk as always. Not that it was his fault. I could see no visible improvement, but I didn't really expect to. I got up out of my chair and took his hands, testing his forearms for stiffness. The "cogwheeling" was gone. I saw his face move more freely. Decreasing the dose worked then to help his stiffness without any obvious worsening or improvement of his thoughts. Well, I would probably leave well enough alone for now with respect to the medications.

"So now, Mrs. Dube, it's time to get to some of the more difficult stuff. I need to ask your son about his experience at Mlondolozi." My knowledge of the place was all second-hand. Dr. Mark Winston had taken a field trip down there and remarked on the horrible conditions of the place, which made the spartan surroundings of the Harare Psychiatric Unit look positively like the Ritz-Carlton.

I never visited a jail or prison in Zimbabwe and, in retrospect, I wish that I had. It's clear to me now that, during my stint in Zimbabwe, I was subconsciously trying to cleanse myself from the emotional sullying that my psyche had suffered by working as a psychiatrist in the San Francisco county jail. I didn't want to mingle with the criminal element in Africa any more than I had to. Working with San Francisco's sociopaths had probably knocked a good five years off my career as a psychiatrist.

I proceeded to ask about Mlondolozi from every angle I could conjure, with Grace Dube patiently translating my questions into Ndebele. Nothing. Nada. Zippo. I observed only a continuation of that pleasantly vacant stare and insipid grin. Again, I considered whether he might be retarded or had had a stroke. But, from the information that I had already gathered, I doubted it. I was fairly fixated on the notion that he had been brutalized in those cells of Mlondolozi. The clock was ticking as I banged my head against a proverbial wall. I was pretty much ready to give up for the week.

Grace Dube could sense my frustration and, no doubt, experienced a sense of helplessness as well. "I am sorry, *chiremba*. He is no help."

"He can't help it. He is very sick. For now, continue the trifluoperazine and, next week, I will try some other ways to unlock him. Wish me luck." Before I bid them adieu, I engaged in some pleasantries. "How is it living with your relatives in Highfield?"

"Well, things are difficult. My sister has fallen ill. Her husband has lost his job. I'm not so sure we can stay there much longer. I can only afford to pay a small amount of rent and I'm afraid we'll have to leave. I don't want that. He's not ready."

"He may never be ready," I thought to myself, biting my tongue. I started to think, "Well at least he's got enough to eat, clean clothes, and a family who loves him," assuming that he existed in a world of blissful ignorance.

On this day, I wasted no time in strolling over to the far reaches of the rutted hospital parking lot, where a number of Harare's ever-present street vendors sold single cigarettes and candies out of battered cardboard boxes. I wasn't going to subject myself to another bout of wracking my mind without a nicotine fix. I needed to do a walking meditation of sorts, particularly since I would soon be venturing into nonverbal realms to try and unlock Mr. Dube from his uneasy, muzzled state of mind. After handing the salesman a pocketful of spare change, the equivalent of about seven cents each for two menthol cigarettes, I struck a match from the vendor's matchbox and ignited the tip of my generic fag. I inhaled deeply, in search of a buzz, careful to stand behind the thick trunk of a baobab tree, away from the bus stop, out of sight of my student nurses, medical students, and residents. Just because I could keep my filthy habit to two smokes a day didn't mean it provided a good example to the citizenry.

As the nicotine unlocked my brain, I tried to recall what I knew about hypnosis, art therapy, and music therapy as ways to try and get at nonverbal, and often unconscious, material in the mind. Hypnosis seemed like a stretch, given that it would have to be done through an interpreter. Plus, I was afraid that Mr. Dube's mind might just float away and never come back if I gained full access to its more disturbed reaches. Music therapy also seemed impractical. But art therapy could be as simple as using a pencil and piece of clean white (or, in the case of Zimbabwe, yellowish-brown) paper. Instructing Mr. Dube to draw a picture might, just might, allow me a chance to get into that troubled mind. Granted, I had had little more than an orientation to the nuances of art therapy while I was in my training. But, voilà! I had a plan, albeit a half-baked one, for the next visit.

The week of our fourth visit was marked by cooling rains, which sprang from cigar-shaped thunderheads pierced by occasional swords of lightning, accompanied by noisy waves of rolling and cracking. The day before brought a rainbow that seemed to stretch over the entire city of Harare. I saw this after getting soaked on my walk home from the medical school. It had not rained yet on this Thursday morning, but I could spy a forbidding wall of black forming over the western horizon.

As we sat down once again in the early afternoon, I could smell the moisture in the air. Scientists might attribute it to the buildup of ozone or other chemicals prior to a rainstorm, but the rest of us would easily and naturally just say, "Gee, it smells like rain." For some reason, both Grace and Thomas looked well scrubbed on this day, even emitting a scent of soap. I wished I felt as fresh as the air and the Dubes smelled because I was frazzled from a really crazy morning in which two of my residents had bolted early, not even bothering to tell me their excuses.

Nonetheless, I remembered the basics of my tentative treatment plan and looked toward the corner of my consulting table to make sure that I had a half-dozen sheets of paper and a couple of colored pencils. I felt vaguely confident despite the overall sense of consuming pessimism I felt about this case. I supposed, at the time, that I could not tolerate any other feeling once he and his mother assumed the position across from me in that spacious consulting room. I had always possessed an almost extrasensory capacity for the perception of suffering in others, even before I went to medical school. But now, as a trained professional, allegedly qualified to help, my observation of suffering in others made me inordinately uncomfortable when I could do little to alleviate it. So, at least in the moment, I borrowed a "can-do, will-do" type of mindset.

After exchanging greetings, I inquired about his sleep, thinking, ability to communicate, stiffness, and other side effects. It appeared that he was slightly worse again—sleeping more, smiling less, but with no recurrence of the muscle tightness. "Oh, great," I thought, "now I don't even know what I'm doing with the medications. Is he slowly getting depressed because I stopped his antidepressant medication? Is he withdrawing further inward, into a disturbed world of psychosis since I reduced his antipsychotic medication?"

I went on to explain my rationale for trying art therapy. I started by drawing a version of a house with a driveway and tree nearby and a shining sun and birds flying in the sky, kind of a typical scene drawn by scores and scores of ordinary grade-schoolers over the years. I showed him my picture and then asked him, through his mother-translator of course, to draw me a picture of what his house looked like. I handed him a piece of tablet paper and a red colored pencil. I was temporarily emboldened with confidence as he pulled his chair up to the table as if to have a better surface on which to write. He picked up the pencil and held it in his hand. Thank God for overlearning. He proceeded to put the tip of the pencil down to the paper, staring at the tip of the pencil and the middle of the paper for ten minutes straight while I daydreamed, fidgeting and scratching myself. I wanted to scream, but instead I re-explained to him, via his mother, that I wanted him to draw a picture of his house in whatever way he saw his own house.

To make a painfully long story short, over the next thirty minutes all I could muster out of Thomas Dube was a couple of lines drawn on the paper and a lot of seemingly bemused smiles. Nary a word, not even a shake of the head or a nod, could be mustered from Mr. Dube. During this time, I even changed the assignment, drawing a picture of a mountain with a stream and asking him to draw a picture of a beautiful place. Once again, Grace Dube could sense my frustration, although I made every effort to hide it.

Here I was, a biological type of psychiatrist who liked to be active, ask a lot of questions, get to the bottom of matters, prescribe medications, carefully assess their benefits and side effects, adjust accordingly. I was not the type of psychiatrist who liked to sit around and contemplate my navel and wait, wait, wait. I was a man of action, at least for a psychiatrist.

I didn't know what to do. I could only accomplish so much by adjusting his medications. How could I initiate "talk therapy" with someone I could not even talk to? I failed in my first (and only) attempt to gain access to his unconscious mind. I didn't even have an adequate history to make a diagnosis with certainty. I didn't have the training or the resources to initiate a complicated course of behavioral therapy that might begin to reprogram Mr. Dube's day-to-day routine. Mr. Dube had unwittingly pushed me to my limits as a psychiatrist in a mere four sessions and drove me to endless rounds of asking "what-if?" questions.

What if Mr. Dube had commited such a crime in California? It is likely that he would have been found mentally incompetent to stand trial, transferred to a forensic state hospital, restored to competency with proper treatment, avoided getting beaten or raped on a regular basis, eventually found guilty, and served three years on the psychiatric wing of a state prison.

What if Mr. Dube had been routed to a place like the P.U. after becoming psychotic and assaulting his fellow citizen? It is likely that he would have undergone a reasonable psychiatric evaluation and been started on appropriate medication. He probably would have improved or even stabilized over a period of several weeks.

What if Mr. Dube had been able to do his time in spartan but humane prison conditions and received no "treatment"? It's hard to say, but he probably would be much healthier now than he was after regular beatings and possibly rapes compounded his emotional problems.

What if I could send Mr. Dube to a committed, sensitive, experienced colleague who could perform specialized psychological testing and provide psychotherapy? It is likely that I would have a much clearer sense of Mr. Dube's diagnosis and possible that Mr. Dube might become unlocked and slowly get better.

What if I had the resources and experience to conduct an interview of the patient under the influence of intravenous sodium amobarbital (the so-called Amytal interview designed to access unconscious psychological material much like hypnosis)? I might know much more definitively whether psychological, physical, and sexual trauma at Mlondolozi had indeed induced Mr. Dube's frozen state of mind or whether he suffered from merely a very severe case of schizophrenia.

Despite my frustration at the lack of progress over the course of the first four sessions, I felt it was my clinical duty to continue to meet with Thomas and Grace Dube for a few more weeks. I did not want to them to feel abandoned by me, although I knew that Mrs. Dube had already perceived my sense of hopelessness about her son's case. I saw Mr.

Dube three more times before I referred them back for follow-up with the psychiatric sister out in Shurugwi. These final meetings were an amalgam of me checking Mr. Dube's progress, or lack of it, with the medications, futilely attempting another crack at "art therapy," and amiably chatting with Grace Dube, giving her as much support as I could muster at the time. My "completion" of an evaluation and round of therapy was hastened by the ongoing disintegration of the lives of Grace Dube's relatives, who teetered on the brink of eviction from their concrete two-room house in the densely populated suburb of Highfield. Grace and Thomas Dube would be returning to a much more rural lifestyle in their *musha*, located about 15 kilometers outside of Shurugwi.

I wrote a summary of my less-than-brilliant findings to Sister Guvamombe, Mr. Dube's psychiatric nurse out in the bush clinic. What I told her is essentially what I have detailed above. The illness seemed to be a combination of an underlying psychotic illness greatly complicated by an extended bout of "shellshock." The most practical advice I could give to Sister Guvamombe was how to closely monitor the risks and benefits and side effects of the TFPZ and how to monitor Thomas closely for depression. Big deal.

At our last visit, I profusely complimented Grace Dube on how well she was caring for her son and how well she was coping with an incredibly difficult situation. Breaking the Westernized medico-legal tenets governing the practice of medicine and psychiatry, I more or less apologized to her for being unable to do much for her son, other than to pay attention, give a damn, and at least give it the old college try. I felt deflated and dejected. Just before they left, with my letter to Sister Guvamombe in Grace Dube's purse, I took Thomas Dube's right hand in my right hand and lifted it up and squeezed it and looked him in the eye and said, "God bless you!" and "Good luck!" Not particularly religious or superstitious, I mouthed these platitudes, feeling hollow and helpless. "*Fambai zvakanaka*," I bid farewell. There was nothing else left to say.

"*Chisarai chakanaka, chiremba*," said Grace Dube. "Thank you for your help. God bless you and your family."

CHAPTER NINE

"A Sleepy Guy with a Head Full of Weed and Thorazine."

Samuel Rugare: A Case of *Mbanje* Madness

"O God, that men should put an enemy in their mouths to steal their brains."

—William Shakespeare
Othello

Agricultural laborers, almost always black, are indispensable to the operation of commercial farms in Zimbabwe, usually run by white men. Commercial farmer J. C. W. Hawthorne, who managed a farm just outside of Mvurwi, two hours north of Harare by car, relied on men like Samuel Rugare to perform the backbreaking work that kept things running smoothly down on the farm. Samuel Rugare had been an ideal employee for eight years.

Why?

His labor came cheap. He worked for only ZW$300 (in 1994, about US$40) a month and "room and board," which consisted of a straw mat on the dirt floor of a shack and three squares a day of *sadza* with a few greens, maybe some gristle, and no meat.

He was reliable. The twenty-six-year-old Shona man had not missed a day of work, on a six-day workweek, during eight years on the job. More physically demanding jobs are hard to imagine. Samuel chopped cotton, baled tobacco, weeded soybeans, and stooped over to pick greens six days a week. While many of Zimbabwe's commercial farm workers were laid off during the leaner times, Samuel Rugare was always kept on the job during the early rainy season of November through January and the winter months of July and August when less work needed to be done. Samuel proved himself to be physically strong while being emotionally reserved. These attributes made him a compliant and highly efficient worker. Samuel was a devout Christian who did not make trouble. On Sundays, he would attend Methodist services in the sleepy rural village of Mvurwi and then visit his mother, who lived with Samuel's eldest sister in a hut on a plot of land on the outskirts of town.

But what Mr. Hawthorne and Samuel's brothers did not know was that, after church every Sunday, Samuel would pluck a pile of aromatic leaves for his daily use from the spreading stems of a wildly budding marijuana bush in his mother's backyard. The dense shrub, hidden in a jumble of blackberry bushes, grew helter-skelter behind the outhouse. For some reason, probably because they did not partake of *mbanje*, Samuel's brothers and his mother did not know the true nature of the tangle of vegetation.

By the time they carted Samuel off to the P.U. to see Yours Truly, they still were not sure about Samuel's affinity for cannabis, although they possessed an inkling. It all started when Samuel became too physically ill to work on the farm. At first, his elder brothers, Charles and Steady, thought that their brother had come down with tuberculosis or, even worse, the "slim disease" of AIDS. Short of breath and coughing most of the time, the muscular Samuel Rugare was nearly bed-bound with crippling fatigue for a week and a half. Already lean, he was losing weight at the rate of half a stone (a stone being the British equivalent of 14 pounds) per week. They took him that first week to the mission hospital near Mvurwi. The good doctors there diagnosed a "walking pneumonia," prescribed antibiotics, and sent him home. But Samuel could only get up from bed long enough to find his way to the outhouse behind the commercial farm's barracks, where unbeknownst to anyone, he continued to smoke his daily ration of *mbanje*.

One day, in the second week, he made what seemed to be a miraculous recovery. He bounded up out of bed one morning about 5:00 a.m. to go out and take his place in the fields. The sight of a healthy Samuel Rugare back at work made Mr. Hawthorne smile. His smile would soon fade as he watched Samuel Rugare launch into a profane tirade, running through the fields, swinging at both his mates and supervisors alike, running his mouth at 60 miles a minute with a goofy grin plastered on his face. Mr. Hawthorne quickly found Samuel's brother Steady, reliable as his name, picking weeds on a row of soybeans.

"Steady, it's your brother Sam," said Mr. Hawthorne. "Something's not quite right. He looks, well, he looks a bit mad."

"Sir?"

"Could you come and help me talk to him?"

The two went over to the next field only to find Samuel beginning to disrobe. Steady also found his brother Charles before they approached their brother. Before Steady or Charles could say anything, Samuel took a punch at Steady, his usually trusted brother. It took both Charles and Steady to restrain their bigger, more muscular brother Samuel in a bear hug. They dragged him, kicking and screaming, off to a small shaded yard behind the barracks. Mr. Hawthorne followed behind—at a good distance so as not to risk injury. Samuel eventually calmed down. Mr. Hawthorne encouraged the elder Rugare brothers to take their youngest brother again to the hospital, this time for a psychiatric evaluation. But they insisted on taking him to the *n'anga,* which they did.

The *n'anga* said that he had discovered a bewitchment—a deceased great-aunt of the boys who had put a hex on poor Samuel for stealing candy from the general store while still a teenager. So, after the brothers went to the general store to make amends, paying the storekeeper the equivalent of a week's wages, they assumed that the great-aunt would cease and desist in her attempts to physically and psychologically paralyze Samuel Rugare. But the mad behavior persisted and worsened. The brothers took Samuel to live temporarily with their sister's family on the outskirts of Mvurwi. It was there that they became so desperate and fearful that they tied Samuel to the trunk of a thick baobab tree with rope. They had also taken to occasionally punching him about the body and the head to tire him out. Only then would Samuel grab a few hours of sleep before his exhaustion would pass, only to resume once again on a path of mania. They did not want to involve the police. They obviously knew very little of modern psychiatry. Once again they consulted their boss, who suggested that the brothers take Samuel all the way to Harare to see a consultant psychiatrist. Mr. Hawthorne graciously agreed to drive the brothers to Harare, provided that Samuel, hobbled by rope and cord, traveled in the back of his pickup truck where he couldn't do any damage.

By sheer chance alone, they arrived at the P.U. on one of my clinic days, shortly after I had gotten settled in my luxurious corner office at the clinic. These dramatic out-of-town arrivals created a flurry of activity at the P.U. There was absolutely no organized system for triaging such patients to the appropriate place for care so the effect would be random and willy-nilly, all of us simply hoping for the best. Sometimes the patient would be carted straight to Casualty where the doctor would "section" him and admit him straightaway to the inpatient psych ward. Other times, the truck would pull up into the driveway of the ward and the nurses would tuck the patient into a bed. And at other times, the driver would simply park in front of the clinic.

Samuel's arrival was nothing less than spectacular, and not in a good way, as far as I was concerned. The nurses called me out to see him in the back of the pickup truck because they were afraid to release him from the shackles. I couldn't believe my eyes. Samuel Rugare looked like an animal in the bed of the truck. For starters, he was nearly hog-tied; his hands were tied behind his back with thick rough rope and his ankles lashed together with what appeared to be electrical cord. The man's face was bruised, his eyes nearly swollen shut, lids puffy. Blood oozed from a small cut on the bridge of his nose. He was shirtless, wearing filthy dark green cotton cutoffs, cinched at the waist with the same scratchy rope that bound his hands. Although he should have been depleted from bouncing around in the bed of a pickup truck for two hours, the man kept yelling, nearly foaming at the mouth, and thrashing around.

The only thing like this I had seen in San Francisco was when the police would bring to the emergency room someone so agitated that he had to have his hands and feet bound together behind him with a piece of plastic. The practice ceased, however, after a few people died in police custody, in most cases probably of drug intoxication, underlying medical problems, and, how to say it politely, being bound in such a way as to make it difficult to breathe. I had also seen the occasional "five points," where all four extremities were strapped to the bed and a strap cinched over the chest. Doctors and nurses at San Francisco General Hospital routinely strapped patients to beds with leather belts or washable Velcro ties. To watch a patient get forcibly restrained, his often soiled body then recumbent on a clean white sheet, was downright cheery compared to the sight of Samuel Rugare in the back of a pickup truck. He looked like he had just been prepped for a lynch mob, Mississippi-style, circa 1920. Two lean and muscular Shona men, sheepishly observing the scene, surrounded the pickup bed. A ham-fisted white man with muttonchop sideburns popped out of the cab of the truck where he had been lounging and taking indifferent puffs on a cigarette.

"Doctor, I can explain," said the white man.

"I hope so," I said. "It doesn't look good so far."

"Good morning, my name is Mr. Hawthorne. I am the commercial farmer who employs all of these guys," he continued, gesturing to the three black-skinned men. "The man in the back there, his name is Samuel Rugare. As you can see, he needs your professional services. And these are his older brothers, Charles and Steady."

I put my hand out to the men, slipping in a quick one-line "*mangwanani*" to each of them. "Your brother doesn't look too good. What happened?"

"I can explain," interrupted Mr. Hawthorne. "I tried to convince them to take their brother to the hospital, but instead they insisted on taking him to one of their mumbo-jumbo witchdoctors. Most of my people do what I say or else I just fire 'em. But these buggers are two of my best workers. I can't fire 'em. I'd be in serious trouble without 'em."

I looked at the brothers, who remained motionless, their hands crossed in front of them like they were praying, eyes slanted downward at the ground, as if they were studying patterns of the yellow dirt there. "Okay," I said. "Go on."

"I'm sure you know by now just how superstitious these people are," continued Mr. Hawthorne. "Where are you from? Britain?"

"No, the United States," I said. I don't think Mr. Hawthorne knew it, but he wasn't making any points with me. "Okay, go on."

"Well, Samuel was running wild in the fields—taking off his clothes, talking nonsense, striking other people, mumbling about the spirits. Obviously he was too unwell to work. I begged them to take him to the hospital. They didn't. He got worse. So they had him tied to a tree for the last two days, force-feeding him, beating him from time to time to calm him down. These goddamned apes, strong buggers, really hurt him, I think. Finally, they came to me and asked me to drive him down here. I was reluctant, but it was the first sense that they had spoken, so I agreed to it and here we are."

J. C. W. Hawthorne was a fairly typical white Zimbabwean. He considered himself an African by virtue of his family having tilled the land for four generations after arriving here from England in the late 1800s. Well-meaning and hard-working, a man like Mr. Hawthorne would never consider himself a "racialist," as the British say. He was just accustomed to being in charge. He viewed his fellow citizens, black Zimbabweans, as overwhelmed and undereducated and bedeviled in some way, not necessarily less than human, but definitely needing guidance from educated white men like himself. He saw them through a prism of condescension, tabbing them as "superstitious" when he considered their traditional beliefs in spirituality. "It wasn't their fault that the poor buggers were born black," he might say. If he were a missionary or even a serious Christian, he would try to convert all of them to pure Christianity, forsaking all of the traditional ways. But Hawthorne was a businessman, a pragmatist. The predominant brand of colonialism under the old flag of Southern Rhodesia was that of paternalism. Ironically, it echoed the black Shona male's view of himself as "king of the hill" within the patriarchal Shona culture.

I didn't particularly like most of the white Zimbabweans that I came across. I saw most of them as knee-jerk racists. For the most part, they seemed bitter at having lost political power, and bitterness as a bulwark of your personality does not engender a whole lot of sympathy. The old ladies could be particularly acerbic in verbally whipping "the boys," Shona men in their twenties and thirties who manned the cash registers and bagged their groceries at the supermarkets. To me, their attitude smacked of an acculturated paranoia: "These black people took away our power and are actually running things" —and doing it badly, if one were to take the word of the embittered "Rhodies," as the white Zimbabweans were mockingly nicknamed.

"Thank you, Mr. Hawthorne," I said to him, for some reason just now reaching out to shake his hairy hand. "If you could please stand by while I speak to Samuel's brothers," I said. "But first, let's get Samuel out of those chains."

"Are you sure you want to do that?" said Hawthorne. "He's quite agitated."

"Don't worry, Mr. Hawthorne, we're professionals here," I said with a touch of irony that, of course, nobody caught. Samuel Rugare continued to struggle against the ropes, although he was tiring. "I take it he hasn't gotten any medications?" I asked of the brothers, who shrugged.

"I believe he only received antibiotics from the hospital," offered Mr. Hawthorne.

"Sister, could you bring 200 milligrams of CPZed?" I asked Sister Mada.

"By mouth or injection?"

"We'll try tablets first, Sister. And bring back Innocent and Lovemore, we'll need their help in getting this guy over to the seclusion room."

"Yes, *chiremba*," said Sister Mada, who waited for further instructions before retreating.

"We'll try to give him some medications by mouth while he's still restrained. Then we'll escort him to the seclusion room. We'll throw a mattress on the ground in there, let him get caught up on some of his sleep. In the meantime, I'll try to talk to him." I pointed to one of the brothers, who stood by, and said, "Steady, is that right? Are you Steady?"

"Yes, sir."

"Steady, I want you to translate for me," I said. Normally, an objective health-care professional is the best interpreter, but, in this case, I needed to maximize any type of trust that I could establish with the crazed Samuel Rugare. "Do you speak good English?"

"Yes, sir."

Turning toward the form of Samuel in the back of the pickup truck, I started: "Good morning, Samuel, I am Dr. Linde. I am a psychiatrist and this is the Psychiatric Unit of Harare Hospital. This is meant to be a safe place for you."

Steady translated my opening remarks. Samuel looked toward me, but he did not say anything.

"Do you think he understands?"

Steady spoke to his brother again in Shona, but he got no response. "It's hard to tell. I think so, but he doesn't say."

"Let's continue. I would like to take you out of those ropes, but I want you to take some medication first. Then you will go to rest in your own room." Emergency psychiatry is a land of euphemisms. "We are here to help you. This is a hospital. I am a doctor. These are nurses here." I am reminded of the New Yorker cartoon, with the psychiatrist and the ever-present patient on the couch, the beleaguered psychiatrist saying, "I medicate first and ask questions later."

Steady interpreted for me once again and the big man tied in ropes this time nodded as he surveyed the situation. By now, Sister Mada was hustling up the path with some tablets, a big plastic glass of water and our two middle-aged security guards du jour, Innocent and Lovemore. With no further ado, Sister Mada hopped up on the bed of the pickup and approached Samuel Rugare, who sat upright. Sister made a motion with her hand toward his mouth, which he opened. Sister plopped the two tablets on the back of Samuel's tongue and then offered the cup to his lips. He drank greedily, probably bone-dry from the ride down. The up-and-down movement of his Adam's apple indicated that Samuel had swallowed the tablets.

"Sister, let's untie his feet first and then we can walk him to the seclusion room. Do you feel safe going alone with Innocent and Lovemore?"

"Oh, yes. He seems quite settled already." Mr. Rugare, seemingly docile, maybe even grateful, followed Sister Mada and the two security guards slowly through the gravel parking lot toward the driveway leading to the P.U., where Samuel Rugare was to settle onto a thin, but clean mattress in the cement-block Hilton, to slumber for nearly twenty-four hours. It was a deep sleep of Thorazine and exhaustion. After Samuel had departed with his new entourage, the throng of visitors, clinic patients, hospital employees, and passersby who had stopped by started to disperse from the scene. This accident of the mind had drawn its share of rubberneckers.

I motioned for Hawthorne and the brothers to follow me into my consulting room. The white farmer begged off, but not before telling the two that he was driving back to Mvurwi in exactly one hour. He jumped in the cab of the truck, lighting a cigarette simultaneously.

I was glad to meet with the two brothers alone. We slid our way along the hallway, trying not to kick too many shins or get our rear ends too close to someone's nose, as we made our way to my corner office. Before I started with the usual litany of questions, I felt compelled to ask the brothers about their treatment plan of desperation, namely tying their brother to a tree for days and beating him.

"We thought he was possessed. We didn't know what to do," said Steady.

"What about seeing a *profita* or your church pastor?"

"I thought about it, but . . . but I was too ashamed. We didn't know what else to do," he continued.

This response had me a little bit dumbfounded. These two young Shona men presented themselves to me as quiet, thoughtful, respectful—not Neanderthals. By now, I should have known about the unpredictability of the human mind and human behavior. Or was I missing something subtle yet again in the Shona culture?

"What about taking him to the hospital?"

"We didn't, we didn't think he was sick. We thought he was possessed."

"Well, it's madness all right. And next time, heaven help us if there is a next time, please bring him to the hospital. If he's violent, it's okay to restrain him from hurting others, but instead of punching your brother, we can give him medications to slow him down. It's more effective and more humane. How many days was he tied up?"

"Two days. It was terrible, not something I want to repeat," said Steady.

With that aside, I put the brothers through my customary array of questions, trying to sort through my usual differential diagnosis for an episode of psychosis: schizophrenia, manic-depressive illness, stress-induced psychosis, medically induced psychosis, or substance-induced psychosis. Playing the role of medical detective when admitting a newly psychotic patient to the hospital continued to be highly satisfying to me—it was a job for which I was actually trained. The abrupt onset of Samuel's disturbed behavior suggested a stress-induced or substance-induced or medically caused psychosis instead of manic-depressive illness or schizophrenia, illnesses in which the onset is more gradual. I could find no evidence of a family history, no previous episode of madness, no overwhelming stressor, no serious medical illness. In every culture, the use of substances to alter consciousness can sometimes tip a person over the edge. Thus, drugs are a common cause of psychosis. In San Francisco, methamphetamines, cocaine, Ecstasy, and hallucinogens are the usual suspects, but in Zimbabwe, tetrahydrocannabinol (THC), the active ingredient of marijuana, was the prime culprit.

Before I could get around to the question of drugs, Charles Rugare pretty much sealed it for me as he produced a baggie of pungent green buds. "What about this?" he asked.

"Hmm. Where did you get that?"

"When I went to Samuel's barracks to pack, I was looking for his stash of money that we keep for emergencies. I didn't find any, but I did find this bag buried in the bottom of a jar filled with ground nuts."

"Do you know how much Samuel smokes?"

"It is not something that we know about," said Steady with a slight grimace. "We do not smoke. We were brought up Christian, Methodist, and we were taught not to take drink or smoke or use drugs."

"Well, I could ask him about it when I talk to him later. It is quite possible that the abuse of this *mbanje* might be the cause of his *kupenga* (koo-PENG-ah)," I said, using the well-recognized Shona word for madness. "That's the good news and the bad news. The good news is that the madness should only last for a few days. With some rest and medications, we will know in a few days whether it's from the *mbanje* or if there is some other underlying, more permanent cause of his madness."

"And the bad news, *chiremba*?"

"The bad news is that you have to keep him from smoking *mbanje* ever again. And that can be difficult."

"Ah, don't worry, *chiremba*, we can keep him from smoking."

"Knowing your powers of persuasion, I'm sure that you can," I said, chuckling.

"Doctor?" asked Steady, struggling to understand my American brand of humor.

"Never mind. If you need to get back to work, your brother is in good hands. If you could come back a week from today, then I will know for certain if your brother will be good enough to go home."

"We will return then."

"I would say there's a good chance that your brother will be better. If it's from the *mbanje* only, then I can guarantee it," I added.

Although cannabinoid receptors have recently been cloned and identified in both human and rat brains, it is not clear that binding at these receptors causes psychosis. Scientists do not understand how marijuana might make someone psychotic. Nonetheless, researchers have generated a few hypotheses that may explain the psychotogenic properties of Zimbabwean weed: First, the marijuana in subtropical southern Africa may be more potent than elsewhere. Second, the Zimbabweans may simply smoke huge amounts of it because of its easy availability and affordability. Or third, the Zimbabweans may process it in some way to enhance the high. For example, the Binga people of northern Zimbabwe, whose traditional culture incorporates the use of marijuana into their day-to-day lives much like the Rastafarians, feed marijuana plants to their barnyard animals, collect the resultant feces, and smoke it as part of their religious rituals. In a society stung with problems of unemployment, hunger, illness, and stress, cannabis provides a temporary respite for the suffering masses.

Among mind-altering substances used in Zimbabwe, cannabis was king. No wonder Bob Marley and his *rastafarai* played prominently at Zimbabwe's Independence in 1980. Celebrating the people's snatching of freedom from colonial overseers, Bob Marley no doubt was there to play for this newfound unfettering from dominance. In certain political contexts, cannabis represents freedom from oppression and its use presents an opportunity to escape from what might be a dreadful day-to-day reality.

The next morning, a Friday, I arrived at the P.U. to do my ward rounds. Since I always saw the new admissions first, Samuel Rugare was my first patient. Sister Shuga was on duty to assist me. Short and plump, with an ever-present smile and a good-natured laugh never too far from her lips, Sister Shuga was good company, even when we weren't dancing the *kwassa kwassa*. But, on this November morning, we had far too many patients to have any time for dirty dancing. So after a simple round of "*mangwananis*" we got down to business.

"*Chiremba*, the patient is still in seclusion, sleeping."

"Did he sleep all night?"

"Oh, yes."

"Is he taking fluids well?"

"Two pitchers of water last night before going to sleep."

"Is he still breathing?"

"Of course," giggled Sister Shuga.

"Well, what is it? Nine o'clock?" I asked. "Let's go see him, get him up to eat breakfast, get him out of seclusion, if we can."

Sister Shuga led the way back into a maze of cement floors and brick walls toward the seclusion room door. We both peeked through the judas hole. Samuel Rugare was balled up into the fetal position lying on his side on the mattress. He had covered himself with a woolen blanket with the texture of sandpaper. I noted the even rise and fall of his chest about twelve times per minute. I hated to wake him, but the morning's mental status examination would go a long way to determining how fast Samuel would recover from his bout of madness. If drugs were the cause, then Samuel would be much, much better from just one dose of medication and some sleep.

We entered. Sister Shuga gently called to him in Shona while she shook his muscular shoulder. "I am orienting him, *chiremba*." He was still dirty, smelling strongly of body odor, needing a bath, wearing those shabby green cutoffs. The cuts on his lips and face oozed a small amount of blood on the meager mattress, creating smears of deep purple. He awoke with a start. Sister Shuga backed off a little. She told him, in Shona, where he was, what day and time it was, and who these suspicious people were above his head.

"Sister, now that you oriented him, I want him to repeat the answers back to you."

She asked him the orientation questions in Shona and he responded slowly. She told me his answers: "To 'where?' He says Harare, a hospital. To 'when?' He says Friday, the morning, in July sometime, he does not know the date or the year, but that's not unusual for a rural farm worker. To 'who?' He knows his name and that I am a nurse. He is not sure who you are."

"That's okay. Some days, I'm not so sure, either," I said. "Sister, I think he did pretty well for a sleepy guy with a head full of weed and Thorazine. Good morning, Samuel. My name is Dr. Linde. I am a psychiatrist. You are at the Harare Psychiatric Unit." Sister Shuga interpreted my series of one-liners. Samuel looked up at me quizzically but said nothing.

"This is a hospital. Do you feel safe here?" I asked, inquiring with the simplest of questions that fishes for paranoia.

He answered quickly. "No, they are here also. They have followed me here."

"Who?"

"I don't know. I just know that they have been following me for the last two weeks."

"Why? What do they want to do?"

"They are testing me, and I am failing. That is why you punish me here."

"What do you mean by punish?"

"Those strong drugs. They make me weak, so I cannot defend myself."

"Well, we gave you the medication to calm you down. You have been very sick for the last two weeks and the tablets will calm your mind and your body down. I will give you less of it so it does not make you so weak.

"Do you hear voices of people who are not there?" I continued.

"Only those who are following me."

"What do they say?"

"They say, 'The ancestors are unhappy, you will suffer, but you will survive.' That is why I keep going."

"Do you trust us to help you?" I asked, motioning to Sister Shuga and myself.

"Her? Yes. You? I am not so sure about."

"Fair enough. I have a few more questions. Has anything like this ever happened to you before?"

"*Aiwa.*"

"Do you smoke *mbanje*?"

"*Aiwa.*"

"You know, a little *dagga* to rest your muscles and your mind after working all day?"

Samuel Rugare stared at me, directly but not hostilely, maybe figuring that I knew something that he didn't know that I knew. He paused and looked over at Sister Shuga before telling her in Shona: "Yes, but only once a week, on Saturday night after the day is done."

"See, the only reason I ask is that I have seen many young men like yourself develop *kupenga* from smoking too much *mbanje*. I think that may have caused you to get sick —and when I say sick, I mean tearing off your clothes, fighting with people, talking nonsense, hearing voices, feeling unsafe."

Sister Shuga translated all of this, and the young man nodded and laid back down. He looked exhausted.

"I'll let you rest up. Any questions for me?" By the time I had finished speaking these words, Samuel Rugare was nearly snoring.

"So, Sister, obviously we can take him out of seclusion. I'm going to switch him over to TFPZ, 5 milligrams three times a day for a couple of days, then tapering it until I see him again next Tuesday."

"Yes, *chiremba*."

In some ways, a young Zimbabwean man like Samuel Rugare, who became psychotic from smoking too much or too potent or too modified a type of cannabis, was unfamiliar to me. But in other ways, I have seen literally hundreds of patients just like him—legions of San Franciscans who catapult themselves into an agitated psychosis from exposing too many of their fragile brain's dopamine receptors to too many methamphetamine molecules. San Francisco is America's Mecca of speed and for speeders.

Among Zimbabwe's predominantly poor black people, fashionable drugs such as amphetamines, cocaine, LSD, Ecstasy, heroin, or prescription pills were unavailable due to cost. Even spirits, wine, and beer were pretty much out of reach. Thus I saw very few alcoholics among the Shona. That's not to say that I did not witness some serious abuse of alcohol and the behavioral consequences of that overeager imbibition. What I often observed when I attended concerts and clubs to hear the local music was some jawing and pushing and fighting after midnight, when the patrons had consumed a few too many Castle or Zambezi lagers. But that was an infrequent blowout for most of the brawlers.

According to ritual traditions, the Shona would brew ceremonial beer from grains like millet for their ancestor spirits to drink after "arriving" as spotlighted guests at the Shona's traditional rites, hosted by specialist *n'anga* channelers. This ritual got bastardized, carried on by Shona men who would buy minikegs of thick grainy *chibuku* beer, equivalent to the traditional beer in its consistency, to consume in mass quantities during Sunday afternoon "beer drinks." But when it came to day-to-day use, cannabis was definitely the drug of choice for those Zimbabweans who sought solace, enlightenment, and stress reduction via the chemical route.

The midst of a drug-induced psychotic episode can look identical to that of a nervous breakdown of schizophrenia or manic-depressive illness. In other words, drugs alone can make you as crazy as Samuel was when he was running wild through the fields of Mvurwi. I was not surprised that Samuel continued to have paranoid thoughts and faint auditory hallucinations. The combination of sleep deprivation, poor intake of food and fluids, and too much marijuana had driven him pretty far beyond the brink. I was fairly certain that a few more days of supportive care and low doses of antipsychotic medications would have Samuel back on track.

I evaluated Samuel again five days after he was admitted to the P.U., during my Tuesday morning ward rounds. He looked, sounded, and smelled like a totally normal human being who had found himself transported to hell and back. Today was the last scheduled day for his trifluoperazine—his dose was down to 5 milligrams just once in the morning. He was lucid, well-groomed, and pleasant, but unable to remember much from the previous three weeks. He did, however, clearly remember his wildly inappropriate behavior leading up to his shackling at the hands of his brothers.

"Good morning, my name is Dr. Linde. Do you remember me?"

Samuel's face a blank, he only said, "*Pamwe* (PAHM-way)." Perhaps.

"Do you remember how you were acting before you came to Harare?" Sister Shuga, of course, translated.

"Yes, I do." He hung his head in shame.

"Well, Mr. Rugare, not to make you feel bad, but your disturbed behavior was very likely due to your smoking too much *mbanje*. You've got to stop smoking it because your brain is too sensitive to it. It makes you crazy."

"Yes. When can I go home?"

"Your brothers, Charles and Steady, are coming back on Thursday with Mr. Hawthorne to pick you up. You must tell them where the *mbanje* plant is, so that they can destroy it. You need to refrain from smoking *mbanje* 100 percent."

"Yes. When can I go back to work?"

"How do you feel from a physical standpoint?"

"Fit, sir."

"I would say you can go back next Monday," I said.

"Are you going to tell Mr. Hawthorne what happened?" asked Samuel.

"Don't worry, you won't lose your job." I tried to reassure him, which was no mean trick given his recent paranoia. "Do you trust me?"

"Yes, *chiremba*."

Thursday morning came and midway through the morning, just after teatime, Charles and Steady Rugare, driven by Mr. Hawthorne, arrived at the clinic. I alerted Sister Mada to fetch Samuel from the inpatient ward and bring all of them back when they arrived. The four of them entered my consulting room. Greetings were exchanged. I immediately excused Mr. Hawthorne, who didn't seem to mind, for a few minutes while I talked to the brothers Rugare.

"So, how do you think he looks, Steady?"

"Almost back to his usual self, *chiremba*. What happened?"

Back in San Francisco, in this situation, I would have the patient answer this question for his relative so I could gauge the patient's level of understanding and insight about the situation. But, in this case, I decided to tell him myself since it seemed that Zimbabweans still responded to the authority of the doctor, for better or worse. "Bottom line? Samuel got mad from smoking too much *mbanje*."

"Hah," said Steady, "I told you so," speaking now to his brother Charles who stood by. "Where do you get it?" asked Steady.

Without hesitation, Samuel said, "From a bush in Mother's backyard. It's way back behind the outhouse."

"We must burn it," Steady said.

"Well, however you do it, you must restrict the *mbanje* from Samuel. He became quite mad and is perfectly fine now. There is no need for Samuel to take tablets and no need for Samuel to follow up with a psychiatrist unless any of those problems return."

"I see, *chiremba*," said Samuel. "What are you going to tell Mr. Hawthorne?"

"Well, Steady, Charles, you just sit back, wait and see," I said. "It will be okay, better than okay." I went into the hallway and motioned Mr. Hawthorne back.

"Good morning, Doctor," said a chipper Mr. Hawthorne as he thrust his meaty palm out to shake my hand. "How's my boy?"

"Good morning, Mr. Hawthorne," I said. My average-sized mitt disappeared in Mr. Hawthorne's and he squeezed so hard I thought he might break my hand. I gathered myself. "Samuel Rugare is as good as new."

"What seemed to be the problem?"

"Well," I said, scratching my head and looking up at the ceiling, "the brothers here might have been on the right track. It appeared to be a case of madness stemming from a bewitchment by Samuel's deceased great aunt, the sister of his mother's father's."

"Oh, really," sneered Mr. Hawthorne.

"Oh, yes. I have a witch doctor here that I consult with," I said, only partially lying as I did occasionally run bizarre cases by a local *n'anga*. "My witch doctor said, most definitely, that a bewitchment occurred. Of course, a few days of medication and rest and good food helped matters as well."

The brothers Rugare did not tempt the fates by looking at each other's faces as they would have surely all erupted into a fit of laughter if their eyes met. Each brother stared nonchalantly at Mr. Hawthorne, hats in hand, sitting still in their chairs.

"Oh, you gullible American, believing all of the superstitions held by these buggers."

"Well, you know what they say, Mr. Hawthorne, all of us psychiatrists are crazy."

"Evidently," huffed J. C. W. Hawthorne.

"In any case, Mr. Hawthorne, Samuel is better," I said. "He wants to return to work on Monday and I believe he is fit to return to work on Monday and Monday only. Understand?"

"Yes, Doctor. Thank you," said Mr. Hawthorne. "Anything else I need to know?"

"Oh, no," I said, a blank look on my face, "there's nothing else you need to know. Travel well."

CHAPTER TEN

"So, You Want Another Operation?"

Winston Chivero: Self-Mutilator with a Cause

"Exposure to the magical can be as dangerous to a person as exposure to high levels of radiation. Without proper protection one runs the risk of losing one's self to the very world that radiates these energies."

—Malidoma Patrice Somé
The Healing Wisdom of Africa

As the end of my year in Zimbabwe approached, I found that I had learned a fair amount about the overall influence of spirits within the Shona culture. I was familiar with the different types of divination, traditional healing, sorcery, and witchcraft being practiced in Zimbabwe. I roughly understood the different types of traditional medical practitioners, called, of course, *n'anga* among the Shona, and present in some form in most of the traditional cultures of sub-Saharan Africa. These specialists include traditional birth attendants, bonesetters, *omobaris* (so-called surgeons who performed ritualistic bloodless operations), herbalists, diviners, and the Great Spirit healers. Since I had little contact with my physician colleagues in obstetrics, surgery, or emergency medicine, I did not learn much about the first three types.

Herbalists, as the name implies, mix combinations of plants whose ingestion or application are considered most helpful in the treatment of physical ailments rather than in addressing mental or social problems. Moving up the *n'anga* hierarchy, diviners are thought to have an intrinsic sense of the invisible world, capable of finding lost items, diagnosing the cause of an illness, and probing for any sources of external malice that might underlie an apparent accident or bout of misfortune. The diviners harness the spiritual power generated by the use of possession-trance and other rituals, including that of repetitively tossing and reading "divining dice" (usually large fruit seeds or bones), and gazing at stones to enhance their understanding of a situation. They are also able to "channel" ancestor spirits to pass messages from the Spirit World to the material world. Most diviners are able to prescribe herbal treatments as well. The Great Spirit healers are believed to have the ability to diagnose an evil spirit as the problem, communicate with the spirit, and then command the spirit to leave, much as an exorcist of the Roman Catholic church casts out demons from afflicted Christians.

On the evil side of the good-versus-bad spiritual split in Zimbabwe are the witches, sorcerers, and diviners gone bad, those "who've gone over to the other side." The Shona word for witchcraft or sorcery is *muroyi* (moo-ROH-yee). Different types of spirits in the Shona culture include the *mudzimu* (mood-ZEE-moo), family ancestral spirits; the *mashave* (mah-SHAH-vay), alien spirits; and the *ngozi* (in-GOH-zee), very frightening and dangerous avenging type of spirits often "hired" by witches to perform witchcraft. Witches are also thought to employ animals, called *tokoloshi* (toh-koh-LOH-shee), and birds, called *zvishiri* (zvee-SHEE-ree), to carry out acts of witchcraft.

I would need to marshal all of this newfound knowledge to properly step up to the batter's box and face the curveball that was pitched to me by fate on a warm and humid day in November. Muggy summer was settling in even at Harare's altitude, more than fifteen hundred meters above sea level. The combination of moist breeze and piercing sun threatened to turn the P.U. into a gentle sauna as early as 8:30 a.m. on the day I walked onto the ward to do hospital rounds.

At first I didn't make the connection when the nurse told me that I was about to see a man from Sangani who literally had needles and nails jammed into his lower legs. My memory was immediately jogged, however, when I ripped open the referral letter from an orthopedic surgeon in the rural areas south of Harare. No wonder the case sounded so familiar. I had seen a stranger-than-fiction report about Winston Chivero several months earlier on the Zimbabwean Broadcasting Corporation's (ZBC) nightly newscast.

X-rays confirmed what the Zimbabwean surgeon suspected. The deep tissue under Winston Chivero's left shin harbored a hodgepodge of construction nails and sewing needles. After examining the fresh bloody puncture wounds and the upward angle of entry indicated on the x-ray, the surgeon determined that the wounds were self-inflicted. Time for Winston to see a psychiatrist. Winston, whose shin full of nails and needles brought him national notoriety and a visit to the psychiatrist, denied inserting these foreign objects. His steadfast contention was that the nails and needles were placed in his leg surreptitiously by a witch. I instantly recalled my reaction at the time of the newscast, when I said to my wife, "Guy sounds crazy. Bet I'll be seeing him sometime down the road." By the time he came to me, I wished that I hadn't been so clairvoyant and that there were more psychiatrists working in this part of the world. I hate having to clean up somebody else's mess. But that's why they paid me the big bucks there in Zimbabwe.

Winston's leg had already been operated on twice. His left shin now showed a fresh puncture with new nails aboard. In the second surgery, the doctor could only remove six of eight needles, as the last two were so deeply buried. At his postoperative visit, Wilson's surgical scar was red and cratered. Displeased and suspecting yet another round of self-mutilation, the surgeon repeated the x-ray and discovered two new nails piercing upward into his shin. I can only imagine the surgeon throwing up his hands at the time—angry, disgusted, puzzled. Surgeons generally have little tolerance for such foolishness. They live in a land of dramatic fixes—cut-and-dried, black-and-white. We psychiatrists live in a land of ambiguity with glacial improvements and blankets of fog obscuring all the landmarks.

Tall but thin, shy, subdued, and appearing younger than his twenty years, Winston was already dressed in drab khaki hospital pajamas when I interviewed him the day after his admission to P.U. We stepped into a small interview room just off the nurses' station. Dimly lit, dusty, and ramshackle with scattered old textbooks and a mishmash of medical records handwritten on yellowing tablet paper, the room was made even smaller by the presence of a writing table and four chairs. Although he had completed several years of school and English instruction, Winston spoke primarily Shona so I interviewed him with an experienced psychiatric nurse, Sister Chimhenga, interpreting for me.

First I examined the x-rays and his new wound, being the complete head-to-toe physician that I was. Nickel-sized and a few millimeters deep, the gape was oozing and partly covered with new magenta scabbing. It looked damn fresh and painful to me. "Does it hurt?"

"No."

"How did it happen?"

"I don't know." A long pause.

"Hmm. Really?"

This open-ended query brought no response from Winston. I stared at him for ten seconds or so, knowing that my work was cut out for me on this one. He looked studiously at his bare feet, avoiding my eye contact. Somewhat frustrated, wanting to be a surgical psychiatrist at the moment, I decided to attempt a jab into Winston's mind: "Did you stick those needles into your leg?"

"No."

"It looks like it on the x-ray," I said, my voice even, fantasizing that I was methodically cutting deeper and deeper into Winston's psyche by asking such direct questions. I showed him the film, the new nails clearly showing. "Did you do it?"

He looked at the x-ray with detachment. "No."

"Then how did they get there?"

"I don't know."

Back to square one. Time to slow down. The guns-a-blazing cowboy approach would get me nowhere in this case. An aggressive style of questioning, under the hot glare of a bare lightbulb, rarely worked in the real world. Maybe in the land of cops and robbers, but not in the realm of psychiatry.

I decided to ask questions that were much more innocuous and then obtain a more formal history. With time and with the able assistance of Sister Chimhenga, Winston opened up a little more. He had no significant medical or psychiatric history; he had no girlfriend; he spent time with a few close friends his own age; he worked part-time as a laborer; he was the youngest of seven children who lived at home with his widowed mother. His father had died a few months earlier, possibly of alcoholism. He acknowledged to me that he had enjoyed a close relationship with his father and was unable to express grief after his father's death.

"How is your mood?" I asked. "How do you feel?"

"Bored," Winston said.

"No, I mean your mood. Are you happy? Sad? A little of both?"

He did not hesitate. "Happy." Winston did not appear happy; indeed, his affect was bland. I asked him what it was like to be at the P.U. He told me that it was "boring to be in the hospital" and that he was "bored" by all the attention regarding his condition, including the national television news report. He proceeded to tell me that his family was not at all "bored" by the situation—his mother, in particular, was apparently "very angry" with Winston, his nails, his needles, and his newfound notoriety.

I again asked, "How did those needles get there?"

"A witch." Finally, a response. "A witch put them there."

"How?"

"I don't know."

With more painstaking patience on the part of Sister Chimhenga, the story evolved. Sister Chimhenga was probably the best nurse at the P.U. I'm not embarrassed to inform you, however, that my judgment might have been clouded by the fact that I had a crush on her, though I doubt it. Mature beyond her mid-twenties, whip-smart, funny, compassionate, and warm-hearted, Sister Chimhenga was also beautiful without being a classic beauty. Her skin was a smooth dark chocolate, her smile a mouthful of brilliant white, her figure, how shall I say it, on the pleasant lighter side of the Rubenesque spectrum. Plus, she was a capable and experienced nurse, who helped me to solve the puzzle presented by Winston.

Winston eventually told us that, just prior to the needles appearing in his leg, he had killed his neighbor's owl by a vicious stoning.

Creature of the night and accomplice to witches, the owl is an evil icon within Shona culture. It is highly taboo to kill an owl. According to African beliefs, such an act must carry consequences. The very next morning, after slaying the owl, Winston awoke with an excruciating pain in his left leg. He did not puzzle or obsess over this or bemoan his miserable luck as any red-blooded American would. Oh, no, he accepted his fate. He knew right away. Of course, he didn't know that needles, stuck in his leg, were causing the pain until he got an x-ray at his local clinic. But he knew right away that a witch was the cause of the pain in his leg. It was payback for killing her owl, nothing more, nothing less.

This made for a very complicated situation. Did the witch insert the needles from afar? Some witches were thought to inflict pain or injury purely at a distance—by remote control, so to speak. Or did the witch sneak into Winston's sleeping space and jam the foreign bodies into his leg? This was culturally feasible because it was widely believed that witches met after midnight before traveling off together to stage bizarre and wicked deeds. They are believed to be able to fly long distances after dark and to secretly infiltrate the homes of mere mortals in the wee hours. There are some people who go so far as to assert that a witch can leave her own body asleep in her bed while only her spirit rambles around wreaking havoc.

Who was I to say that a witch didn't surreptitiously insert those needles? By the time winter had turned to spring and then summer in the Southern Hemisphere, I had observed dozens of garden-variety cases of psychosis. By then, I had begun to wonder if both physical and psychological illness could actually occur in response to a bewitchment. I had heard countless patients attribute their psychotic symptoms to a bewitchment but so far found no evidence that such a thing had indeed occurred. So I was pumped up, on the lookout for a case of real bewitchment. That I might possibly bag a clinical case of such extraordinary exotica excited me very much. In Winston's case, in fact, I considered the possibility higher up in my list of possible diagnoses, hoping to discover a truly exotic psycho-spiritual phenomenon.

Of course, before I went floating off into the Spirit World, I needed to keep my American feet on the ground. As a Western-trained psychiatrist, I was compelled to consider the more humdrum possibilities—that Winston inflicted self-harm because he was suicidal or reacting to the commands of an auditory hallucination or punishing himself in response to delusions with guilty themes. But Winston clearly denied a wish to kill himself. His pattern of symptoms and behavior did not clearly fit that of a clinical depression. He denied hearing any voices in his head or outside of his head, now or in the past. And, most importantly, his claim that a witch supernaturally placed the needles in his leg could not be considered delusional because the placement of needles in a mysterious fashion *is* a form of witchcraft considered plausible within Shona culture.

Before he arrived on the steps of the P.U. with referral letter in hand, Winston and his older sister had consulted a hometown *n'anga* who curiously could not divine that a bewitchment had occurred. This confused me because Winston told such a good story and all of the pieces of the puzzle seemed to indicate true witchcraft. Maybe I was looking a little too hard for a real case. However, I did come to understand that some diviners were afraid to identify a witch for two reasons: One, it was technically illegal to even acknowledge the existence of witches and witchcraft (contravening Zimbabwe's Witchcraft Suppression Act, on the books since colonial times); and two, the *n'anga* might fear retribution or having an insufficient magnitude of benevolent powers to counteract and subdue the evil powers of the witch.

Through all of this, I did have enough wits about me to obtain an in-depth cross-cultural translation, consulting Dr. Sekai Nhiwatiwa, a Shona psychiatrist, in her final year of specialty training, with whom I worked. I presented all the details of the case to her. She listened patiently.

"So, Sekai," I ventured cautiously, "could this actually be a bewitchment?"

"I have heard of similar cases," replied Dr. Nhiwatiwa, who had completed some of her training in Great Britain. "One was recently in the news. A newborn who was found to have more than forty pins and sewing needles in her abdomen."

"I didn't hear about that one."

"In Shona culture, we believe that it is possible to be bewitched in such a way," she continued. "But what is very strange about this case is that the *n'anga* could not find the witch. If Winston's story is true, then the *n'anga* should be able to identify it as a bewitchment. That's very fishy."

"You know, the other thing that's suspicious is where the nails are inserted, upward into his left shin," I added.

"Right, right. He's right-handed, that's exactly where someone would push them up into the leg. He probably put them there," concluded Dr. Nhiwatiwa, concurring with my suspicions of self-injury.

I got to thinking. If Winston's own hand had indeed inserted the foreign bodies into his leg, was it possible that a witch could have somehow controlled Winston's body and mind externally to make Winston carry out such an action? Or was it that the needles and nails just suddenly appeared in his leg, a transfer of protons and electrons and energy, like Mr. Spock getting instantaneously beamed from one of the outer galaxies to Captain James T. Kirk's Starship *Enterprise*? When I tried to divine the details of just how a witch might work to make the needles appear, I came up against a brick wall. Either the Shona professionals did not honestly know, or they were afraid to think about it in much detail, not wanting to get burned. No one wants to dabble too much in the Spirit World, particularly if you grew up in a culture that embraced such ideas. It is a risk for that individual, not knowing the true way around the realm of the spirits or the limits of the unseen dimension. These are areas for an experienced *n'anga* to patrol.

Another angle from which to approach Winston's situation was to consider the handful of culture-bound syndromes recognized among Zimbabwe's traditional healers. Winston's behavior could have been explained by a syndrome called *kutanda botso* (koo-TAHN-dah BOAT-soh), described as an acute and brief behavioral disturbance occurring suddenly after an individual breaks a major cultural taboo. In Winston's case the cause— stoning an owl—seemed serious enough, but the time course was all wrong. In this condition, sort of the Western equivalent of a brief psychotic breakdown due to overwhelming stress, the individual generally gets much better in a matter of several days. Winston's behavioral problems had become almost chronic by the time I saw him.

I also tried to understand Winston's case from a purely Westernized view and constructed a few hypotheses, in homage to my psychotherapy training, spun from a traditional psychodynamic perspective. First, it was possible that Winston may have been unconsciously punishing himself by inserting the needles and nails into his leg. Alternatively, he might have been acting out of anger, as a result of unresolved grief over his father's death. Or, as the youngest of seven children, he might even have been trying to hang on to a dependent position in the family by making himself deformed and debilitated. Frankly, these theories didn't hold much water, in my opinion, because in Zimbabwe I was working under the influence of spirits.

To put my thinking about the case into perspective, it may be helpful to understand the way that American psychiatrists and psychologists think about self-injurious behaviors. Self-injury in the United States is often driven by America's dominant culture of narcissism; ironically, it's the self-absorption of many Americans that impels them to hurt themselves. Self-injurious behaviors are not necessarily suicidal. To cut your wrist deep and vertically with the intention of puncturing your ulnar or radial artery is certainly a suicidal act. To superficially lacerate or scratch your wrist in a horizontal position, burn yourself with a lit cigarette, slap yourself, pull out your hair, or scratch yourself are all self-injurious behaviors without suicidal intent. These behaviors are driven from a number of different psychological motivations—to punish oneself, to redirect anger away from others and toward oneself, to manipulate loved ones, to feel pain rather than emotional numbness. Another motivation is to assume a dependent sick role as a patient in hospitals and clinics.

While Winston's case seemed like a newsworthy novelty on the face of things, I was still dealing with a human life here. I was stuck, so to speak, with the unenviable task of trying to do something, anything, for this poor kid with gaping wounds in his shin. On the layman's face of things, Winston didn't seem to care a whit about his situation.

Despite my seduction by the spiritual possibilities of the case, I found Winston's case ultimately frustrating because I didn't know where to start. How could I devise a treatment plan when I didn't really know what was going on? Welcome to the nebulous world of psychiatry. There's an old maxim that still floats around medical schools and hospitals: Neurologists can diagnose it but can't treat it. Psychiatrists can't diagnose it but they can treat it. The translation here is that while neurologists can often exactly pinpoint the cause of a particular disease, such as a stroke or inoperable brain tumor or spinal cord injury, they often cannot offer much treatment. Psychiatrists, on the other hand, can pick out a few target symptoms and signs from the history and mental status examination, not really knowing the precise diagnosis and cause of illness, and throw a virtual armamentarium of psychiatric medications at the "thing" in question, whatever it might be.

So, in the spirit of that hoary stereotype, during the second week of Winston's hospitalization, I started him on a modest nighttime dose of thioridazine (thigh-oh-RID-ah-zeen), a somewhat kinder and gentler cousin of CPZed called Mellaril in the United States. What was I treating? Beats me. But I rationalized it by thinking: Can it hurt? If his thoughts were delusional, then this mild antipsychotic medication with sedative properties could help. Psychiatrists often prescribe low doses of antipsychotic medications as a "character glue" for patients with borderline personality disorder, those who are not out-and-out psychotic but rather the emotional and mental equivalent of spinning and unraveling balls of twine. "And they call Economics the dismal science?" I thought to myself.

During that second week of hospitalization, Winston, still a patient at P.U. because I didn't know what to do with him except follow the potential benefits and side effects of the magical thioridazine, tipped his close-to-the-vest hand. The psychiatric nurses interrupted my hospital rounds early one afternoon to report evidence of a fresh traumatic injury on Winston's shin. I went out into the courtyard to find Winston splayed cross-legged on the ground with droplets of blood falling from his left shin into the reddish brown dust; they formed a splattering of purplish clots. It looked like he had reinjured himself. Winston looked up at me blankly.

"Holy shit," I silently mouthed to myself. "Let's get an x-ray," I said to the nurses. "Let's send him to x-ray, looks like he either pulled a nail out of there or put something in." I didn't even consider confronting Winston on the spot. I needed to think about the case, get the results back, and strategize what my response would be. No surprise, just a few hours later the radiologist called with the result: In comparing this film to his admission film, this x-ray revealed one less nail, specifically the one that previously resided nearest to the surface. It wasn't too much of a logical leap to conclude that Winston dug a nail out of his shin, causing the wound to bleed again. This illustrates the point that self-removal of a previously inserted foreign object is as much an example of self-injury as is the original act of sticking it in.

Despite the avalanche of circumstantial evidence to the contrary, Winston stuck to his story of being the victim of a bewitchment. However, after consulting with Dr. Nhiwatiwa and thinking more about the case, I had no choice at that point but to believe that Winston was absolutely the one who was manipulating his own shin. I'm embarrassed to say that I was coming around to slapping a good old-fashioned diagnosis lifted straight out of America's *DSM-IV*, on the bedraggled and misunderstood Winston Chivero. For better or worse, Winston's self-mutilation was most consistent with a Western diagnosis of factitious disorder, an unusual psychiatric illness characterized by volitional self-injury or feigning of illness to assume the sick role, motivated unconsciously by psychological factors.

The plain English translation? Winston stuck needles and nails in his leg on purpose: to see doctors, to get hospitalized, and to get operated on for reasons unclear even to his own mind, which in this case refers only to his conscious awareness. And, sorry to say, the reasons for Winston's self-injury remained opaque also to the conscious mind of his treating psychiatrist, who had skipped school on the day that his professors had taught divination, or, at least, mind-reading. Of course, all of you who have attended cocktail parties and mingled with psychiatrists do realize that psychiatrists, particularly psychoanalysts, can and do read minds, contrary to the disavowals and denials that spout from the mouths of doctors of the mind.

So what to do for Winston? I waited until my next scheduled hospital rounds, three days hence, to speak with Winston about his most recent bout of self-injury. This delay was probably a good thing, since my first all-too-human response was to give Winston a minor tongue-lashing—an absolute no-no when it comes to managing factitious disorder. Plus I wanted to integrate somehow Winston's cultural factors in my understanding, or lack of it, of his case. The standard treatment for factitious disorder is to "do no harm" by avoiding unnecessary and potentially harmful procedures. One must avoid direct confrontation, using the power of suggestion that the problem will gradually resolve itself. This treatment allows the patient a "face-saving" way to get better and give up the symptoms. Despite any best efforts from a team of doctors and nurses, the prognosis for a complete recovery is poor. Medications seem to do little, unless a treatable case of depression or anxiety can be identified. Even months of psychotherapy may do little to change what may be a longstanding personality problem and maladaptive way of seeking help—reflexively becoming "a patient" when times get tough.

I struggled mightily, trying to integrate Winston's psychological workings, his perception of what caused the illness, the strictly American diagnosis of factitious disorder, and the possible psycho-spiritual diagnoses suggested by an understanding of Shona culture and phenomenology. The path of diagnosis and understanding of Winston that I was embarking on was consistent with what is now called the new cross-cultural psychiatry, a term coined by the prominent psychiatrist, anthropologist, and author Arthur Kleinman. While these tenets specifically guide the conduct of cross-cultural psychiatric research, the new cross-cultural psychiatry gets translated into the clinical practice of medicine something along these lines: Try to understand the patient's thoughts and behaviors within the specific context of his culture. And, furthermore, try to discover exactly what the patient believed to be the cause of the illness and even what the recommended treatment might be.

Of course this mindset and technique would never work for a ruptured appendix or sky-high blood sugars or a bursting aneurysm, in which case the recommended treatment would depend on the technical acumen of the physician, but in the murky world of psychiatry, it seemed like it was worth a shot. Since the treatment of factitious disorder hinges on giving the patient a sense of control, when I next saw Winston I went out of my way to again find out what he thought should be done about his situation.

Friday rolled around and I evaluated Winston toward the end of rounds, already in the early afternoon, long after I had interviewed three new patients and several others in follow-up. He entered the room. What amazed me was that his facial expressions and manner never seemed to change. He could be dozing in the courtyard, picking at the scab on his leg, eating a plate of *sadza* and greens, talking to a nurse—his way of being in the world remained seemingly complacent. Since psychiatrists assiduously follow an individual's changing mental status examination on a day-to-day basis to determine whether he is improving or not, Winston's unchanging persona made it impossible for me to determine whether he was getting any better.

He sat down at a table, kitty-corner from me, returning the morning greeting that I offered him. I started in, getting translation help from Sister Chimhenga. "So, Winston, on Tuesday, you pulled out a nail from your leg," I started. "The nurses saw that you were picking at your leg and you were bleeding from a gash on your shin. The x-ray showed that a nail was gone. What happened?"

A long pause. Finally, came the answer: "Nothing."

I already had clued in Sister Chimhenga and the other nurses that none of us were to harangue Winston about what appeared to be an obvious case of self-injury. I explained to them the concept of factitious disorder and the way in which a psychiatrist attempts to treat it.

"Well, Winston," I said. "I think that you pulled the nail out of your leg on Tuesday. The nurses' observation, the bleeding, the hole in your leg, the x-ray." My tone was even. I did not express any particular frustration or anger. Although I avoided being confrontational with Winston, I did need him to try to understand the way in which I was seeing things so that any attempt at treatment might work. "Did you pull the nail out of your shin?"

"No," he said immediately.

"Then what happened?"

"The witch did it."

"But you moved away from the witch. You have been staying in Harare now for a few weeks," I countered, knowing that a witch is generally thought to be influential only in his or her home area. "And you told me that a *n'anga* could not identify a witch," I continued.

"The witch is very powerful," stated Winston, looking me in the eye for nearly the very first time since he had been my patient.

"I see," I said. His eyes once again returned to staring at his hands folded in front of him on the rough wooden table. I once again reviewed with him the sort of nonspecific treatments that the *n'anga* offered him to treat his condition. A concoction of herbal tea and local application of a mixture of herbs did not help. A traditional ritual—sounding sort of generic according to my Shona nursing colleagues—also did not help.

"Do you want to see a different *n'anga*, a more powerful *n'anga*?" I asked.

At this, Winston paused, took a deep breath, and sighed. This action signaled the first tiny crack in Winston's seeming imperturbability. "No, a *n'anga* cannot help this situation," he said finally.

"Why not?" I asked. "If you think a witch did this to you, my understanding is that only a *n'anga*, maybe a *profita*, could help this situation."

Winston said nothing. Sister Chimhenga became somewhat animated in speaking to him in Shona for half a minute or more. "*Chiremba*, I was explaining to him what you just said."

"Isn't that right, Sister?" I asked the experienced Sister Chimhenga. "If this is a bewitchment, then most Shona people would think that only a traditional healer could cure it."

"Yes, *chiremba*," said Sister Chimhenga, who again embarked on a kind, but persistent, conversation with Winston, who responded by leaning back in his chair, stretching out his legs, and placing himself in what appeared to be a state of repose. "It is true that sometimes a *n'anga* living far away from the witch may be able to identify the witch or do a better job of treating. I was just telling him that, *chiremba*."

"So, Winston, I am at a loss," I said. "Should I just discharge you home? What would that accomplish?" He just sat there. "What do you think we should do?" I almost pleaded.

"I want the needles out," said Winston. "If they are all taken out, then the power of the witch will be gone."

"So, you want another operation?"

"I want the needles out," he repeated.

The principle of "do no harm" reverberated around my head. The last thing that a physician is supposed to do to a patient with a suspected factitious disorder is a further round of procedures, which are almost always unnecessary. On the other hand, if we could accomplish Winston's stated goal of getting all of the needles out, this might indeed be the "face-saving" way in which Winston could give up his repetitive bouts of self-injury. I was shocked that Winston did not want to consult another *n'anga*. In retrospect, I might have demanded it, but at the time, I put my mind down the path of repeating another operation.

Of the dozen or so cases of factitious disorder that I had seen in medically hospitalized patients in the States, virtually none of them came to a satisfying outcome. The most common scenario was that one of the internists or surgeons, contravening the advice of the psychiatric consultant, would vigorously confront the self-injurious patient and essentially drive the patient from the hospital. Most of these patients would sign out of the hospital prematurely and against medical advice—the much-dreaded "AMA discharge," the "AMA" standing for "against medical advice." The translation for an "AMA discharge" is: "You're on your own, patient, and if something bad happens to you, then it's entirely your own fault from a medicolegal standpoint."

In Winston's case, I faced one of psychiatry's most difficult diagnoses, the degree of difficulty ratcheted upward by unique cultural and spiritual factors.

Winston's belief that the Western biomedical treatment of yet another surgery would solve his spiritual problems, as well as his physical problems, struck me as curious. But, if I could convince a surgeon to perform another operation and the surgeon could remove all of the needles, then it was possible that I might have engineered a rare cure for a case of factitious disorder. Going against my usual inclination, in opposition to my better judgment, influenced by spirits, and operating in a realm over my head, I agreed with Winston. So, I consulted a surgeon at Harare Central Hospital, who, understandably, first thought that maybe I was the crazy one in this situation. Not surprisingly, he was reluctant to do the procedure.

After a long conversation with him, in which I tried to mentally juke him with my psychobabble mumbo-jumbo and formulations, the doctor gave in. Don't get me wrong. I didn't lie to the surgeon. I told him that, of course, in many ways repeating another operation was against my better judgment. I was afraid that another operation wouldn't work. Nonetheless, I told him about my theory of doing what the patient wants as a way to make it succeed, as a way of curing the case of factitious disorder. I also carefully explained that all of the foreign bodies would need to be removed for the surgery to be successful from a psychiatric standpoint. He seemed to clearly understand this point. Either he bought the story or else just got tired of listening to me. The surgeon agreed to do the operation. Of course, this surgery would have to be the last one.

I saw Winston on the postsurgical ward two days after the operation. His state of mind had not changed. His demeanor continued to be placid. I found out that the surgeon was unable to remove all of the nails and needles. I just assumed that the surgeon would not embark on the operation if he could not remove all of the foreign bodies. I assumed that the surgeon could determine that from the x-ray. I assumed wrongly.

Winston wanted to go home, witch and all. He didn't know if he was cured or not, but he was beginning to miss his friends and family. I agreed with him. There was nothing that I could do and this state of affairs aggrieved me. I feared for Winston. He was discharged from the postsurgical ward, and I never saw or heard of Winston Chivero again. My work with him was done. I could do no more. I wasn't sure I had done him any favors. I'm not sure I did him no harm.

The burning question that I was left with was not what? Or how? But why? Why did Winston stick those needles in his leg? A part of me—a dreamy part of me, utterly seduced by the possibilities invoked by the Spirit World—wanted to believe his story. I found the African perspective more interesting, more plausible on the face of things, more useful for understanding the situation. But I could also speculate from the American perspective, searching for the psychodynamic underpinnings to explain his behavior. I got whipsawed by the case and it stayed on my mind. Even after I returned to San Francisco, I continued to think and read about self-injury and factitious disorder, all the while wondering "Whatever happened to Winston?"

The anthropologist M. F. C Bourdillon, author of *The Shona Peoples*, asserts that conflict within a Shona community often precedes a bewitchment. Killing an owl would certainly qualify as a significant source of tension. According to the American psychiatrist A. R. Favazza, who wrote *Bodies Under Siege: Self-Mutilation in Culture and Psychiatry*, self-mutilation is sanctioned within some cultures to serve a higher, spiritual function—preserving harmony within a community, fostering healing, guarding against disease and misfortune.

I wonder now if Winston scapegoated himself for the owl's killing; if he was absolving and protecting his entire community from the expected wrathful response of the witch. In other words, Winston might have inserted the nails and needles, suffered the pain, to ward off a potentially cataclysmic bewitchment engineered by the hand of an irate witch bent on revenge. Classically speaking, his self-injury served a higher, spiritual and cultural function within his local community. He was not the victim of a bewitchment in the traditional sense, but he might have been the victim of witchcraft in an indirect sense because he hurt himself to protect others from witchcraft.

This notion tossed my previous understanding of self-injury on its head. Zimbabwean patients are very different from Americans in this regard. Although Winston might have mutilated himself for the sake of the community, most self-mutilators in the United States cut, bite, pick at, and burn themselves for their own sake in response to psychological conflicts. This fits nicely with the concept of African cultures as being "outer-directed," concerned with the extended family and community, and our culture being "inner-directed," emphasizing self-absorption and the rights of the individual.

So in Winston's case, I went in search of a bewitchment but instead found a case of factitious disorder with the patient assuming the patient role not for his own personal gain, but to save his fellow neighbors. My belief that factitious disorder was indeed a correct diagnosis was reinforced by my Shona colleagues, who believed that the pattern of obvious self-injury in this case did not fit recognized patterns of bewitchment within the Shona culture. This realization left me feeling frustrated and a bit empty. Although I ultimately reported Winston's case, "A Bewitching Case of Factitious Disorder in Zimbabwe," in the journal *General Hospital Psychiatry*, I was far more interested in my transcultural surfing of spirit realms than in padding my curriculum vitae with this rare bird of factitious disorder in a nonindustrial culture.

I wanted to do what was best for my patient, but I also wanted to unearth a real live case of bewitchment. But, since I didn't really know the Shona culture in a deep-down lifetime kind of way, I would be wholly unprepared to recognize a real bewitchment if it came up and hit me over the head. I'm afraid that for an outsider like myself, there would be a better chance of catching lightning in a bottle, which I reckon were about the same odds for "fixing" Winston Chivero when I first started treating him.

CHAPTER ELEVEN

"You Ask a Lot of Questions, You Know That?"

Wonder Kasimonje: Redemption Is Where You Find It

"The white man came to Africa primarily to heal himself. . . . Why should we remain passive while the white man searches the world for the means to save himself? We are together in this struggle. All our souls need rest in a safe home. All people must heal, because we are all sick."

A shaman, as quoted by
Malidoma Patrice Somé
The Healing Wisdom of Africa

During my last month on the job in Zimbabwe, at least twenty of my patients asked for my mailing address in the United States, presumably so they could write and keep me updated on their lives. Since I didn't even have an address in the United States at the time, I gave them my in-laws' address in Arizona. For more than a year-and-a-half, our mail had been collected, sorted, screened, and stored by my wife Laurie's parents. Despite that flurry of interest, only one of my patients, Wonder Kasimonje, actually wrote to me.

Amazingly, nearly six years later, we still correspond by letter, and more recently, by e-mail. During those six years, Wonder has written more than seventy letters and dozens of e-mails to me. Over the course of our correspondence, each of us has weathered tumultuous life changes, surviving bittersweet experiences and feeling the highs of life as well as the lows. Sometimes our lives moved in parallel directions and, at other times, our fortunes diverged. As a wise man once told me: Into each life some rain must fall.

After I moved back to San Francisco, I paid for Wonder's tuition, books, and room and board at a Zimbabwean Bible college. The fees, an incredible bargain at less than US$400 per year, went directly to the school. Wonder endured lean times, suffering from hunger, deprivation, and academic inconsistency on the part of some of his instructors. But he persevered and received his degree after one transfer and three years of study.

In return, Wonder has given me a much more intangible gift. He has grounded me in the ways of Africa, instructing me on the importance of family and faith and keeping on in the face of adversity. He demonstrates an unwavering Christian faith and thereby provides a real-life example of an individual simultaneously steeped in traditional African ways and Christianity, a brand of so-called dualism that is more the rule than the exception in Africa.

By the time Wonder Kasimonje arrived at the clinic of P.U., I was heading into the homestretch of my time in Zimbabwe. It was December, a time of heat and episodic rainstorms. Although I still had two or three months left to work in Zimbabwe, I was already looking forward to the future, which would include several weeks of holiday in Malawi, Botswana, Namibia, and South Africa. I had gone so far as to inquire about available jobs in northern California. I was anxious to return home and begin chipping away at the massive medical school debt Laurie and I had accumulated.

I should have learned a lesson from the African mindset, articulated to me one day by the caretaker of a cottage that was perched atop the Zomba Plateau of Malawi, teetering on the edge of Africa's Great Rift Valley. In the late morning of a steamy February day, Laurie and I were anxious to secure the lodging for that night. We spoke to the caretaker, Stephen, a middle-aged Malawian man (whom the colonialists and missionaries would have referred to as the "boy"), who told us that it was likely that the cottage would be available. In typical American style, we pressed him for a commitment. Stephen, short and sprightly, comported himself as a common man of uncommon wisdom. He demurred, knowing that he could not guarantee it, when finally he said, "See how the day goes. Just see how the day goes. Come back around four."

The simple statement was made with such quiet conviction that we immediately backed off to take a walk, blissfully and mindfully exploring the lush green highlands surrounding the cottage for the next two hours. "See how the day goes." Sage advice indeed—advice that these days I almost never heed.

When I first began treating Wonder Kasimonje, he was living in a halfway house that had been established for people recovering from episodes of serious mental illness. He had previously seen another doctor who had diagnosed him with psychotic depression and started him on medication. On the first day that I saw Wonder, he could have seen any of the four doctors on duty that day, each of whom toiled behind a different door. It was like a game show: Behind door number 4 worked the husky *marungu* doctor. It was a fateful coincidence that he was at the head of the line when my door opened. My immediate impression of Wonder Kasimonje was purely a physical one. He was one of the tallest Shona men I had ever seen, maybe six-foot-three, and razor-thin. His face was drawn tight, whether out of fear, depression, or respect, I did not know. He was just twenty-one years old.

On many of his visits, Wonder was accompanied by one of the staff from the halfway house—Bob Kitchin, a mental health worker from England. I came to know Bob very well before I left Zimbabwe. Carefree and with a big heart, muscular, and balding, Bob Kitchin had learned the best of what it meant to be an African. He could "see how the day goes" and not crumble in the face of life's unpredictability. He didn't sweat the small stuff.

Initially, Wonder sat quietly next to Bob Kitchin, impassive and respectful as I inspected his medical record card. For several weeks, he had been taking both TFPZ and AMT at bedtime. The regimen seemed reasonable, especially since so many of the patients that I saw in Zimbabwe had been inappropriately and prematurely diagnosed with schizophrenia and started on crippling doses of injectable antipsychotic medications.

The halfway house worked out very well for Wonder, who needed the housing, support, and fellowship available there. He was a valuable resident who helped with the daily chores and participated in the activities and groups. Bob noted that Wonder was quiet and kept mostly to himself; he felt that this attribute was driven not by fear but more by Wonder's sense of shyness and respect for others. Bob believed that Wonder's depression was slowly lifting. Wonder remained motionless in his chair but maintained good eye contact with me as Bob spoke.

I inquired about Wonder's symptoms. Yes, he was sleeping better. His spirits were still a little bit down. His appetite and weight were still decreased. He said that he did not hear voices and did not feel paranoid. He was happy at the house. I also inquired about his history. These problems of sadness, not eating, and hopelessness started after Wonder got hit with a lot of stress within his family. He had never experienced anything like this before. Although he respected many of the traditions of the Shona culture, Wonder did not believe in the old ways of witchcraft and described himself as a devout Christian.

Wonder spoke slowly, deliberately, and I could tell that his English skills were very good. He gave only brief answers, and his facial muscles revealed precious little of what he was experiencing inside. But then, almost out of nowhere, came a fountain of questions such as I almost never heard from any patient in Zimbabwe.

"What is my diagnosis?"

"Well, I just met you so it's hard for me to say," I began, hedging. "The card here says psychotic depression."

"What is psychotic depression?"

"Well, it's a serious emotional illness with symptoms of extreme sadness, trouble sleeping and eating, crying, not caring about the future, sometimes thinking of ending your life, and also with symptoms of hearing voices or seeing things or believing things that are not true."

"What causes it?"

"Well, we don't know for sure. It may be from a chemical imbalance in the brain. It may also have to do with suffering severe losses in your life. It may be both at the same time."

"What is it really?"

"You ask a lot of questions, you know that?" I was surprised. Usually I had to actively draw a sense of curiosity out of my patients. This was odd and, frankly, a little time-consuming. But I was intrigued.

"What is the treatment?"

"Talking, getting help from people like Bob here, taking medications. You are taking trifluoperazine, which is a medicine to make voices and fear go away. And you are taking amitriptyline, which is a medicine to help with your sadness and trouble sleeping."

"Take me off my tablets."

"That would be my goal. I think, with time we can taper you off of your medications. In fact, I feel comfortable cutting your dose of trifluoperazine down to 2 milligrams per day right now." The hallucinations and delusions of psychotic depression often resolve within a matter of weeks. When they die down, it is then safe to taper a person off of his antipsychotic medications. I felt more than comfortable doing that for Wonder.

"Why can't I go off all of them now?"

"Because you would be at risk of getting sick again. I don't think you'll need medications long-term. We will work together to taper you off of them. But since you are still early in your recovery and I am just meeting you now for the first time, I am hesitant to make any big changes since you are doing so well."

"Okay," said Wonder reluctantly, glancing at trusted confidante Bob Kitchin, who was nodding his head in agreement with me. I scrawled a quick note on Wonder's card and wrote a two-week prescription, noting to Sister Mada the reduced dose of TFPZ. Wonder and Bob thanked me and took note of the appointment to come back and see me in two weeks. I gave them the tip of showing up at six-thirty or so to be near the head of the line. I had once asked Sister Mada to inform me just how early a patient has to come to be near the head of the line. She said the earliest arrive at five or five-thirty, but that an arrival before seven got you in the first ten or so patients to be seen on that day.

After Wonder walked out, I scratched my head. He was one of the most assertive patients that I had seen in Zimbabwe, albeit in an understated, quiet, and persistent way. Those types of questions were standard issue in the United States but a downright rarity in Zimbabwe. I was more than happy to answer them.

The typical Zimbabwean's laid-back perspective and seeming stoicism is laudable, for it helps him to be resilient and accept the suffering and hardship that is particular to the life of a spiritually rich but economically poor African. However, this mindset can slide into downright passivity and approach a sense of fatalism that can work against an individual who is trying to recover from illness. The middle route, with the patient exhibiting some assertiveness and self-knowledge while continuing to trust the doctor's advice, is the best attitude for getting better.

Although Wonder's visage remained relatively flat throughout that first encounter, I sensed a certain spark, a "life force" in him that seemed nearly impossible to extinguish. What I didn't know then, but could have predicted after that first meeting, was that his curiosity and slight impatience would serve him well in the future. I did not know that he would continue to develop a profound sense of self-awareness; that he would thrive, and not just survive, in his life and endeavors.

The fortnight passed seemingly in an overnight and I was once again seeing Wonder Kasimonje. Christmas had just passed. I was walking with crutches, hobbled by a ligament tear in my left knee, sustained while playing soccer on a slick field with a handful of Kenyan boys on the rainy afternoon of Christmas Eve. Bob and Wonder entered my room. Greetings were exchanged. I saw that Wonder's face shown a little brighter, a bit more relaxed than on our first meeting. His arms swung looser at his sides. His walking was a little less stiff. Was this because he was not suffering the ill side effects of his previously higher dose of TFPZ? Was it because his depression was further lifting?

Immediately noticing the crutches, Wonder asked me about the injury. This was unusual among my patients in Zimbabwe. Out of respect for authority, most of them would not ask personal questions about me, which, within reason, I am generally happy to answer wherever I practice. In that respect, I am different than many American psychiatrists who are taught to reveal little or nothing of a personal nature to their patients.

The reasons for this distancing stance are many. According to the Freudian theory of psychotherapy, self-revealing by the therapist "contaminates" the transference, the relationship between patient and therapist that theoretically recapitulates the patient's relationship with important figures such as mother, father, wife, or husband. The transference is what gets analyzed in traditional psychotherapy. And, at the time of my psychiatric training in the late 1980s and early 1990s, psychiatric residents at Langley Porter Psychiatric Institute were still taught to approach psychotherapy patients from a traditional perspective. I always found this approach to be artificially stiff and off-putting to the patient. I believed that emotional healing of the patient would better occur in the context of a humane and fluid relationship.

I brought Wonder up to speed on the soccer injury and reassured him that I was recovering well. Almost like a reporter, Wonder wanted to know just the facts, to satisfy his curiosity, to then move on to the next point.

"Okay, Dr. Linde, let's talk about me stopping the tablets." This was said matter-of-factly, not in a loud or pressured manner. Wonder wanted to move on with his life and he saw the medications as a stumbling block to his progress as a human being.

"We will talk about it," I said. "I would like to ask you a few more questions first."

"Okay," said Wonder.

"Where were you born?" I asked. "Where did you grow up?"

"I was born and bred in Charter district now known as Chikomba. It is about two to three hours south of Harare by bus. I was born on March 9, 1973."

"How much schooling did you complete?"

"I received my early education at Sadza Primary School and several secondary schools in Chikomba."

"What was your early life like? What was your family like?"

"I grew up in a devout Christian family. I loved writing and singing religious songs from a very early age. I was brought up and educated by my mother. My mother is a potter. The evangelist Elisha Munonyara and his wife Phoebe of the Methodist Church in Zimbabwe encouraged my mother to discipline her family in a godly manner. They used the Bible, Proverbs Chapter 22, Verse 6. This verse is about how to discipline children. It reads: 'Train up a child in the way he should go, Even when he is old he will not depart from it.'"

I was impressed with Wonder's willingness to talk so much about his early life. I was relieved to hear that he grew up in a devout Christian family. Individuals with strong religious beliefs tend to cope better and recover more fully from serious illness. But, more importantly, this knowledge reassured me that Wonder's firmly held beliefs were consistent with his religious upbringing and not a symptom of relapsing mental illness. Many patients suffering from relapses of schizophrenia or manic-depressive illness may espouse extreme religious beliefs that can slide over into the realm of delusion. Classically, manic patients suffer from religious delusions and often hear auditory hallucinations of the two extremes—Jesus Christ or Satan—exhorting them to do good or evil, as the case may be. I needed to consider the possibility that Wonder's depression might have been the first onset of bipolar disorder, in which sustained episodes of depression and mania alternate during a patient's lifetime.

"Do you still write?" I asked.

Wonder, who had been articulate and quick with his answers to this point, faltered momentarily, his eyes falling to my table, almost as if he took those few seconds to study the pattern of its wood. "No, *chiremba*. I have not felt up to it." I noticed his face drooping somewhat.

"Listen, Wonder, you are still recovering from a serious illness." I tried to reassure him. "You are definitely making progress. I can see it in your face, your stride, your manner of speaking. You are going to continue to get better. Your creativity will come back. Creativity is sometimes the last thing to come back after such a serious illness." Wonder nodded almost imperceptibly, his gaze still fixed downward.

I continued: "Are you hearing any voices? Such as hearing other people talking even when you know that you are all alone?"

"No."

"Are you suspicious of others, afraid of being followed or in danger?"

"No."

"Are you sleeping well at night?"

"Yes."

"How many hours?"

"Seven or eight."

"Bob, do you or any of the other staff notice anything unusual about Wonder's behavior? Anything bizarre?"

"No, absolutely nothing."

"Great," I said, slightly smiling at Wonder, who still sat quietly across from me. "That's good news. It means that we can stop the antipsychotic. Let's meet again in three weeks. Same time, same place. Maybe, just maybe, we can look at tapering the amitriptyline. It makes me nervous to think about doing that, but I know how you feel about it. It's important that you continue taking it for now."

When Wonder and Bob returned, three weeks later, it was clear to me that Wonder continued to improve with his treatment. He felt more energy and had regained some of his interest in music and writing, though he had not resumed his creative activities as of yet. He was slowly gaining weight and he was starting to plan his next step. He had to leave the halfway house in another month or so. He was looking at his options, which included boarding at a mission just outside of Harare. Wonder was indeed resourceful and social. He had become friends with a Catholic priest from Switzerland, Father John Hummel, who provided counseling and friendship as he recovered from his depression.

At this visit, I decided to take a calculated risk and completely taper him off of his amitriptyline over the next week. I considered this a bit of a gamble since the standard of care was to maintain patients on antidepressant medications for six months after a bout of such serious depression. It had really been only two months since he started the treatment. However, I knew that he would be observed at the halfway house for the next month, so if he began to deteriorate, then the staff could bring him back in and we could restart the medications. I would also be able to evaluate him again in three weeks to see how he was coping with the transition from a halfway house to the community and to determine if he was stable enough to continue in his life without having to take psychiatric medications.

That meeting three weeks hence would coincide with my very last week working at the P.U. I couldn't say that my interest in Wonder was any greater than my curiosity in any other patient that I had seen more than once. But, as I mentioned already, I did notice and admire a certain healthy stubbornness in the youthful Wonder Kasimonje.

Although I had already told Wonder that I would be leaving Zimbabwe for good, he acted surprised when I reminded him of that fact during our last meeting. Things were going along swimmingly for Wonder. He felt nearly back to his usual best self. At our final visit, he presented himself in a subdued fashion that could have been mistaken for depression. But now that I knew him a little better, I considered Wonder to be a thoughtful, reflective young man who demonstrated a quiet confidence with his calm countenance. What I may have first construed as fear or respect, both responses to the external world, was really a reflection of his genuine internal self.

"Well, Wonder, you have done very well for yourself," I started. "I see no evidence that you need those psychiatric tablets. Now, at some point in the future, if you find yourself again feeling unwell—sad, not taking care of yourself—you will need again to consult a doctor before things get too bad." This was my standard proviso to my patients recovering from any of the major mental illnesses, many of which are chronic, episodic, and relapsing in nature.

Wonder sat on a small wooden chair just across from me, his long legs tucked awkwardly under the table, his knees nearly knocking the underside of it when he shifted in his chair.

"Have you made plans for your next accommodation?" I asked.

"Yes, Father John Hummel helped me find a place of religious sisters outside of Harare. For now I will stay there and study and do chores in return for room and board."

"That sounds fine. What are your plans for the longer term?"

"I don't know yet, but I trust that God has a plan for my life and that if I place my faith and trust in God, then He will provide for me."

"I need to remind you. This is our last visit. I am moving back to the United States."

"Is it true? Are you really leaving?"

I know that he did not intend to inflict guilt with those questions, but I felt some just the same. I knew that I needed to go back to the United States for many different reasons. Separations are difficult for me and I needed to resist the urge to be defensive or give a knee-jerk response to assuage my own guilt.

"Yes. It is difficult for me to say goodbye to people like you and all of the nurses. I will miss this place very much. But I must go. It is time."

"Can I write to you?"

"Sure." I said, not giving it much of a thought. I wrote the address on a piece of scratch paper and handed it to Wonder.

"Thank you," he said. "I will write you."

"I will be on holiday for the next couple of months so I won't get it until May or so," I said, thinking to myself, "Really now, what are the chances he'll write?"

"Thank you for taking me off the tablets," said Wonder, holding out his hand to shake mine. "And thank you for your help."

I shook his hand and said, "You're welcome." With that, Wonder took his leave.

I didn't give him much more thought over the next few weeks as I feverishly made plans to pack up my life in Zimbabwe, go on holiday for a few weeks, and think about starting nearly from scratch again somewhere back in the United States. Part of my departure from Zimbabwe included saying farewell to my expatriate friends, fellow doctors and nurses, and, of course, my patients. Always a little restless in my school and work history, I had already said goodbye to many different important people in my life and seemed to do okay in moving on to the next phase. I'm afraid to say that my attitude generally is "out of sight, out of mind." On the other hand, I can get quite emotionally involved with those I work with, so the process of separating from them is difficult for me in the moment. As any psychiatrist worth his salt knows: Any parting is a minipreview of the human's ultimate departure from this life—going to the grave. That's why parting is not necessarily such a sweet sorrow for those of us who would rather avoid pain than face it.

The nurses over at the P.U. threw a party for me during my last week on the unit, complete with all of the psychiatric inpatients, nurses, security guys, aides, and even a few administrators present. We ate *sadza* and greens with gusto and danced to African music that blared from a boombox—*kwassa-kwassa* bounced off the concrete walls. This party was emotional for me because I had labored on the front lines of acute-care psychiatry with these nurses. They were fun, knowledgeable, good teachers. At the party, they gave me a heartfelt card and plaque in the shape of the nation of Zimbabwe with the bigger cities and tourist destinations highlighted on it. Within the psychiatric sisters beat a big collective heart, enlarged from years of giving selflessly to the sick and the poor and the forgotten people of the society. Sure, the sisters needed their jobs to support their families, but, in general, they worked as nurses because they were dedicated to caring for patients, showing themselves to be much more altruistic than the doctors in Zimbabwe.

The matron was still pleading with me to stay. She promised many things—converting the cramped solarium of the clinic into an office for me. Trying to get me more pay, more vacation. I remained firm. I had debt to pay. I also harbored grandiose visions that I would develop into some superstar and find fulfillment from a career in psychiatry. In retrospect, though, I can see that I peaked professionally in Zimbabwe. I would never find the practice of psychiatry in the United States as fulfilling.

As promised, Wonder Kasimonje wrote a letter to me, posted not long after I departed Zimbabwe. It arrived care of my in-laws in Arizona. It was an aerogramme dated April 19, 1995, sent from a post office box in Chegutu, a town 75 kilometers from Harare in the Mashonaland West Province. Wonder had taken up residence with some religious sisters of the Roman Catholic Church in a mission called "*Maria Chiedza* (Mary of the First Light of Dawn)." Wonder's spiritual benefactor, Father John Hummel, had helped him find this lodging after his departure from the halfway house.

Wonder wrote: "I am still studying. I mostly devour books on spiritual matters. My goal is to never stop learning. . . . I am still off tablets. I feel very well. Full of health. Our invisible father-mother God is in control and he is everywhere. . . . I thank you once again. I wish you all the best. I look forward to hear from you soon. From Wonder Kasimonje."

I received the letter during an extended visit to my in-laws, taking some rest and relaxation, hiking bone-dry canyons, visiting the Native American monuments so abundant in northern Arizona, eating well, sleeping late. But while recreating, my mind rebelled against me, repeating a personal mantra of self-torture and American impatience—"No job, no car, no home. Got to find a job, a car, a home. No job, no car, no home. Got to find a job, a car, a home."

So much for me learning anything about life while I worked in Africa. I couldn't allay my Americanized brand of anxiety to "see how the day goes." Instead I nervously snapped up a job back at San Francisco General Hospital, where I worked prior to my departure to see the world and work as a doctor in Africa.

After arriving back in San Francisco and finding a nice three-bedroom Victorian flat in a competitive market, I received another letter from Wonder dated July 20, 1995, from Chegutu. It was a typical message from Wonder. It included several key elements in crystal-clear penmanship: a description of the season, an update on his studies and writing, a personal message, and a commentary on the political and economic climate in Zimbabwe.

Wonder wrote: "Thanks so much for writing. I received your letter recently. I was most happy to hear from you after a long time. Here in Zimbabwe we are in winter. The weather is windy and cool. I am keeping well at the place I reside. . . . I am still doing my lonely occupation, writing poems and short stories. Writing and reading can ease my mind and heart. I am still an unpublished writer. Inside my hut there are many books, mostly on spiritual matters. 'A room without books is like a body without a soul.' I surround myself with good thoughts and I don't think I fret. God cares so much. . . . Doctor, when replying to this letter, enclose your photo. I will send you mine in the next mail. Give my love to your work mates, friends, family, including your wife. . . . Keep up your spirit, Dr. Linde. I pray to our spiritual parent God to bless you with spiritual blessings. I remain awaiting and in contact. Yours faithfully, Wonder Kasimonje."

He penned another dispatch from Chegutu dated September 29, 1995, in which he wrote: "Physically I am not there with you but spiritually we are united in Christ. United we shall fight Satan and his empire in our lives because Satan wants us to suffer and lose our faith, which is a futile endeavor on his part because we have Christ on our side. One man can conquer millions if he has Christ. God is all in all and nothing else. I hope you are a very *devoted* Christian. . . . I have fair insight that you are a writer. This is based on your expressive use of language in your letter. Keep the fire burning. Don't look down because you fall. Failure is a word I don't accept. There is nothing either good or bad but thinking makes it so. . . . As a budding writer my ideas come from walking, talking, listening, observing, doing, reading, believing, disagreeing, dreaming, scheming, asking, an open mind. My thoughts are more powerful than words but no psychotic features. I surround myself with good thoughts."

Wonder's attempt to identify with me, on an intimate and personal level, as a Christian and a writer left me momentarily shaken, but I felt ultimately uplifted by his encouragement. I also noted that Wonder unwittingly but wisely practiced techniques of cognitive-behavior therapy on himself to prevent himself from dwelling on demoralizing thoughts that might drag him back into the depths of depression. He also communicated to me that he was not sliding into a psychotic break with all of these expansive thoughts. Although he was no longer my patient, I noted his powers of self-observation and his need to reassure.

By November, Wonder had moved to "The Manger," a convent located in Mabelreign, a suburb of Harare. How he had lost his place on the farm in Chegutu was a mystery to me. Again, Father John Hummel helped Wonder find his new lodging. In January of 1996, Wonder moved once again, for unclear reasons, this time to his half-brother's house in the high-density suburb of Glen View in Harare. I could only speculate about whether he was moving on good terms or otherwise. Despite the frequent moves, Wonder had become a published writer during this period of time. "I am still writing poems, short stories, jokes, etc.," he wrote. "Sometimes I contribute to *Kwayedza,* our local mother language newspaper. They pay me $15.00 per story. . . . Poetry is my first love. I will keep on writing poems until the last hour. I have a pregnant book of poems titled 'Lunatic's Bag.' More of my poems are on spiritual matters. Some of my poems are broadcast on the radio. . . . Dr. Linde, I love and respect you greatly. I am against overdependency. My goal is to work hard. To work is to pray. Hands to work and hearts for God. . . . May our father-mother God be with you. Peace in your family is always within reach. I remember you with authentic prayers. I close with best wishes. Lovingly, Wonder Kasimonje."

During this time Wonder asked me to be his benefactor, the financial sponsor of his education. I wondered if his letters were written partially with the intention of reassuring me that I would not be fueling the whims of a crazy man if I did indeed send him money to further his education.

Zimbabwe's system of higher education is a pyramidal one in which only the very best students, with the highest test scores, qualify for a university-level education. Many good students like Wonder, excluded from the opportunity to obtain a university education, continue with studies at technical or religious colleges. I struggled with the decision only briefly before determining that I would pay for his tuition, books, and basic living expenses. I also sent him US$10 or US$20 by mail from time to time as I knew that his pay for writing poems and stories, the equivalent of a little more than US$1 per story, would hardly keep him in clothes, soap, pens, and writing paper. One of Wonder's mantras to reassure me emerged during this time: "I am against overdependency."

As the year turned into 1996, some hardship came my way, and I came face to face with my limitations in trying to do "something special" in the realm of American psychiatry. I hardened my heart and became somewhat withdrawn and cynical. But Wonder remained buoyant. While I possessed a searing sense of entitlement, Wonder maintained his perspective by being thankful for the little that he had; where I struggled with the lukewarm Christian faith of being a "retired" Catholic, Wonder had sprung forward in his life, guided by a God intimate to him. His first letter of 1996 was written from the Pentecostal Bible College in Harare. In it he drew a diagram of a cluster of grapes that illustrated the "fruit of the spirit."

"Where there is love, there is joy. Where there is love, there is peace. Where there is love, there is longsuffering. Where there is love, there is meekness. Where there is love, there is temperance. Where there is love, there is gentleness. Where there is love, there is goodness. Where there is love, there is faithfulness," wrote Wonder. "The fruit here is love and the rest are ingredients in the fruit. The ingredients are important because they make the fruit sweet. If one part of the fruit decays the fruits loses its normal taste. Thus our lifestyle within the body of Christ can either enhance the body or can cause corruption."

I was humbled by his respectful request for a small amount of pocket money. While I bitched about having to save for a down payment on a home in San Francisco, Wonder Kasimonje was just making sure he had enough money to buy soap for himself a month or two down the road. Why am I so starved for good news and excessive prosperity when Wonder and other Africans plod on with so little?

That year I received a notice from the Pentecostal Bible College that Wonder's tuition and fees for the year would be about ZW$3000. As the currency slid to a rate of approximately ZW$10 to US$1, I figured that a check of US$300 ought to cover the cost. What a bargain, I thought.

By May, Wonder seemed to be establishing himself as a student and resident at Pentecostal Bible College. I received a favorable reply from the headmaster, thanking me for the fees paid and also giving me a report that Wonder had indeed settled in well. However, in his letter dated May 4, 1996, Wonder began to sound the alarm about worsening poverty and social problems in Zimbabwe.

"Worse than better, Zimbabwe is a destitute country. People are willing to be dishonest (corruption). Due to undue hardship caused by Economic Structural Adjustment Programme (ESAP), a number of people are extremely suffering. Some are in danger of depression. It really pains. We cannot talk about it any more. God will give his final judgment."

The dispatches described a slowly collapsing country throughout the year. "It's now a dog biting a dog situation.

Survival of the fittest. 'Nepotism and corruption' is now a slogan for Zimbabweans."

While Wonder struggled, I was fighting a few demons of my own back here in the land of milk and honey. Laurie and I found ourselves in a marital crisis, needing couples counseling to sort things out and repair the matter bit by bit. My mother was diagnosed with a rare abdominal cancer with a poor prognosis and spent five days in the hospital with a burst appendix. I flew back to Minnesota and stayed with her during a few of those hospital nights, monitoring her delirium in person, reorienting her, trying to stave off shots of sedatives to calm her. One of my best friends from medical school, a family practice doctor with a wife and a young daughter, suffered a serious closed head injury and neck fracture in a motor vehicle accident in which he was flung through his truck's sunroof, catapulted dozens of feet into an Oregon forest. In addition, I was in the midst of studying and preparing for my oral board examination in psychiatry, scheduled for January 1997. I was taking it for the second time after I had suffered a mild form of professional humiliation by failing in my first attempt.

Adversity knows no boundaries, no skin color, no socioeconomic targets. Wonder continued to write of Zimbabwe's imploding economy and mushrooming AIDS crisis. "Cost of living is very high in Zimbabwe. Nurses and some of the doctors are on strike. They are demanding more money. Life here is getting worse rather than better. Life in Zimbabwe is no longer stable because of the cost of living. Nearly everything is up. Survival of the fittest. . . . Death rate in Zimbabwe is high. Day by day people are dying. AIDS/HIV is now a king. People are not fearing of AIDS. They don't believe that AIDS is there and there is no medicine for it. I'm missing some of my relatives. It really pains but birth is as sure as death."

Faithfulness, persistence, perseverance, endurance, even stubbornness—these were the attributes that propelled Wonder forward in his life. He was able to make the best of his situation and create opportunities out of adversity. During this time, Wonder continued to write poetry that he recited on the radio. He came to consider himself a developing pastoral poet.

The act a symptom of his everlasting hope, Wonder secured a small plot of land 40 kilometers east of Harare in the Goromonzi Rural area. Talk about chutzpah! Here was a guy with no money, no permanent address, pretty much alone in the world, in his early twenties, barely getting enough to eat or put clothes on his back, who felt confident enough about his future to buy a piece of land! He even had the audacity to plan to build a small home and till the plot to feed himself and others.

While Wonder operated from a base of faith and endurance, on the other side of the globe both literally and figuratively, Paul Linde functioned in a mindset of existential angst and restlessness, feeling like a dangling protagonist of Saul Bellow's fiction.

In his critical introduction to *The Portable Saul Bellow*, literary critic Gabriel Josipovici writes: "The hero dangles because he won't fit into the world the way people seem to want him to, but he lacks the drive or egocentricity or madness of the Protestant hero or the Romantic rebel that would lead him to create an alternative world. He can't sit still, but he can't find the confidence in himself to make a move. In fact, as the hero stands back from the world, objects start to gain in clarity, but this, far from helping him to act, inhibits action more and more, for the multiplicity of detail assaulting his senses only bewilders and confuses him. . . . It is as though he were too close to the world to make sense of it anymore."

Dissatisfied with my full-time job at San Francisco General, I impulsively dumped half of it to start an outpatient practice across town in a medical office building near a private hospital. I did this without thinking too much. I just knew I needed a change. I thought that I needed to experience private-practice psychiatry before I junked all of psychiatry.

In spite of a lack of faith, my life took a turn for the better in 1997. My mother's cancer did go into a temporary remission. Laurie and I did repair our marriage. We saved enough money for a down payment on a home in a nice neighborhood in San Francisco. We decided to have kids, not realizing yet that we were up for some more adversity in terms of trouble getting pregnant and miscarriages. Despite all of the good things happening in my life, I still fidgeted and gyrated and obsessed and ruminated while Wonder, with his certain faith in God, plowed ahead with his life despite having virtually nothing in terms of material comfort or opportunities. Paul Linde, bloated with relative prosperity and chances in life, pissed and moaned and whined and stumbled forward. Was my unhappiness due to a lack of faith?

Wonder continued to provide an eyewitness account of the torturous unraveling of Zimbabwe as the year 1997 turned into 1998. The seeds of destruction took the form of a currency crisis; the fruits arising in the form of ongoing strikes, rising prices, and, eventually, food riots. Rereading his letters now, I am struck by how optimistic Wonder remained while Zimbabwe was falling apart. I am continually struck with the sharp contrast between Zimbabwe's crumbling and Wonder's blossoming, his hopefulness in the face of bleakness.

"Life here in Zimbabwe is busy and people are angry, hungry, and dissatisfied," he wrote. "Last month security guards went on strike. Also, urban council workers all over the country went on strike. The Zimbabwean dollar is now worthless. More people are dying day by day because of AIDS.

"I myself am fit and fine. I am planning to build my own home in rural area. Afterwards I want to marry. I commit my plans to God the author and finisher of our life."

In another letter he wrote, "Three days ago, there was a strike in Harare and Chitungwiza (food protest). The demonstrators were unhappy about sharp price increases of basic food commodities. There was public violence and theft during the strike period. Now things are back to normal. The cost of living is still very high. People are crying all over the country because of inflation. Life here in Zimbabwe is now undue hardship. Two weeks ago, the weather was too hot. We received heavy rains a few days ago. Some parts of the country are affected by drought so people are ailing because of El Niño.

"I am staying in Goromonzi at my homestead. I have already built a toilet, bedroom and a kitchen at window's level. I want to get married *too soon*. My main aim is to stay at my homestead and do farming. I am also willing to minister to people through writing. God bless you abundantly. May we continue to live in his direction, the Holy Ghost. I am praying for you and more power from God. In his love, Wonder Kasimonje."

By October of 1998, Wonder's life and my life were headed in opposite directions. He was cranking up to finish his last term with six courses to graduate in November. I was grieving yet another miscarriage and my mother's entry into home hospice care. I went back to Minnesota twice before my mother died on November 21, 1998. It was painful to watch her wither away, but absolutely inspiring to witness her courage in facing death and withstanding tremendous pain and suffering. Knowing her courage was no coincidence, I couldn't help but notice her very strong Catholic faith. At the time, I didn't make a connection between her faith and Wonder's faith. It's not until nearly two years later, as I write this, that I see they are the same.

Wonder knew none of the details of my losses when he wrote me this letter on October 8, 1998: "Greetings in Jesus' holy name. I trust in our Lord and Saviour Jesus Christ that you are well. Myself I am very well. Praise God for the measure of health we have and look forward to the day when we will enjoy perfect wholeness. How is your mother these days? I pray that she may enjoy good health and that all may go well with her. God's desire is that all remain in good health. We have a heavenly Father who cares for each of us. . . . I got published in August of this year. I have five Shona poems published and an English short story titled "The Lethal Herb." I really like to write poems and short stories. I hope you are also enjoying writing articles. Keep up the standard." As Wonder ascended to his graduation, I plummeted to my mother's death.

In the wake of my mother's death, I seriously reevaluated my career and, following my heart, planned a transition from the practice of psychiatry to a writing life. I dumped my private practice—too much work, which I did not particularly enjoy, for too little money—and kept a half-time job doing emergency psychiatry at The General. It was then that I decided to write a book about my experience in Zimbabwe.

As if on cue, I heard from Wonder, "I have a fair insight that you will get published. Can you try to write a story about me from the time when I was staying at halfway home, leaving there, stopping tablets, staying with religious sisters, and going to college to study theology and having a plot of land?"

In addition to writing religious articles, columns, and poetry, Wonder continued to perform good works, sheltering unfortunate boarders in his modest home in Goromonzi while expanding his farm:

"I am staying with an ailing young man and a young boy who lost his father when he was very young. My zeal is for Zimbabweans to work hard and to give God a chance. In hardship, duties of Christians are to pray for peace and love. The Devil is working clockwise to disturb peace in the world. My main aim is to accommodate orphans at my homestead. It really pains me to see the number of children in Zimbabwe having no parents because of AIDS. I got seven bags of maize from my field. I am keeping two goats, hens, and a number of rabbits."

Over the course of the next year, Wonder continued to supply firsthand accounts of Zimbabwe's biblical suffering, the result of both natural and manmade disasters. Floods, fuel shortages, corruption, AIDS, and an economy in a tailspin combined to sully the fates of many of his fellow countrymen. He closed one of his last snail-mail letters to me by giving me his e-mail address. "I don't have my personal computer. I am doing computer lessons in Harare. That's where I check for my e-mail messages and for sending." Wonder was still trying to improve himself and better his skills—again persevering through some of his nation's most difficult times.

I began to consider the close connection between faith and trust as demonstrated by the average Zimbabwean. In addition to being steadfast in the face of adversity, most Zimbabweans were trusting of authority figures, in general, and doctors, in particular. This was true even of my paranoid patients. This trust is likely an offshoot of colonialism and the British medical system, which is more hierarchical than ours. Many of the patients that I saw were accustomed to taking orders without question from those in positions of authority, particularly if those individuals had white skin.

I did my best not to be corrupted by this power and to consider my work in Zimbabwe as a privilege. I appreciated my experience while I was there. And I continue to think fondly and often of my time at the ramshackle P.U. Why? I enjoyed a lot of freedom in how I conducted my practice in Zimbabwe. There were no right answers. I didn't worry about getting sued. No lawyer was going to come by and second-guess me. Blaming other individuals for your problems is not a big part of the Shona culture. Very few, if any, personal-injury attorneys practiced in Zimbabwe. None could be seen pimping themselves with toll-free numbers on either of Zimbabwe's two television stations.

I didn't have to worry about submitting bills and fighting with managed care and insurance companies to get paid. No insurance company reviewer was going to swoop through and ask to see my records, to determine if they were going to pay for my services or not. I worked for little money, paid in the increasingly worthless local currency, the equivalent of about US$10,000 per year—enough to live comfortably in Zimbabwe for the time, but nothing in comparison to what I would have made back in the States. My patients did not have to pay to come see me.

Most of all, I liked the unpredictability of the place, never knowing what would roll in, what sort of seemingly impossible situation I might be faced with on any given day.

I also enjoyed the intellectual challenge of solving psychiatric puzzles on a day-to-day basis, of being presented with limited information and then embarking on a process of scrambling, asking dozens of questions through an interpreter with the clock ticking, the grains of sand falling through the bottleneck of an hourglass.

I enjoyed working around a lot of people, figuratively high-fiving and literally sidestepping the clientele every time I entered the courtyard of the P.U. I worked closely with the nurses and got to know them professionally and personally. They taught me about themselves and the culture. I felt comfortable enough with them to joke around with them, dance the slightly naughty steps of the *kwassa-kwassa* with Sister Shuga and mildly flirt with Sister Chimhenga. I cope better with a stressful work environment by joking around as much as possible and getting serious only when necessary. I think the nurses appreciated that rhythm and style of work.

Being around the energy of Africans on a day-to-day basis made me feel revitalized. And the patients that I saw, despite living with the triple burden of poverty, hardship, and mental illness, were grateful and generally satisfied with their lives. Of course, this was true because of their possession of the African mindset, with its acceptance of suffering, maintenance of low expectations, and willingness to "see how the day goes." But the relative contentment of my patients also arose from the unwavering support of their extended families. This reality of life in Africa lies in sharp contrast to the situation in America, where family members are more likely to ostracize and shun their mentally ill relatives.

In Zimbabwe, I worked as a stranger in a strange land and experienced daily adventure. The whole experience appealed to my sense of sacrifice, martyrdom, and reverse status. I drove a 1982 Renault LeCar, dressed like a casual bum at work, wore dusty shoes, spoke plainly, and did as little administrative work as possible. I was doing something real, something that made a difference, in my work-life. The job there was perfect for me—sequestered away from the shackles of the academic, teaching only as much as I wanted to, performing no research, attending no committee meetings. Expectations for me were low, given the chaos and entropy on display there. I had a chance to harness that chaos, an uphill struggle all the way.

My experiences in Zimbabwe left an indelible mark on me. On a near-daily basis, I mentally transport myself back to that time and that place, to be with those people. Those memories, plus Wonder's regular correspondence, keep Zimbabwe close to my heart. Around the time I began to correspond with Wonder by e-mail I figured out that I wanted the last chapter of my book to be about him and our relationship. I had totally forgotten that Wonder had, in fact, requested that I write about him way back in March of 1999. I felt ambivalent about writing about Wonder. His story inspired me, but I wanted to respect his privacy and not give the impression to him or to anybody else in Zimbabwe that I was "using" my patients to advance my writing career.

Africans are very sensitive to opportunists coming to Africa to gratify their own needs, in the process contributing nothing to the Africans. This scenario recapitulates Africa's painful colonial history. I didn't go to Africa to collect stories about crazy people. I went over there to get a job as a psychiatrist, to experience the culture, and to help people if I could. In Zimbabwe, I didn't have to be perfect. I could just do the best that I could every day, with the best of intentions, in a way that felt ethically pure to me. I knew that I had a skill to offer to the Zimbabwean health-care system and my

Zimbabwean patients—namely the services and consultation of an attending psychiatrist. Several hundred psychiatrists and other therapists ply their craft in the city of San Francisco, ministering to about seven hundred thousand denizens. About ten psychiatrists, most of them foreigners, do their work in the nation of Zimbabwe, providing bare-bones care for more than ten million people. I provided a service that no one else was willing or able to provide. I found that damn rewarding.

Not wanting to be a neocolonialist, I was very careful to ask Wonder explicitly for his permission for me to write about my experience working with him as a patient. I wanted to use his real name and describe his treatment and our developing friendship since then. In corresponding by e-mail, I tried to be overly explicit in explaining my intentions. In doing so, I was acting like a "cover-your-ass" American psychiatrist, keenly aware of lawyers peering over my shoulder. I had totally forgotten about the African mindset in which a sense of community, friendship, loyalty, honor, and adopting a humanistic approach to the world were so much more important than assuming a legalistic stance.

I was worried that Wonder would deny me permission. I was worried that he would demand the right of refusal of me to publish certain attributes of our friendship. I was worried that he would want me to pay him to quote from his letters. My worries were entirely "Americocentric" and I don't think Wonder even caught my drift when I wrote such explicit questions to him. With little fanfare, Wonder gave me his blessing to proceed. When I later sent him a copy of the chapter, he pretty much just told me that he liked it. And I was worried about him trying to control the process?

What had happened to my African way of thinking? To see how the day goes? That mentality dissolved the day I returned to the States, when the tires of the Northwest Airlines DC-10 touched down in Minneapolis from London the day after the Oklahoma City bombing in April of 1995.

I had not properly learned to live my life with an African mindset. I needed remedial work. Oh, sure, I met lots of interesting patients and learned a few things about the Shona culture and about practicing psychiatry in a foreign land, but I was still an American through and through.

Control or be controlled. Ruminate, worry, obsess. Fight like hell for your individual rights. Piss and moan. Accumulate capital. Get what you deserve. Piss on the other guy. Kill or be killed. To really learn the lessons of Africa I think that I would have to go back and never leave the continent again. I'm not sure if I'm ready to do that. Or maybe even be born into a different family, with a different skin color, in a different tribe, in a different era. Recycle this life for a new one.

Although it wasn't easy to start work in the midst of a strike or learn the ropes of living and working in Zimbabwe, I was able to accomplish those tasks. To master the last one, that of thinking like an African, might require a more radical shift—that I become an African. And to do that I might have to come around again.

ABOUT THE AUTHOR

Paul R. Linde is a board-certified psychiatrist who works as an emergency psychiatrist at San Francisco General Hospital. He is an Associate Clinical Professor of Psychiatry at the University of California–San Francisco School of Medicine, where he finished his specialty training. In addition to working in Africa, he has traveled extensively throughout the world.

The fourth of five children, Paul grew up in Hastings, Minnesota. He currently lives with his wife and two sons in San Francisco. His work has appeared in *DoubleTake*, *JAMA*, and the *San Jose Mercury News* as well as numerous other newspapers and academic journals.